AF447521

9 798330 425822

Siddur Ner Tamid: Hoshanot
© 2024 Eitz Echad LLC
All rights reserved.

Editing, format design and layout, artwork were all made in-house by Eitz Echad in the United States of America.

WWW.EITZECHAD.COM

❧ <u>Foreword: On Hoshanot</u> ❧

The Hoshanot prayers provide modern Jews with a window into ancient days. During the time of the Beit HaMikdash, during Sukkot, the Kohanim would place willow branches next to the altar. The heads of the willow branches were bent over the altar to increase joy during Sukkot. The Kohanim would then sound the shofar. They would then proceed to circle the altar once and would recite the Hoshana prayer. They would cry out, "Please G-d, bring salvation now. Please G-d bring success now." On Hoshana Rabbah, i.e., the great Hoshana, the seventh day of Sukkot, the Kohanim would circle the altar seven times perhaps reminiscent of Yehoshua's circling of Jericho seven times before its walls fell.

Today the Hoshanot prayers in the Sephardic tradition have evolved into much longer pieces recalling G-d's salvation for the Jewish people in times past and plea for G-d to remember us just as in days of old. Today we have no Temple, but the practice of circling the altar, now the Bima, has been transferred to the synagogue. Circling the Bima is no longer limited to the Kohanim but is practiced by every Jewish man.

Perhaps this is reflective of the reality that a cry for salvation and favor is needed from every Jew. We long for the day that the Kohanim will be restored to their rightful place and responsibility. Until that day, we must consider that each one of us carries the responsibility to search for G-d while He may be found and to plea for all Israel. The High Holidays, Rosh Hashanah and Yom Kippur are certainly the high point of this period, but the desire to cry for G-d's favor should always be foremost in our minds through Sukkot and beyond.

L'shalom,

Rabbi Dr. Juan Marcos Bejarano Gutierrez
Chavurah Zohar Yisrael
B'nei Anusim Center for Education

ב"ה

Introduction: About the Hoshanot

The intention of creating the Siddur Ner Tamid series came about as a congregational need for helping those with Converso or B'nei Anusim backgrounds (Spanish and Portuguese Jews who accepted Christianity in order to avoid death) to be able to join in with Jewish practice as well as be able to have a great resource to learn and grow with minimal hinderance. While in exile, the Sephardic B'nei Anusim have faced a difficult task of re-entering the world of Judaism and becoming members of often reluctant and even suspicious Jewish communities. Citing Yosef Karo, author of the Shulchan Arukh, in a letter to a community in Kandiyah, Greece:

"...We have heard that Jews who had lived in Spain and were forced to convert have now come to your kehillah in order to live freely as Jews and keep all the mizvot openly. Instead, you remind them of the sins they committed in Spain and, when a disagreement arises between them and the people of your kehillah, you claim these blessed baalei teshuvah are meshumadim (converts to Christianity). This is a terrible sin, because you are slamming the door in the faces of baalei teshuvah. The Mordechai (a Rishon from Ashkenaz) recorded in his sefer that Rabbenu Gershom decreed that any Jew who does not openly accept ba'alei teshuvah should himself be considered menuddeh (not part of the Jewish people). Therefore, from today and henceforth, may every person be exceptionally careful in his dealings with these ba'alei teshuvah, and never again refer to them as meshumadim. And if, has veshalom (may Hashem forbid), the word escapes someone's lips, be he young or old, let him sit completely alone for an entire day and with his own mouth confess his ugly sin. And further, he must undertake never to do so again...Written this 15th of Tammuz, here in Sefat, in the year 5328, (1568), David ben Zimra, Yosef Caro, Moshe miTrani and Yisrael de Kuriel."

- quoted from The Story of Maran Bet Yosef: R Yosef Caro, Author of the Shulhan Aruch (The Sephardic Heritage Series), Artscroll, 1986.

We therefore feel it is our duty and a great mitzvah to bring these souls, as well as anyone closer to the light of Torah and Judaism. We've done our best to bring as much of the Hoshanot transliterated as possible and to cover the most communities. We also included Hoshanot for Shabbat Day for the communities that say them on that day as well.

May this work continue to help those in need and may we continue to feel the importance of כל ישראל ערבים זה לזה / "All Yisrael are responsible for one another", caring for one another within the community, outside of the community, within Eretz Yisrael, and all over the world, a responsibility to all of עם ישראל / the people of Yisrael.

Kelil
President of Eitz Echad

Table of Contents

Hoshanot for the First Day
הושענות ליום ראשון

Erchatz Benikayon Kapai

אֶרְחַץ בְּנִקָּיוֹן כַּפָּי

Va'asovevah Et-Mizbachacha

וַאֲסֹבְבָה אֶת־מִזְבַּחֲךָ

Adonai: Lashmia' Bekol Todah

יְהוָה: לַשְׁמִעַ בְּקוֹל תּוֹדָה

Ulesaper Kol-Nifle'oteicha.

וּלְסַפֵּר כָּל־נִפְלְאוֹתֶיךָ:

I will wash my hands in innocence, and I will encircle your altar, Hashem. That I may make the voice of thanksgiving to be heard, and tell of all Your wondrous works. (Ps. 26:6-7)

Hosha'ana. Hosha'ana:

הוֹשַׁעְנָא. הוֹשַׁעְנָא:

Please save us. Please save us:

Lema'anach Eloheinu.

לְמַעַנְךָ אֱלֹהֵינוּ.

Lema'anach Bore'enu.

לְמַעַנְךָ בּוֹרְאֵנוּ.

Lema'anach Go'alenu.

לְמַעַנְךָ גּוֹאֲלֵנוּ.

Lema'anach Doreshenu:

לְמַעַנְךָ דּוֹרְשֵׁנוּ:

For Your sake, our God. For Your sake, our Creator. For Your sake, our Redeemer. For Your sake, our Seeker.

Lema'anach Adir Adirim.

לְמַעַנְךָ אַדִּיר אַדִּירִים.

Lema'anach Borei Ruach

לְמַעַנְךָ בּוֹרֵא רוּחַ

Veyotzer Harim.

וְיוֹצֵר הָרִים.

Lema'anach Gedol Ha'etzah

לְמַעַנְךָ גְּדוֹל הָעֵצָה

Mashpil Umerim.

מַשְׁפִּיל וּמֵרִים.

Lema'anach Dover Tzedek

לְמַעַנְךָ דּוֹבֵר צֶדֶק

Magid Meisharim.	מַגִּיד מֵישָׁרִים.
Lema'anach Hayodea' Va'ed Im	לְמַעַנְךָ הַיּוֹדֵעַ וָעֵד אִם
Yisater Ish Bemistarim.	יִסָּתֵר אִישׁ בְּמִסְתָּרִים.
Lema'anach Vehu Be'echad Umi	לְמַעַנְךָ וְהוּא בְאֶחָד וּמִי
Yeshivenu Amarim.	יְשִׁיבֶנּוּ אֲמָרִים.
Lema'anach Zach Venaki	לְמַעַנְךָ זַךְ וְנָקִי
Umitbarer Im Barim.	וּמִתְבָּרֵר עִם בָּרִים.
Lema'anach Chofes Matzpun	לְמַעַנְךָ חוֹפֵשׂ מַצְפּוּן
Vechoker Kol-Chadarim.	וְחוֹקֵר כָּל־חֲדָרִים.
Lema'anach Tipechah Yemino	לְמַעַנְךָ טִפְּחָה יְמִינוֹ
Shamayim Ve'asah Me'orim.	שָׁמַיִם וְעָשָׂה מְאוֹרִים.
Lema'anach Yasad Eretz Batzurot	לְמַעַנְךָ יָסַד אֶרֶץ בַּצּוּרוֹת
Bika Ye'orim. Lema'anach Kabir	בִּקַּע יְאוֹרִים. לְמַעַנְךָ כַּבִּיר
Koach Mechubad Ba'urim.	כֹּחַ מְכֻבָּד בָּאוּרִים.
Lema'anach Lo Yitamu Shenotav	לְמַעַנְךָ לֹא יִתַּמּוּ שְׁנוֹתָיו
Ledor Dorim:	לְדוֹר דּוֹרִים:

For Your sake, Mightiest of the mighty. For Your sake, Creator of the wind and the Former of mountains. For Your sake, Great in counsel, Who humbles and lifts high. For Your sake, Speaker of righteousness, declaring uprightness. For Your sake, Knower and Witness, whether a person hides in secret places. For Your sake, He Who is One, and Who will return us with utterances. For Your sake, Pure and Innocent and Who is pure with the pure. For Your sake, Liberator of the hidden and Searcher of all chambers. For Your sake, He Who spread out the sky with His right hand and made the luminaries. For Your sake, He Who founded the earth with its boundaries, carving the rivers in rocks. For Your sake, the Great in Power, honored with lights. For Your sake, His years will never end for generations of generations:

Hosha'ana. Hosha'ana:

הוֹשַׁעְנָא. הוֹשַׁעְנָא:

Please save us. Please save us:

Ana El Echad Ushemo Echad.

אָנָּא אֵל אֶחָד וּשְׁמוֹ אֶחָד.

Umi Yeshivenu Vehu Ve'echad.

וּמִי יְשִׁיבֵנוּ וְהוּא בְאֶחָד.

Kara Shamayim Va'aretz

קָרָא שָׁמַיִם וָאָרֶץ

Vaya'amdu Ke'echad.

וַיַּעַמְדוּ כְּאֶחָד.

Hoshi'enu Bachagigat Yom

הוֹשִׁיעֵנוּ בַּחֲגִיגַת יוֹם

Echad:

אֶחָד:

Please, God, Who is One and His name is One. And Who will return us, He is One. He called heaven and earth, and they stood as one. Save us on the celebration of the first day:

Ana Zechor Av Yarash Et

אָנָּא זְכוֹר אָב יָרַשׁ אֶת

Ha'aretz Vehayah Echad.

הָאָרֶץ וְהָיָה אֶחָד.

Hechin Lamoredim Lev Echad

הֵכִין לַמּוֹרְדִים לֵב אֶחָד

Vederech Echad. Likro Chulam

וְדֶרֶךְ אֶחָד. לִקְרֹא כֻלָּם

Beshem Adonai Ule'ovdo

בְּשֵׁם יְהֹוָה וּלְעָבְדוֹ

Shechem Echad. Hoshi'enu

שְׁכֶם אֶחָד. הוֹשִׁיעֵנוּ

Bachagigat Yom Echad:

בַּחֲגִיגַת יוֹם אֶחָד:

Please remember, a father [Avraham] inherited who inherited the land and was one man. Who prepared for the rebels one heart and one way. To they would all call in the name of Hashem, and to serve Him, shoulder to shoulder, as one. Save us on the celebration of the first day:

Ana Zechor Ben Yachid Hayah

אָנָּא זְכוֹר בֶּן יָחִיד הָיָה

Lifnei Aviv Echad. Sheneihem

לִפְנֵי אָבִיו אֶחָד. שְׁנֵיהֶם

Benisayon Halechu Ke'echad.

בְּנִסָּיוֹן הָלְכוּ כְּאֶחָד.

Natata Kofer Tachtav Ayil

נָתַתָּ כֹּפֶר תַּחְתָּיו אַיִל

Echad. Hoshi'enu Bachagigat

אֶחָד. הוֹשִׁיעֵנוּ בַּחֲגִיגַת

Yom Echad:

יוֹם אֶחָד:

Please remember, the only son [Yitzchak] who was before his father as one. Both of them went through the test as one. You provided a ram as a substitute, one ram. Save us on the celebration of the first day:

Ana Zechor Av Hosif Chelek

אָנָּא זְכוֹר אָב הוֹסִיף חֵלֶק

Shechem Echad. Kivah Lehaflit

שְׁכֶם אֶחָד. קִוָּה לְהַפְלִיט

Hamachaneh Ha'echad. Asaf

הַמַּחֲנֶה הָאֶחָד. אָסַף

Banav Lekabel Malchut

בָּנָיו לְקַבֵּל מַלְכוּת

Shamayim Peh Echad.

שָׁמַיִם פֶּה אֶחָד.

Hoshi'enu Bachagigat Yom

הוֹשִׁיעֵנוּ בַּחֲגִיגַת יוֹם

Echad:

אֶחָד:

Please remember a father [Ya'akov], who added one more portion [to Yosef]. Who hoped to save one of the camps, and gathered his sons to accept the kingship of heaven with one voice. Save us on the celebration of the first day:

Ana Hamashmi'enu Shetayim

אָנָּא הַמַּשְׁמִיעֵנוּ שְׁתַּיִם

Bekolot Uverakim Ke'echad.

בְּקוֹלוֹת וּבְרָקִים כְּאֶחָד.

Hamanchilenu Torah Achat

הַמַּנְחִילֵנוּ תּוֹרָה אַחַת

Umishpat Echad. Hoshi'enu

וּמִשְׁפָּט אֶחָד. הוֹשִׁיעֵנוּ

Bachagigat Yom Echad:

בַּחֲגִיגַת יוֹם אֶחָד:

Please, Who let us hear two [mitzvot] in thunder and lightning as if one. Who endowed us with one Torah and one Law. Save us on the celebration of the first day:

Hosha'ana. Hosha'ana: הוֹשַׁעְנָא. הוֹשַׁעְנָא:

Please save us. Please save us:

El Yish'acha Tzameti. Va'e'eroch אֵל יִשְׁעֲךָ צָמֵאתִי. וָאֶעֱרֹךְ

Negdecha. Sameach Nefesh נֶגְדֶּךָ. שַׂמֵּחַ נֶפֶשׁ

Avdecha: Na'or Attah Adir. עַבְדֶּךָ: נָאוֹר אַתָּה אַדִּיר.

Heyeh Lanu Lishu'ah. הֱיֵה לָנוּ לִישׁוּעָה.

Samechenu Kimot Initanu Shenot שַׂמְּחֵנוּ כִּימוֹת עִנִּיתָנוּ שְׁנוֹת

Ra'inu Ra'ah: Yeshu'ot Chomot רָאִינוּ רָעָה: יְשׁוּעוֹת חוֹמוֹת

Vachel. Shiyt Lesurah וָחֵל. שִׁית לְסוּרָה

Vegalmudah. Yismach Har- וְגַלְמוּדָה. יִשְׂמַח הַר-

Tziyon Tagelenah Benot צִיּוֹן תָּגֵלְנָה בְּנוֹת

Yehudah: Yadecha Hosif Shenit. יְהוּדָה: יָדְךָ הוֹסִיף שֵׁנִית.

Chish Lenochalei Dat Ari'el. חִישׁ לְנוֹחֲלֵי דַת אֲרִיאֵל.

Yagel Ya'akov Yismach יָגֵל יַעֲקֹב יִשְׂמַח

Yisra'el: Tzaveh Yeshu'ot Ya'akov. יִשְׂרָאֵל: צַוֵּה יְשׁוּעוֹת יַעֲקֹב.

Asher Leyish'acha Kemehim. אֲשֶׁר לְיִשְׁעֲךָ כְּמֵהִים.

Vetzadikim Yismechu Ya'altzu וְצַדִּיקִים יִשְׂמְחוּ יַעַלְצוּ

Lifnei Elohim: Chevel לִפְנֵי אֱלֹהִים: חֶבֶל

Nachalatecha Toshia'. נַחֲלָתְךָ תּוֹשִׁיעַ.

Vetzidkatecha Yeshanenu. וְצִדְקָתְךָ יְשַׁנְּנוּ.

Veyismechu Chol-Chosei Vach וְיִשְׂמְחוּ כָל-חוֹסֵי בָךְ

Le'olam Yeranenu: Kore'im לְעוֹלָם יְרַנֵּנוּ: קוֹרְאִים

Beshimcha. Teshovev Leveit בְּשִׁמְךָ. תְּשׁוֹבֵב לְבֵית

Menuchah. Sason Vesimchah	מְנוּחָה. שָׂשׂוֹן וְשִׂמְחָה
Yassigu Venasu Yagon	יַשִּׂיגוּ וְנָסוּ יָגוֹן
Va'anachah: Bishu'atecha	וַאֲנָחָה: בִּישׁוּעָתֶךָ
Yeranenu. Veranei Falet	יְרַנֵּנוּ. וְרָנֵּי פַלֵּט
Bechikam. Yismach Yisra'el	בְּחִכָּם. יִשְׂמַח יִשְׂרָאֵל
Be'osav Benei-Tziyon Yagilu	בְּעֹשָׂיו בְּנֵי־צִיּוֹן יָגִילוּ
Vemalkam: Rav Lehoshia'. Yariv	בְּמַלְכָּם: רַב לְהוֹשִׁיעַ. יָרִיב
Rivam Veyatzik Limtzikam.	רִיבָם וְיָצִיק לִמְצִיקָם.
Yismach Tzadik Ki-Chazah	יִשְׂמַח צַדִּיק כִּי־חָזָה
Nakam: Veyede'u Ki Yadecha	נָקָם: וְיֵדְעוּ כִּי יָדְךָ
Zot. Teshu'atecha Leshanen. Ki	זֹאת. תְּשׁוּעָתְךָ לְשַׁנֵּן. כִּי
Simachtani Adonai Befo'olecha	שִׂמַּחְתַּנִי יְהֹוָה בְּפָעֳלֶךָ
Bema'asei Yadeicha	בְּמַעֲשֵׂי יָדֶיךָ
Aranen: Imratecha Takim Yesha	אֲרַנֵּן: אִמְרָתְךָ תָקִים יֶשַׁע
Lehachish Lifduyim. Ranu	לְהָחִישׁ לִפְדוּיִם. רָנוּ
Leya'akov Simchah Vetzahalu	לְיַעֲקֹב שִׂמְחָה וְצַהֲלוּ
Berosh Hagoyim: Loveshei	בְּרֹאשׁ הַגּוֹיִם: לוֹבְשֵׁי
Bigdei Rikmah. Yaronnu Bechol-	בִּגְדֵי רִקְמָה. יָרֹנּוּ בְּכָל־
Afikim. Simchu B'Adonai Vegilu	אֲפִיקִים. שִׂמְחוּ בַּיהֹוָה וְגִילוּ
Tzadikim: Yir'u Anavim	צַדִּיקִים: יִרְאוּ עֲנָוִים
Veyismachu. Behoshi'acha	וְיִשְׂמָחוּ. בְּהוֹשִׁיעֶךָ
Evyonai. Yismach Lev Mevakshei	אֶבְיוֹנַי. יִשְׂמַח לֵב מְבַקְשֵׁי
Adonai: Kore'ei Mikra Kodesh.	יְהֹוָה: קוֹרְאֵי מִקְרָא קֹדֶשׁ.
Yesha Yikre'u Befetzach. Sova	יֶשַׁע יִקְרְאוּ בְּפֶצַח. שָׂבַע
Semachot Et-Paneicha Ne'imot	שְׂמָחוֹת אֶת־פָּנֶיךָ נְעִמוֹת
Bimincha Netzach: Barishon	בִּימִינְךָ נֶצַח: בָּרִאשׁוֹן
Bechagam Kehayom. Hosha Tzur	בְּחַגָּם כְּהַיּוֹם. הוֹשַׁע צוּר
Benivo. Zeh-Hayom Asah	בְּנִיבוֹ. זֶה־הַיּוֹם עָשָׂה

Adonai Nagilah Venismechah Vo: יְהֹוָה נָגִילָה וְנִשְׂמְחָה בֹו:

I thirst for Your salvation. And I will arrange [my service] before you. Rejoice the soul of Your servant: You are radiant and mighty. Be our salvation. Rejoice us like the days you humbled us, the years we have seen evil. Salvations of walls, and and ramparts; Set for wandering and exile. Let Mount Tziyon rejoice, let the daughters of Yehudah be glad. Let Your hand add a second time. Hasten Ariel [the Alter] for the inheritors of the Law. Let Ya'akov rejoice, let Yisrael be glad: Command the salvations of Ya'akov, who yearn for Your salvation like water. And the righteous shall rejoice and exult before God: The inheritance of Your lot You will save, and Your righteousness will renew us. And all who trust in You will rejoice, forever they will sing. Those who call on Your name, return them to the house of rest. Joy and gladness shall be achieved, and sorrow and sighing shall flee. Of Your salvation, they will sing. And the cries of deliverance in their mouths. Let Yisrael rejoice in it's Maker, let the sons of Tziyon rejoice in their King. The One Who is Great to save will contend with their opponents and oppress their oppressors. The righteous shall rejoice, for they will have seen vengeance. And they will know that this is Your hand. Your salvation to sharpen. For You have made me rejoice, Hashem, in Your deeds; at the works of Your hands I sing for joy. Your word establishes salvation, to hasten the redeemed. Let Ya'akov rejoice and exult at the head of the nations: Those dressed in embroidered garments sing joyously in all the streams. Rejoice in Hashem and be glad, you righteous: Let the humble see and be glad. In Your salvation, the needy rejoice. The heart of those who seek Hashem rejoice: Those who proclaim the holy convocations shall call salvation at the opening. Full of joy in Your presence, delights at your right hand forever: On the first day of their celebration, bring salvation, O Rock, with your utterance: This is the day that Hashem has made; let us rejoice and be glad on it.

Hosha'ana. Hosha'ana: הוֹשַׁעֲנָא. הוֹשַׁעֲנָא:

Please save us. Please save us:

Ana Hoshi'ah Na.   אָנָּא הוֹשִׁיעָה נָּא.

Ana Hoshi'ah Na: אָנָּא הוֹשִׁיעָה נָּא:

Please save us now. Please save us now:

Ana El Acharon Verishon. Ametz   אָנָּא אֵל אַחֲרוֹן וְרִאשׁוֹן. אַמֵּץ

Am Netzurim Ke'ishon.   עַם נְצוּרִים כְּאִישׁוֹן.

Betza'akam Hosha'ana   בְּצַעֲקָם הוֹשַׁעֲנָא

Velachashon. Hayom Beyom   בְּלַחֲשׁוֹן. הַיּוֹם בְּיוֹם

Rishon. Hoshi'ah Na: רִאשׁוֹן. הוֹשִׁיעָה נָּא:

Ana Hoshi'ah Na.   אָנָּא הוֹשִׁיעָה נָּא.

Ana Hoshi'ah Na: אָנָּא הוֹשִׁיעָה נָּא:

Please, God, Who is the last and the first, strengthen the guarded
nation like the apple of the eye, when they cry, "Please save us!", in
their whisper [prayer]. Today, on the first day, please save us: Please
save us now. Please save us now.

Ana Geda Ninei Dishon. Ge'al   אָנָּא גְּדַע נִינֵי דִשׁוֹן. גְּאַל

Meyachadeicha Velachashon.   מְיַחֲדֶיךָ בְּלַחֲשׁוֹן.

Uneteh Lanu Shalom Kemeimei   וּנְטֵה לָנוּ שָׁלוֹם כְּמֵימֵי

Fishon. Hayom Beyom Rishon.   פִישׁוֹן. הַיּוֹם בְּיוֹם רִאשׁוֹן.

Hoshi'ah Na: הוֹשִׁיעָה נָּא:

Ana Hoshi'ah Na.   אָנָּא הוֹשִׁיעָה נָּא.

Ana Hoshi'ah Na: אָנָּא הוֹשִׁיעָה נָּא:

Please cut off the branches [descendants] of Dishon. Redeem those Who declare Your Oneness in a whisper. And extend peace to us like the waters of the Pishon. Today, on the first day, please save us: Please save us now. Please save us now.

Ani Vahu Hoshi'ah Na.	אֲנִי וָהוּ הוֹשִׁיעָה נָּא.
Ani Vahu Hoshi'ah Na:	אֲנִי וָהוּ הוֹשִׁיעָה נָּא:

Ani VaHu, please save us now. Ani VaHu, please save us now.

Kehosha'ta Yeruyei Haye'or.	כְּהוֹשַׁעְתָּ יְרוּיֵי הַיְאוֹר.
Be'uzecha Hana'or. Vetavrik	בְּעֻזְּךָ הַנָּאוֹר. וְתַבְרִיק
Ma'or. La'alutim Ke'ishon: Gam	מָאוֹר. לַעֲלוּטִים כְּאִישׁוֹן: גַּם
Attah Kemo Chen. El Shachak	עַתָּה כְּמוֹ כֵן. אֵל שַׁחַק
Shochen. Pedut Le'amecha	שׁוֹכֵן. פְּדוּת לְעַמְּךָ
Hachen. Nehalach Beyom	הָכֵן. נְהַלֶּלְךָ בְּיוֹם
Rishon. Ken Hosha'ana:	רִאשׁוֹן. כֵּן הוֹשַׁעְנָא:
Ani Vahu Hoshi'ah Na.	אֲנִי וָהוּ הוֹשִׁיעָה נָּא.
Ani Vahu Hoshi'ah Na:	אֲנִי וָהוּ הוֹשִׁיעָה נָּא:

As you brought salvation to those cast into the river with your illuminated strength. And shown light, for those seedlings like the pupil of the eye. Now also, God Who swells in the skies, prepare redemption for your people. We will praise You on the first day, so, please save us: Ani VaHu, please save us now. Ani VaHu, please save us now.

Kehosha'ta Segel. Degel Mul	כְּהוֹשַׁעְתָּ סֶגֶל. דֶּגֶל מוּל
Degel. Verosh Mo'adei Regel.	דֶּגֶל. וְרֹאשׁ מוֹעֲדֵי רֶגֶל.
Dishanta Dishon: Peduyei Aviv.	דִּשַּׁנְתָּ דִישׁוֹן: פְּדוּיֵי אָבִיב.

Nekuvei Am Chaviv. Sovevei Dat	נְקוּבֵי עַם חָבִיב. סוֹבְבֵי דַת
Saviv. Nehalach Beyom Rishon.	סָבִיב. נְהַלֵּךְ בְּיוֹם רִאשׁוֹן.
Ken Hosha'ana:	כֵּן הוֹשַׁעְנָא:
Ani Vahu Hoshi'ah Na.	אֲנִי וָהוּ הוֹשִׁיעָה נָּא.
Ani Vahu Hoshi'ah Na:	אֲנִי וָהוּ הוֹשִׁיעָה נָּא:

As you brought salvation to the chosen ones, banner by banner, and with the first of the pilgrimage festivals [Pesach], you generously enriched: The redeemed of the Spring, the people who are called beloved, the ones who surround the Law around. We will praise You on the first day, so, please save us: Ani VaHu, please save us now. Ani VaHu, please save us now.

Moshia' Chosim. Hoshia'	מוֹשִׁיעַ חוֹסִים. הוֹשִׁיעַ
Emunai. Am Bedatecha	אֱמוּנַי. עַם בְּדָתְךָ
Doreshim. Zera	דוֹרְשִׁים. זֶרַע
Eitanai: Hapa'am Hazot.	אֵיתָנַי: הַפַּעַם הַזֹּאת.
Odeh Et Adonai:	אוֹדֶה אֶת יְהֹוָה:

Savior of those who take refuge, save my faithful, the people who seek Your Law, the seed of my mighty-ones: This time, I will thank Hashem.

Retzeh Na Shav'atam. She'eh	רְצֵה נָא שַׁוְעָתָם. שְׁעֵה
Na Litfilatam. Bapa'am	נָא לִתְפִלָּתָם. בַּפַּעַם
Rishonah. Heyeh Na Eyalutam.	רִאשׁוֹנָה. הֱיֵה נָא אֱיָלוּתָם.
Am Asher Beyom Kippur.	עַם אֲשֶׁר בְּיוֹם כִּפּוּר.
Mipesha Peditam. Omerim	מִפֶּשַׁע פְּדִיתָם. אוֹמְרִים
Umehalelim. Ein Kadosh	וּמְהַלְּלִים. אֵין קָדוֹשׁ

K'Adonai: Hapa'am Hazot, כַּיהוָה: הַפַּעַם הַזֹּאת.

Odeh Et Adonai: אוֹדֶה אֶת יְהוָה:

Please favor their cries, please accept their prayers, on this first occasion, please be their protection. The people who on Yom Kippur, You redeemed from their transgression, saying and praising, there is none Holy like Hashem: This time, I will thank Hashem.

Kehosha'ta Me'az Adatecha. כְּהוֹשַׁעְתָּ מֵאָז עֲדָתֶךָ.

Ken Hoshi'ah Et-Amecha כֵּן הוֹשִׁיעָה אֶת־עַמֶּךָ

Uvarech Et-Nachalatecha. וּבָרֵךְ אֶת־נַחֲלָתֶךָ.

Nehalach Beyom Rishon. נְהַלֶּךְ בְּיוֹם רִאשׁוֹן.

Ken Hosha'ana: כֵּן הוֹשַׁעֲנָא:

As You saved Your congregation from then, so save Your people and bless Your inheritance. We will praise You on the first day, so please save us.

Ani Vahu Hoshi'ah Na. אֲנִי וָהוּ הוֹשִׁיעָה נָּא.

Ani Vahu Hoshi'ah Na: אֲנִי וָהוּ הוֹשִׁיעָה נָּא:

    Ani VaHu, please save us now. Ani VaHu, please save us now.

Kakatuv: Hoshi'ah Et-Amecha כַּכָּתוּב הוֹשִׁיעָה אֶת־עַמֶּךָ

Uvarech Et-Nachalatecha וּבָרֵךְ אֶת־נַחֲלָתֶךָ

Ure'em Venase'em Ad-Ha'olam: וּרְעֵם וְנַשְּׂאֵם עַד־הָעוֹלָם:

Vene'emar: Veyihyu Devarai Eleh וְנֶאֱמַר: וְיִהְיוּ דְבָרַי אֵלֶּה

Asher Hitchananti Lifnei אֲשֶׁר הִתְחַנַּנְתִּי לִפְנֵי

Adonai Kerovim El-Adonai יְהוָה קְרֹבִים אֶל־יְהוָה

Eloheinu Yomam Valayelah	אֱלֹהֵינוּ יוֹמָם וָלַיְלָה
La'asot Mishpat Avdo Umishpat	לַעֲשׂוֹת מִשְׁפַּט עַבְדּוֹ וּמִשְׁפַּט
Amo Yisra'el Devar-Yom	עַמּוֹ יִשְׂרָאֵל דְּבַר־יוֹם
Beyomo: Lema'an Da'at Kol-	בְּיוֹמוֹ: לְמַעַן דַּעַת כָּל־
Amei Ha'aretz Ki Adonai Hu	עַמֵּי הָאָרֶץ כִּי יְהוָה הוּא
Ha'elohim Ein Od: Lo-Yamush	הָאֱלֹהִים אֵין עוֹד: לֹא־יָמוּשׁ
Sefer Hatorah Hazeh Mipicha	סֵפֶר הַתּוֹרָה הַזֶּה מִפִּיךָ
Vehagita Bo Yomam Valaylah	וְהָגִיתָ בּוֹ יוֹמָם וָלַיְלָה
Lema'an Tishmor La'asot Kechol-	לְמַעַן תִּשְׁמֹר לַעֲשׂוֹת כְּכָל־
Hakatuv Bo Ki-Az Tatzliach Et-	הַכָּתוּב בּוֹ כִּי־אָז תַּצְלִיחַ אֶת־
Derachecha Ve'az Taskil: Halo	דְּרָכֶךָ וְאָז תַּשְׂכִּיל: הֲלוֹא
Tziviticha Chazak Ve'ematz Al-	צִוִּיתִיךָ חֲזַק וֶאֱמָץ אַל־
Ta'arotz Ve'al-Techat Ki Imecha	תַּעֲרֹץ וְאַל־תֵּחָת כִּי עִמְּךָ
Adonai Eloheicha Bechol Asher	יְהוָה אֱלֹהֶיךָ בְּכֹל אֲשֶׁר
Telech:	תֵּלֵךְ:

As it is written: Save Your people and bless Your inheritance, and shepherd them and exalt them forever. And says: May these words of my supplication before Hashem be close to Hashem our God, day and night, to do justice to His servant and justice to His people Yisrael, each matter day by day. So that all the peoples of the Earth may know that Hashem is God, there is no other. Do not let the Book of this Torah depart from your mouth, meditate on it day and night, in order that you may keep and do according to all that is written in it, for then you will succeed in your ways and then you will be wise. Have I not commanded you? Be strong and courageous, do not be afraid and do not be dismayed, for Hashem your God is with you wherever you go.

Hoshanot for the Second Day
הושענות ליום השני

Erchatz Benikayon Kapai

אֶרְחַץ בְּנִקָּיוֹן כַּפָּי

Va'asovevah Et-Mizbachacha

וַאֲסֹבְבָה אֶת־מִזְבַּחֲךָ

Adonai: Lashmia' Bekol Todah

יְהֹוָה: לַשְׁמִעַ בְּקוֹל תּוֹדָה

Ulesaper Kol-Nifle'oteicha.

וּלְסַפֵּר כָּל־נִפְלְאוֹתֶיךָ:

I will wash my hands in innocence, and I will encircle your altar, Hashem. That I may make the voice of thanksgiving to be heard, and tell of all Your wondrous works. (Ps. 26:6-7)

Hosha'ana. Hosha'ana:

הוֹשַׁעֲנָא. הוֹשַׁעֲנָא:

Please save us. Please save us:

Lema'anach Eloheinu.

לְמַעֲנָךְ אֱלֹהֵינוּ.

Lema'anach Bore'enu.

לְמַעֲנָךְ בּוֹרְאֵנוּ.

Lema'anach Go'alenu.

לְמַעֲנָךְ גּוֹאֲלֵנוּ.

Lema'anach Doreshenu:

לְמַעֲנָךְ דּוֹרְשֵׁנוּ:

For Your sake, our God. For Your sake, our Creator. For Your sake, our Redeemer. For Your sake, our Seeker.

Lema'anach Adir Adirim.

לְמַעֲנָךְ אַדִּיר אַדִּירִים.

Lema'anach Borei Ruach

לְמַעֲנָךְ בּוֹרֵא רוּחַ

Veyotzer Harim.

וְיוֹצֵר הָרִים.

Lema'anach Gedol Ha'etzah

לְמַעֲנָךְ גְּדוֹל הָעֵצָה

Mashpil Umerim.

מַשְׁפִּיל וּמֵרִים.

Lema'anach Dover Tzedek

לְמַעֲנָךְ דּוֹבֵר צֶדֶק

Magid Meisharim.	מַגִּיד מֵישָׁרִים.
Lema'anach Hayodea' Va'ed Im	לְמַעֲנָךְ הַיּוֹדֵעַ וָעֵד אִם
Yisater Ish Bemistarim.	יִסָּתֵר אִישׁ בְּמִסְתָּרִים.
Lema'anach Vehu Be'echad Umi	לְמַעֲנָךְ וְהוּא בְּאֶחָד וּמִי
Yeshivenu Amarim.	יְשִׁיבֵנוּ אֲמָרִים.
Lema'anach Zach Venaki	לְמַעֲנָךְ זַךְ וְנָקִי
Umitbarer Im Barim.	וּמִתְבָּרֵר עִם בָּרִים.
Lema'anach Chofes Matzpun	לְמַעֲנָךְ חוֹפֵשׂ מַצְפּוּן
Vechoker Kol-Chadarim.	וְחוֹקֵר כָּל־חֲדָרִים.
Lema'anach Tipechah Yemino	לְמַעֲנָךְ טִפְּחָה יְמִינוֹ
Shamayim Ve'asah Me'orim.	שָׁמַיִם וְעָשָׂה מְאוֹרִים.
Lema'anach Yasad Eretz Batzurot	לְמַעֲנָךְ יָסַד אֶרֶץ בַּצּוּרוֹת
Bika Ye'orim. Lema'anach Kabir	בִּקַּע יְאוֹרִים. לְמַעֲנָךְ כַּבִּיר
Koach Mechubad Ba'urim.	כֹּחַ מְכֻבָּד בָּאוּרִים.
Lema'anach Lo Yitamu Shenotav	לְמַעֲנָךְ לֹא יִתַּמּוּ שְׁנוֹתָיו
Ledor Dorim:	לְדוֹר דּוֹרִים:

For Your sake, Mightiest of the mighty. For Your sake, Creator of the wind and the Former of mountains. For Your sake, Great in counsel, Who humbles and lifts high. For Your sake, Speaker of righteousness, declaring uprightness. For Your sake, Knower and Witness, whether a person hides in secret places. For Your sake, He Who is One, and Who will return us with utterances. For Your sake, Pure and Innocent and Who is pure with the pure. For Your sake, Liberator of the hidden and Searcher of all chambers. For Your sake, He Who spread out the sky with His right hand and made the luminaries. For Your sake, He Who founded the earth with its boundaries, carving the rivers in rocks. For Your sake, the Great in Power, honored with lights. For Your sake, His years will never end for generations of generations:

Hosha'ana. Hosha'ana: הוֹשַׁעְנָא. הוֹשַׁעְנָא:

Please save us. Please save us:

Ana El Echad Umevayesh   אָנָּא אֵל אֶחָד וּמְבַיֵּשׁ

Omerim Shenayim. Bachatzi   אוֹמְרִים שְׁנָיִם. בַּחֲצִי

Hashem Bere Olamot Be'otiyot   הַשֵּׁם בָּרָא עוֹלָמוֹת בְּאוֹתִיּוֹת

Shenayim. Yatzar Hakol Ba'avur   שְׁנָיִם. יָצַר הַכֹּל בַּעֲבוּר

Adam Ve'ezro   אָדָם וְעֶזְרוֹ

Shenayim. Hoshi'enu   שְׁנָיִם. הוֹשִׁיעֵנוּ

Bachagigat Yamim Shenayim: בַּחֲגִיגַת יָמִים שְׁנָיִם:

Please, God, Who is One and Who humiliates those who say two. With half of the Name, He created worlds with two letters. He formed everything for the sake of man and his help, two. Save us on the celebration of two days:

Ana Zechor Av Benah Beveit El   אָנָּא זְכֹר אָב בָּנָה בְּבֵית אֵל

Mizbechot Shenayim.   מִזְבְּחוֹת שְׁנָיִם.

Benisayon Halach Im Ne'arim   בְּנִסָּיוֹן הָלַךְ עִם נְעָרִים

Shenayim. Ukerato Min-   שְׁנָיִם. וּקְרָאתוֹ מִן־

Hashamayim Pe'amim   הַשָּׁמַיִם פְּעָמִים

Shenayim. Hoshi'enu   שְׁנָיִם. הוֹשִׁיעֵנוּ

Bachagigat Yamim Shenayim: בַּחֲגִיגַת יָמִים שְׁנָיִם:

Please remember the father [Avraham] who built two altars in Bet-El. He went through trials with two youths. And You called him from heaven two times. Save us on the celebration of two days:

Ana Zechor Ben Hichmir   אָנָּא זְכֹר בֵּן הִכְמִיר

Rachamai Av Ba'amirot   רַחֲמַי אָב בַּאֲמִירוֹת

Shenayim. Chananto Goyim   שְׁנָיִם. חֲנַנְתּוֹ גוֹיִם

Shenayim Ule'umim Shenayim.   שְׁנַיִם וּלְאֻמִים שְׁנָיִם.

Vayvarech Heveh Gevir   וַיְבָרֶךְ הֱוֵה גְבִיר

Pe'amim Shenayim. Hoshi'enu   פְּעָמִים שְׁנָיִם. הוֹשִׁיעֵנוּ

Bachagigat Yamim Shenayim: בַּחֲגִיגַת יָמִים שְׁנָיִם:

Please remember the son who aroused the mercy of his father with two utterances. You favored him with two nations and two peoples. And he [Ya'akov] blessed him "to be a lord [over his brother]' two times. Save us on the celebration of two days:

Ana Zechor Hayah Tza'ir   אָנָּא זְכֹר הָיָה צָעִיר

Venachal Pi Shenayim. Ve'asah   וְנַחַל פִּי שְׁנָיִם. וְעָשָׂה

Mat'amim Gedayim Shenayim.   מַטְעַמִּים גְּדָיִים שְׁנָיִם.

Avar Bemaklo Et Hayarden   עָבַר בְּמַקְלוֹ אֶת הַיַּרְדֵּן

Vehayah Lemachanot   וְהָיָה לְמַחֲנוֹת

Shenayim. Hoshi'enu   שְׁנָיִם. הוֹשִׁיעֵנוּ

Bachagigat Yamim Shenayim: בַּחֲגִיגַת יָמִים שְׁנָיִם:

Please remember [Ya'akov] who was younger and inherited twice. And he made great delicacies from young goats, two. He crossed the Yarden with his staff and was two camps. Save us on the celebration of two days:

Ana Hamashmi'enu Torah Al-   אָנָּא הַמַּשְׁמִיעֵנוּ תּוֹרָה עַל־

Yedei Ro'im Shenayim.   יְדֵי רוֹעִים שְׁנָיִם.

Hamanchilenu Aseret Devarim   הַמַּנְחִילֵנוּ עֲשֶׂרֶת דְּבָרִים

Al Luchot Shenayim. Hama'azin   עַל לֻחוֹת שְׁנָיִם. הַמַּאֲזִין

Ume'id Banu Edim	וּמֵעִיד בָּנוּ עֵדִים
Shenayim. Hoshi'enu Bachagigat	שְׁנָיִם. הוֹשִׁיעֵנוּ בַּחֲגִיגַת
Yamim Shenayim:	יָמִים שְׁנָיִם:

Please, the One Who made us hear the Torah through two shepherds. Who bequeathed to us the Ten Commandments on two tablets. Who listens and bears witness for us with two witnesses. Save us on the celebration of two days:

Hosha'ana. Hosha'ana:	הוֹשַׁעֲנָא. הוֹשַׁעֲנָא:

Please save us. Please save us:

Elohim Eli Attah Ashacharecha.	אֱלֹהִים אֵלִי אַתָּה אֲשַׁחֲרֶךָ.
Me'eretz Shivyi Ufezuri. Esa	מֵאֶרֶץ שִׁבְיִי וּפְזוּרִי. אֶשָּׂא
Einai El-Heharim Me'ayin Yavo	עֵינַי אֶל־הֶהָרִים מֵאַיִן יָבֹא
Ezri. Bechol-Libi Derashticha	עֶזְרִי: בְּכָל־לִבִּי דְרַשְׁתִּיךָ
Hidaresh Li Me'aretz. Ezri Me'im	הִדָּרֵשׁ לִי מֵאֶרֶץ. עֶזְרִי מֵעִם
Adonai Oseh Shamayim	יְהֹוָה עֹשֵׂה שָׁמַיִם
Va'aretz. Gevuratecha Orerah	וָאָרֶץ: גְּבוּרָתְךָ אוֹרְרָה
Lene'enakim Beyad Rodam.	לְנֶאֱנָקִים בְּיַד רוֹדָם.
Havah-Lanu Ezrat Mitzar Veshave	הָבָה-לָנוּ עֶזְרַת מִצָּר וְשָׁב
Teshu'at Adam: **some add:** (Ge'Im	תְּשׁוּעַת אָדָם: יֵשׁ הַמּוֹסִיפִים: (גָּאִים
Be'orecham Migezerot	בְּאוֹרְחָם מִגְּזֵרוֹת
Semechim Legizrati. Hachazek	שְׂמֵחִים לִגְזֵרָתִי. הַחֲזֵק
Magen Vetzinah Vekumah	מָגֵן וְצִנָּה וְקוּמָה
Be'ezrati): Gemol Al-Avdecha	בְּעֶזְרָתִי): גְּמוֹל עַל-עַבְדֶּךָ
Echyeh Chavosh Lenafshi	אֶחְיֶה חֲבוֹשׁ לְנַפְשִׁי

Ha'anushah. Retzeh Adonai	הָעֲנוּשָׁה. רְצֵה יְהֹוָה
Lehatzileni Adonai Le'ezrati	לְהַצִּילֵנִי יְהֹוָה לְעֶזְרָתִי
Chushah: Davekah Le'afar	חוּשָׁה: דָּבְקָה לֶעָפָר
Nafshenu Betigrat Kameicha	נַפְשֵׁנוּ בְּתִגְרַת קָמֶיךָ
Lenegdecha. Kumah Ezratah	לְנֶגְדֶּךָ. קוּמָה עֶזְרָתָה
Lanu Ufedenu Lema'an	לָּנוּ וּפְדֵנוּ לְמַעַן
Chasdecha: Himatze Li Vekare'i	חַסְדֶּךָ: הִמָּצֵא לִי בְקָרְאִי
Tzur Yish'i Vego'ali. Shema-	צוּר יִשְׁעִי וְגוֹאֲלִי. שְׁמַע-
Adonai Vechaneni Adonai	יְהֹוָה וְחָנֵּנִי יְהֹוָה
Heyeh-Ozer Li. Ve'e'eneh	הֱיֵה-עוֹזֵר לִי. וְאֶעֱנֶה
Chorefi Davar Be'uzecha El	חוֹרְפִי דָבָר בְּעֻזְּךָ אֵל
Ozer. Yatom Attah Hayita Ozer:	עוֹזֵר. יָתוֹם אַתָּה הָיִיתָ עוֹזֵר:

God, You are my God; I earnestly seek You from a land of captivity and dispersion. I will lift my eyes to the mountains, where does my help come from? I have sought You with all my heart, answer me from the heavens. My help is from Hashem, Who created Heaven and earth. Awaken your might and help those who groan under the hand of their oppressor. Grant us help against the oppressor; salvation from man is in vain. **some add:** (Proud in their path, they rejoice in My decree. Take up shield and buckler, and come to my defense.) Show favor to your servant that I shall live, bandage my humbled soul. May Hashem desire to save me. Hasten, Hashem, hasten to my aid. Our souls have clung to the dust in the face those who rise against You. Arise to help us and redeem us for the sake of Your loving kindness. Answer me when I call, Rock of my salvation, and my Redeemer. Hashem, hear and favor me. Hashem, be a Helper to me. I will answer those who reproach me with Your strength, God, my Helper. You are Helper to the fatherless.

Zeruyim Bekatzvei Eretz Asher
בְּקַצְוֵי אֶרֶץ אֲשֶׁר זְרוּיִים

Beheichal Devircha Yinhu.
בְּהֵיכַל דְּבִירְךָ יִנְהוּ.

Nafshenu Chiketah L'Adonai
נַפְשֵׁנוּ חִכְּתָה לַיהֹוָה

Ezrenu Umaginenu Hu:
עֶזְרֵנוּ וּמָגִנֵּנוּ הוּא:

Charedim Bekatzvei Eretz
חֲרֵדִים בְּקַצְוֵי אֶרֶץ

Mehagot Geronam Nichar.
מֵהָגוֹת גְּרוֹנָם נִחַר.

Ezrati Umefaleti Attah Elohai
עֶזְרָתִי וּמְפַלְטִי אַתָּה אֱלֹהַי

Al-Te'achar: Taruf Balua'
אַל-תְּאַחַר: תָּרוּף בָּלוּעַ

Befihem Umisham Tzidkatecha
בְּפִיהֶם וּמִשָּׁם צִדְקָתְךָ

Atanen. Ki-Hayita Ezratah Li
אֲתַנֵּן. כִּי-הָיִיתָ עֶזְרָתָה לִּי

Uvetzel Kenafeicha Aranen:
וּבְצֵל כְּנָפֶיךָ אֲרַנֵּן:

Yodea' Vechoker Kelayot
יוֹדֵעַ וְחוֹקֵר כְּלָיוֹת

Uma'aseh Yadav Uma'alo. Ki-
וּמַעֲשֵׂה יָדָיו וּמַעֲלָלוֹ. כִּי-

Yatzil Evyon Meshavea' Ve'ani
יַצִּיל אֶבְיוֹן מְשַׁוֵּעַ וְעָנִי

Ve'ein-Ozer Lo: Kalu Einai
וְאֵין-עוֹזֵר לוֹ: כָּלוּ עֵינַי

Meyachel She'eh Et Shav'ati.
מְיַחֵל שְׁעֵה אֶת שַׁוְעָתִי.

Chushah Le'ezrati Adonai
חוּשָׁה לְעֶזְרָתִי אֲדֹנָי

Teshu'ati:
תְּשׁוּעָתִי:

The scattered in the ends of the earth scream in Your sanctuary. Our souls wait for Hashem, He is our Help and our Shield. Those trembling at the ends of the earth, from weeping, their throats are parched. You are my Helper and Refuge, God, do not delay. Torn and swallowed in their mouths, and from there Your righteousness I will tell, for You have been my Help and I will sing under the shadow of Your wings. You, Who knows and searches the depths of the heart and the work of hands and actions, For He will deliver the poor from the oppressor and the needy when there is no one to help. My eyes fail from longing to see my salvation. Hasten to my aid, my Lord, my Salvation.

Lech Ani Hoshi'eni Mishgabi	לָךְ אֲנִי הוֹשִׁיעֵנִי מִשְׂגַּבִּי
Umerim Roshi. Hineh Elohim	וּמֵרִים רֹאשִׁי. הִנֵּה אֱלֹהִים
Ozer Li Adonai Besomechei	עוֹזֵר לִי אֲדֹנָי בְּסוֹמְכֵי
Nafshi: Misho'eihem Tashiv	נַפְשִׁי: מְשׁוֹאֵיהֶם תָּשִׁיב
Nafshi Veshoveveni. Ezrati	נַפְשִׁי וְשׁוֹבְבֵנִי. עֶזְרָתִי
Hayita Al-Titesheni Ve'al-	הָיִיתָ אַל־תִּטְּשֵׁנִי וְאַל־
Ta'azveni. Neveh Kadeshech	תַּעַזְבֵנִי: נְוֵה קָדְשֵׁךְ
Keme'az Teshachlel Uteyaker	כְּמֵאָז תְּשַׁכְלֵל וּתְיַקֵּר
Yeker. Ya'zereha Elohim Lifnot	יֶקֶר. יַעְזְרֶהָ אֱלֹהִים לִפְנוֹת
Boker: Seridei Yehudah Tevaker	בֹּקֶר: שְׂרִידֵי יְהוּדָה תְּבַקֵּר
Uvetzel Kenafeicha Nichyeh.	וּבְצֵל כְּנָפֶיךָ נִחְיֶה.
Yadav Rav Lo Ve'ezer Mitzarav	יָדָיו רָב לוֹ וְעֵזֶר מִצָּרָיו
Tihyeh: Ir Mo'adenu Asher	תִּהְיֶה: עִיר מוֹעֲדֵנוּ אֲשֶׁר
Misham Nitza'enu. Ezrenu	מִשָּׁם נִצַּעְנוּ. עֶזְרֵנוּ
Elohei Yish'anu Ki Vach	אֱלֹהֵי יִשְׁעֵנוּ כִּי בָךְ
Nosha'anu: Paroach Tifrach	נוֹשַׁעְנוּ: פָּרֹחַ תִּפְרַח
Vetagel Michyah Betitam	וְתָגֵל מִחְיָה בְּתִתָּם
Kolam. Ki Ezrat Avoteinu.	קוֹלָם. כִּי עֶזְרַת אֲבוֹתֵינוּ.
Attah Hu Me'olam:	אַתָּה הוּא מֵעוֹלָם:

I am Yours, save me my Stronghold, Who lifts up my head. Behold, God is my Helper; Hashem supports my soul. Rescue my soul from their destruction and let me be restored, for You have been my Help. Do not forsake or abandon me. Your holy dwelling, from the beginning, is majestic and precious. God will help her when morning dawns. The remnant of Yehudah, You will visit, and will be sheltered under Your wings and live. His hands are mighty for Him, and will be His help against his enemies. Our appointed city from which we were exiled, help us, God of our salvation, for through You we are saved. May it blossom and rejoice and reveal life as they raise their voices. For You have been the help of our ancestors forever.

Tzur Yom Rishon Bekachtenu	צוּר יוֹם רִאשׁוֹן בְּקַחְתֵּנוּ
Leromemecha. Ozrenu Elohei	לְרוֹמְמֶךָ. עָזְרֵנוּ אֱלֹהֵי
Yish'enu Al-Devar Kevod-	יִשְׁעֵנוּ עַל־דְּבַר כְּבוֹד־
Shemecha: Kesher Agudah	שְׁמֶךָ: קֶשֶׁר אֲגֻדָּה
Ashlim Lehodot Shimcha Azarti.	אַשְׁלִים לְהוֹדוֹת שְׁמֶךָ אָזַרְתִּי.
Bo Vatach Libi Vene'ezareti:	בּוֹ בָטַח לִבִּי וְנֶעֱזָרְתִּי:

Rock of the first day, when You gather us to exalt You, help us, God of our salvation, for the sake of Your glorious name: I will complete the union to give thanks to your name, I have girded myself. In Him my heart trusted, and I was helped:

Ratzti Bechapot Temarim Ratzah	רָצִתִּי בְּכַפּוֹת תְּמָרִים רָצָה
Leha'avir Shimtzah. Elohim	לְהַעֲבִיר שִׁמְצָה. אֱלֹהִים
Lanu Machaseh Va'oz Ezrah	לָנוּ מַחֲסֶה וָעֹז עֶזְרָה
Vetzarot Nimtza: Shokedei Anaf	בְּצָרוֹת נִמְצָא: שׁוֹקְדֵי עֶנַף
Avot Peri Ve'arvei Nachali.	עֲבוֹת פְּרִי וְעַרְבֵי נַחֲלִי.
Vadonai Elohim Ya'azor-Li: Ta'as	וַאדֹנָי אֱלֹהִים יַעֲזָר־לִי: תַּעַשׂ
Imanu Ot Letovah Veyit'asherun	עִמָּנוּ אוֹת לְטוֹבָה וְיִתְאַשְּׁרוּן
Becha Bechireicha. Am Nosha	בָּךְ בְּחִירֶיךָ. עַם נוֹשַׁע
B'Adonai Magen Ezrecha:	בַּיהוָה מָגֵן עֶזְרֶךָ:
Vetere Oyavti Vetevosh Asher	וְתֵרֶא אוֹיַבְתִּי וְתֵבוֹשׁ אֲשֶׁר
Ge'altanu. Ki-Atah	גְאַלְתָּנוּ. כִּי־אַתָּה
Adonai Azartanu Venichamtanu:	יְהוָה עֲזַרְתָּנוּ וְנִחַמְתָּנוּ:

I have hurried with palm branches, he desired to remove my disgrace. God is a refuge and strength for us, a very present help in trouble: the branches of the tree are thick with fruit and the willows of the brook. And Hashem-Elohim will help me: perform a sign for our good, and let Your chosen ones prosper in You. A people saved by Hashem, Your protective Shield: and let my enemy see and be ashamed because You have redeemed us. For You, Hashem, have helped us and comforted us.

Hosha'ana. Hosha'ana:	הוֹשַׁעֲנָא. הוֹשַׁעֲנָא:

Please save us. Please save us:

Ana Hoshi'ah Na.	אָנָּא הוֹשִׁיעָה נָּא.
Ana Hoshi'ah Na:	אָנָּא הוֹשִׁיעָה נָּא:

Please save us now. Please save us now:

Ana Yotzeri Daresheni.	אָנָּא יוֹצְרִי דָּרְשֵׁנִי.
Vechimei Olam Chafesheni.	וְכִימֵי עוֹלָם חָפְּשֵׁנִי.
Umadei Hodecha Talbisheni.	וּמַדֵּי הוֹדְךָ תַּלְבִּישֵׁנִי.
Hayom Beyom Sheni. Hoshi'ah	הַיּוֹם בְּיוֹם שֵׁנִי. הוֹשִׁיעָה
Na: Ana Hoshi'ah Na.	נָּא: אָנָּא הוֹשִׁיעָה נָּא.
Ana Hoshi'ah Na:	אָנָּא הוֹשִׁיעָה נָּא:

Please, my Creator, seek me. And as in ancient days, search for me. And with your glory, clothe me. Today, on the second day. Please save us: Please save us now. Please save us now:

Ana Sov Na Vehanfisheni.	אָנָּא סֹב נָא וְהַנְפִישֵׁנִי.
Umimeimei Metzulah	וּמִמֵּימֵי מְצוּלָה הַמְשֵׁנִי. פְּנֵה
Hamsheni. Peneh Eli Ve'al	אֵלִי וְאַל תְּבִישֵׁנִי. הַיּוֹם בְּיוֹם
Tevisheni. Hayom Beyom Sheni.	שֵׁנִי. הוֹשִׁיעָה נָּא: אָנָּא
Hoshi'ah Na: Ana Hoshi'ah Na.	הוֹשִׁיעָה נָּא. אָנָּא הוֹשִׁיעָה
Ana Hoshi'ah Na:	נָּא:

Please, turn now and revive me. And from the depths of the waters, draw me. Turn to me and do not put me to shame. Today, on the second day. Please save us: Please save us now. Please save us now:

Ani Vahu Hoshi'ah Na. Ani	אֲנִי וָהוּ הוֹשִׁיעָה נָּא. אֲנִי וָהוּ
Vahu Hoshi'ah Na:	הוֹשִׁיעָה נָּא:

Ani VaHu, please save us now. Ani VaHu, please save us now:

Kehosha'ta Yegi'ei Neshem.	כְּהוֹשַׁעְתָּ יְגִיעֵי נֶשֶׁם.
Umukei Gev Vageshem.	וּמֻכֵּי גֵו וָגֶשֶׁם.
Vaye'shemu Ashem. Atzim	וַיֶּאְשְׁמוּ אָשֵׁם. אָצִים
Lenakesheni: Sochachei Filul,	לְנַקְּשֵׁנִי: סוֹחֲחֵי פִלּוּל.
Petzot Lecha Hilul, Lesalselach	פְּצוֹת לְךָ הִלּוּל, לְסַלְסְלָךְ
Bemilul. Nehalach Beyom	בְּמִלּוּל. נְהַלֶּלְךָ בְּיוֹם
Sheni. Ken Hosha'ana.	שֵׁנִי. כֵּן הוֹשַׁעֲנָא.
Ani Vahu Hoshi'ah Na.	אֲנִי וָהוּ הוֹשִׁיעָה נָּא.
Ani Vahu Hoshi'ah Na:	אֲנִי וָהוּ הוֹשִׁיעָה נָּא:

As you saved those who labored for breath, wounded physically and in body. Condemn those who hasten to entangle me. So too, save those who whisper prayers, who open their mouths to You in praise to exalt You with words. We shall praise You on the second day. So save us. Ani VaHu, please save us now. Ani VaHu, please save us now:

Kehosha'ta Yotze'ei Chanes.	כְּהוֹשַׁעְתָּ יוֹצְאֵי חָנֵס.
Bemofet Vanes. Veshichata Ones.	בְּמוֹפֵת וָנֵס. וְשִׁחַת אוֹנֵס.
Choshek Lechabesheni: Seridei	חוֹשֵׁק לְכַבְּשֵׁנִי: שְׂרִידֵי

Adatecha. Sovevei Te'udatecha.	עֲדָתֶךָ. סוֹבְבֵי תְעוּדָתֶךָ.
Potzechei Afudatecha. Nehalach	פּוֹצְחֵי אֲפוּדָתֶךָ. נְהַלֶּלְךָ
Beyom Sheni. Ken Hosha'ana.	בְּיוֹם שֵׁנִי. כֵּן הוֹשַׁעֲנָא.
Ani Vahu Hoshi'ah Na.	אֲנִי וָהוֹ הוֹשִׁיעָה נָּא.
Ani Vahu Hoshi'ah Na:	אֲנִי וָהוֹ הוֹשִׁיעָה נָּא:

As you saved those who escaped the snare, with wonder and miracle, and destroyed the oppressor who wanted to subdue me: The remnants of Your congregation, those who surround Your testimony, those who break open Your ephod [Torah]. We shall praise You on the second day. So save us. Ani VaHu, please save us now. Ani VaHu, please save us now:

Chaletah Penei Adoneiha. Am	חָלְתָה פְּנֵי אֲדוֹנֶיהָ. עַם
Atzur Berov Pachad. Vesovevah	עָצוּר בְּרוֹב פַּחַד. וְסוֹבְבָה
Beveit Eloheiha. Shetei Fe'amim	בְּבֵית אֱלֹהֶיהָ. שְׁתֵּי פְּעָמִים
Belev Yachad. Ve'anetah Ki	בְּלֵב יַחַד. וְעָנְתָה כִּי
Tovim Hashenayim Min	טוֹבִים הַשְּׁנַיִם מִן
Ha'echad:	הָאֶחָד:

She became pale in her Lord's presence. The people were confined in great fear, and she encircled her God's house two times with a united heart. And she answered that two are better than one:

Tov Tikach Mimenu. Yadecha	טוֹב תִּקַּח מִמֶּנּוּ. יָדְךָ
Te'atzemenu. Miyomayim	תְּעַצְּמֵנוּ. מִיּוֹמַיִם
Techayenu. Uvashelishi	תְּחַיֵּנוּ. וּבַשְּׁלִישִׁי
Tekimenu. Ha'el Asher Mimenu.	תְּקִימֵנוּ. הָאֵל אֲשֶׁר מִמֶּנּוּ.
Kol-Davar Lo Nichchad.	כָּל־דָּבָר לֹא נִכְחַד.
Ve'anetah Ki Tovim Hashenayim	וְעָנְתָה כִּי טוֹבִים הַשְּׁנַיִם
Min Ha'echad:	מִן הָאֶחָד:

Accept goodness from us. Your hand will strengthen us. You will revive us in two days. And on the third day, raise us up. The God from Whom nothing is hidden. And she answered that two are better than one:

Kehosha'ta Me'az Adatecha.	כְּהוֹשַׁעְתָּ מֵאָז עֲדָתֶךָ.
Ken Hoshi'ah Et-Amecha	כֵּן הוֹשִׁיעָה אֶת־עַמֶּךָ
Uvarech Et-Nachalatecha.	וּבָרֵךְ אֶת־נַחֲלָתֶךָ.
Nehalach Beyom Sheni.	נְהַלֶּךְ בְּיוֹם שֵׁנִי.
Ken Hosha'ana:	כֵּן הוֹשַׁעֲנָא:

As You have saved, since then, Your congregation, so save Your people and bless Your inheritance. We will praise you on the second day. So, please save us:

Ani Vahu Hoshi'ah Na. Ani	אֲנִי וָהוּ הוֹשִׁיעָה נָּא. אֲנִי וָהוּ
Vahu Hoshi'ah Na:	הוֹשִׁיעָה נָּא:

    Ani VaHu, please save us. Ani VaHu, please save us:

Kakatuv: Hoshi'ah Et-Amecha	כַּכָּתוּב הוֹשִׁיעָה אֶת־עַמֶּךָ
Uvarech Et-Nachalatecha	וּבָרֵךְ אֶת־נַחֲלָתֶךָ
Ure'em Venase'em Ad-Ha'olam:	וּרְעֵם וְנַשְּׂאֵם עַד־הָעוֹלָם:
Vene'emar: Veyihyu Devarai Eleh	וְנֶאֱמַר: וְיִהְיוּ דְבָרַי אֵלֶּה
Asher Hitchananti Lifnei	אֲשֶׁר הִתְחַנַּנְתִּי לִפְנֵי
Adonai Kerovim El-Adonai	יְהֹוָה קְרֹבִים אֶל־יְהֹוָה
Eloheinu Yomam Valayelah	אֱלֹהֵינוּ יוֹמָם וָלַיְלָה
La'asot Mishpat Avdo Umishpat	לַעֲשׂוֹת מִשְׁפַּט עַבְדּוֹ וּמִשְׁפַּט

Amo Yisra'el Devar-Yom

Beyomo: Lema'an Da'at Kol-

Amei Ha'aretz Ki Adonai Hu

Ha'elohim Ein Od: Lo-Yamush

Sefer Hatorah Hazeh Mipicha

Vehagita Bo Yomam Valaylah

Lema'an Tishmor La'asot Kechol-

Hakatuv Bo Ki-Az Tatzliach Et-

Derachecha Ve'az Taskil: Halo

Tziviticha Chazak Ve'ematz Al-

Ta'arotz Ve'al-Techat Ki Imecha

Adonai Eloheicha Bechol Asher

Telech:

עַמּוֹ יִשְׂרָאֵל דְּבַר־יוֹם

בְּיוֹמוֹ: לְמַעַן דַּעַת כָּל־

עַמֵּי הָאָרֶץ כִּי יְהֹוָה הוּא

הָאֱלֹהִים אֵין עוֹד: לֹא־יָמוּשׁ

סֵפֶר הַתּוֹרָה הַזֶּה מִפִּיךָ

וְהָגִיתָ בּוֹ יוֹמָם וָלַיְלָה

לְמַעַן תִּשְׁמֹר לַעֲשׂוֹת כְּכָל־

הַכָּתוּב בּוֹ כִּי־אָז תַּצְלִיחַ אֶת־

דְּרָכֶךָ וְאָז תַּשְׂכִּיל: הֲלוֹא

צִוִּיתִיךָ חֲזַק וֶאֱמָץ אַל־

תַּעֲרֹץ וְאַל־תֵּחָת כִּי עִמְּךָ

יְהֹוָה אֱלֹהֶיךָ בְּכֹל אֲשֶׁר

תֵּלֵךְ:

As it is written: Save Your people and bless Your inheritance, and shepherd them and exalt them forever. And says: May these words of my supplication before Hashem be close to Hashem our God, day and night, to do justice to His servant and justice to His people Yisrael, each matter day by day. So that all the peoples of the Earth may know that Hashem is God, there is no other. Do not let the Book of this Torah depart from your mouth, meditate on it day and night, in order that you may keep and do according to all that is written in it, for then you will succeed in your ways and then you will be wise. Have I not commanded you? Be strong and courageous, do not be afraid and do not be dismayed, for Hashem your God is with you wherever you go.

Hoshanot for the Third day
הושענות ליום השלישי

Erchatz Benikayon Kapai　　אֶרְחַץ בְּנִקָּיוֹן כַּפָּי

Va'asovevah Et-Mizbachacha　　וַאֲסֹבְבָה אֶת־מִזְבַּחֲךָ

Adonai: Lashmia' Bekol Todah　　יְהוָה: לַשְׁמִעַ בְּקוֹל תּוֹדָה

Ulesaper Kol-Nifle'oteicha.　　וּלְסַפֵּר כָּל־נִפְלְאוֹתֶיךָ:

I will wash my hands in innocence, and I will encircle your altar, Hashem. That I may make the voice of thanksgiving to be heard, and tell of all Your wondrous works. (Ps. 26:6-7)

Hosha'ana. Hosha'ana:　　הוֹשַׁעֲנָא. הוֹשַׁעֲנָא:

Please save us. Please save us:

Lema'anach Eloheinu.　　לְמַעַנְךָ אֱלֹהֵינוּ.

Lema'anach Bore'enu.　　לְמַעַנְךָ בּוֹרְאֵנוּ.

Lema'anach Go'alenu.　　לְמַעַנְךָ גּוֹאֲלֵנוּ.

Lema'anach Doreshenu:　　לְמַעַנְךָ דּוֹרְשֵׁנוּ:

For Your sake, our God. For Your sake, our Creator. For Your sake, our Redeemer. For Your sake, our Seeker.

Lema'anach Adir Adirim.　　לְמַעַנְךָ אַדִּיר אַדִּירִים.

Lema'anach Borei Ruach　　לְמַעַנְךָ בּוֹרֵא רוּחַ

Veyotzer Harim.　　וְיוֹצֵר הָרִים.

Lema'anach Gedol Ha'etzah　　לְמַעַנְךָ גְּדוֹל הָעֵצָה

Mashpil Umerim.　　מַשְׁפִּיל וּמֵרִים.

Lema'anach Dover Tzedek　　לְמַעַנְךָ דּוֹבֵר צֶדֶק

Magid Meisharim.	מַגִּיד מֵישָׁרִים.
Lema'anach Hayodea' Va'ed Im	לְמַעַנְךָ הַיּוֹדֵעַ וָעֵד אִם
Yisater Ish Bemistarim.	יִסָּתֵר אִישׁ בְּמִסְתָּרִים.
Lema'anach Vehu Be'echad Umi	לְמַעַנְךָ וְהוּא בְּאֶחָד וּמִי
Yeshivenu Amarim.	יְשִׁיבֵנוּ אֲמָרִים.
Lema'anach Zach Venaki	לְמַעַנְךָ זַךְ וְנָקִי
Umitbarer Im Barim.	וּמִתְבָּרֵר עִם בָּרִים.
Lema'anach Chofes Matzpun	לְמַעַנְךָ חוֹפֵשׂ מַצְפּוּן
Vechoker Kol-Chadarim.	וְחוֹקֵר כָּל־חֲדָרִים.
Lema'anach Tipechah Yemino	לְמַעַנְךָ טִפְּחָה יְמִינוֹ
Shamayim Ve'asah Me'orim.	שָׁמַיִם וְעָשָׂה מְאוֹרִים.
Lema'anach Yasad Eretz Batzurot	לְמַעַנְךָ יָסַד אֶרֶץ בַּצּוּרוֹת
Bika Ye'orim. Lema'anach Kabir	בִּקַּע יְאוֹרִים. לְמַעַנְךָ כַּבִּיר
Koach Mechubad Ba'urim.	כֹּחַ מְכֻבָּד בָּאוּרִים.
Lema'anach Lo Yitamu Shenotav	לְמַעַנְךָ לֹא יִתַּמּוּ שְׁנוֹתָיו
Ledor Dorim:	לְדוֹר דּוֹרִים:

For Your sake, Mightiest of the mighty. For Your sake, Creator of the wind and the Former of mountains. For Your sake, Great in counsel, Who humbles and lifts high. For Your sake, Speaker of righteousness, declaring uprightness. For Your sake, Knower and Witness, whether a person hides in secret places. For Your sake, He Who is One, and Who will return us with utterances. For Your sake, Pure and Innocent and Who is pure with the pure. For Your sake, Liberator of the hidden and Searcher of all chambers. For Your sake, He Who spread out the sky with His right hand and made the luminaries. For Your sake, He Who founded the earth with its boundaries, carving the rivers in rocks. For Your sake, the Great in Power, honored with lights. For Your sake, His years will never end for generations of generations:

Hosha'ana. Hosha'ana:	הוֹשַׁעְנָא. הוֹשַׁעְנָא:

Please save us. Please save us:

Ana Ha'el Hanikdash Bikdushot	אָנָּא הָאֵל הַנִּקְדָּשׁ בִּקְדֻשּׁוֹת
Sheloshah. Bara Bema'aseh	שְׁלֹשָׁה. בָּרָא בְּמַעֲשֵׂה
Vereshit Bechol-Yom Sheloshah.	בְרֵאשִׁית בְּכָל־יוֹם שְׁלֹשָׁה.
Uveshishi Uvashevi'i Sheloshah	וּבְשִׁשִּׁי וּבַשְּׁבִיעִי שְׁלֹשָׁה
Sheloshah. Hoshi'enu	שְׁלֹשָׁה. הוֹשִׁיעֵנוּ
Bachagigat Yamim Sheloshah:	בַּחֲגִיגַת יָמִים שְׁלֹשָׁה:

Please, God, Who is sanctified with three sanctifications. Who created in the acts of creation each day with three. And on the sixth and seventh, three and three. Save us on the celebration of three days:

Ana Zechor Av Ra'ah Mal'achim	אָנָּא זְכֹר אָב רָאָה מַלְאָכִים
Sheloshah. Vaymaher	שְׁלֹשָׁה. וַיְמַהֵר
Lehas'idam Se'im Sheloshah.	לְהַסְעִידָם סְאִים שְׁלֹשָׁה.
Halechu Ito Ba'alei Berit	הָלְכוּ אִתּוֹ בַּעֲלֵי בְּרִית
Sheloshah. Hoshi'enu	שְׁלֹשָׁה. הוֹשִׁיעֵנוּ
Bachagigat Yamim Sheloshah:	בַּחֲגִיגַת יָמִים שְׁלֹשָׁה:

Please, remember the father [Avraham] who saw three angels. And he hurried to prepare for them three semi [measures]. Three allies went with him. Save us on the celebration of three days:

Ana Zechor Ben Huchan	אָנָּא זְכֹר בֶּן הוּכַן
La'akedah Leyamim Sheloshah.	לַעֲקֵדָה לְיָמִים שְׁלֹשָׁה.
Karat Berit Im Melech	כָּרַת בְּרִית עִם מֶלֶךְ
Umere'ehu Vesar Tzeva'o	וּמֵרֵעֵהוּ וְשַׂר צְבָאוֹ

Sheloshah. Bizchuto Nachalu Vanav Ketarim Sheloshah. Hoshi'enu Bachagigat Yamim Sheloshah:

שְׁלֹשָׁה. בִּזְכוּתוֹ נָחֲלוּ בָּנָיו כְּתָרִים שְׁלֹשָׁה. הוֹשִׁיעֵנוּ בַּחֲגִיגַת יָמִים שְׁלֹשָׁה:

Please, remember the son [Yitzchak] who was prepared for the binding for three days. He made a covenant with the king, and his friend, and the army chief, three. By his merit, his sons inherited three crowns. Save us on the celebration of three days:

Ana Zechor Av Chazah Sulam Be'olim Veyoredim Sheloshah. Ufitzel Barehatim Maklot Sheloshah. Vayshalach Banav Letzo'an Pe'amim Sheloshah. Hoshi'enu Bachagigat Yamim Sheloshah:

אָנָּא זְכֹר אָב חָזָה סֻלָּם בְּעוֹלִים וְיוֹרְדִים שְׁלֹשָׁה. וּפִצֵּל בָּרְהָטִים מַקְלוֹת שְׁלֹשָׁה. וַיִּשְׁלַח בָּנָיו לְצֹעַן פְּעָמִים שְׁלֹשָׁה. הוֹשִׁיעֵנוּ בַּחֲגִיגַת יָמִים שְׁלֹשָׁה:

Please, remember the father [Ya'akov] who saw a ladder with ascending and descending, three [angels]. And he carved with a chisel three sticks. And he sent his sons to Zoan three times. Save us on the celebration of three days:

Ana Hago'alenu Al-Yedei Achim Sheloshah. Hassam Banu Ma'alot Kohanim Leviyim Veyisra'el Sheloshah. Hamanchilenu Torah Nevi'im Uchetuvim Sheloshah.

אָנָּא הַגּוֹאֲלֵנוּ עַל־יְדֵי אַחִים שְׁלֹשָׁה. הַשָּׂם בָּנוּ מַעֲלוֹת כֹּהֲנִים לְוִיִם וְיִשְׂרָאֵל שְׁלֹשָׁה. הַמַּנְחִילֵנוּ תּוֹרָה נְבִיאִים וּכְתוּבִים שְׁלֹשָׁה.

Hoshi'enu Bachagigat Yamim Sheloshah:

הוֹשִׁיעֵנוּ בַּחֲגִיגַת יָמִים שְׁלֹשָׁה:

Please, our Redeemer, through brothers who were three. He placed among us three levels: Kohanim, Levi'im, and Yisrael. He gave to us the Torah, Nevi'im, and Ketuvim, three. Save us on the celebration of three days:

Hosha'ana. Hosha'ana:

הוֹשַׁעְנָא. הוֹשַׁעְנָא:

Please save us. Please save us:

Ametzeni Elohai Bemo'adi Vachagigi. Amarai Ha'azinah Adonai Binah Hagigi:

אַמְּצֵנִי אֱלֹהַי בְּמוֹעֲדִי וַחֲגִיגִי. אֲמָרַי הַאֲזִינָה יְהוָה בִּינָה הֲגִיגִי:

Behityatzevi Lefaneicha Kedal Sho'el Ledorshecha. Benase'i Yadai El-Devir Kodshecha:

בְּהִתְיַצְבִי לְפָנֶיךָ כְּדַל שׁוֹאֵל לְדָרְשֶׁךָ. בְּנַשְׂאִי יָדַי אֶל־דְּבִיר קָדְשֶׁךָ:

Genon Nochalei Dat Peliliyah. Gedol Ha'etzah Verav Ha'aliliyah: Devarecha Hakem Lameyachalei Retzonecha. Dor Doreshav Mevakshei Faneicha:

גְּנוֹן נוֹחֲלֵי דַת פְּלִילִיָּה. גְּדָל הָעֵצָה וְרַב הָעֲלִילִיָּה: דְּבָרְךָ הָקֵם לִמְיַחֲלֵי רְצוֹנֶךָ. דּוֹר דֹּרְשָׁיו מְבַקְשֵׁי פָנֶיךָ:

Hemyat Kore'eicha Leshochareicha Shachar. Adonai Hakshivah Va'aseh Al-Te'achar:

הֶמְיַת קוֹרְאֶיךָ לְשׁוֹחֲרֶיךָ שַׁחַר. אֲדֹנָי הַקְשִׁיבָה וַעֲשֵׂה אַל־תְּאַחַר:

Ufihem Lo Yichlu Miyichud Shemecha. Attah Adonai Lo-

וּפִיהֶם לֹא יְכְלוּ מִיִחוּד שְׁמֶךָ. אַתָּה יְהוָה לֹא־

Tichla Rachameicha: Zechar-	תִּכְלָא רַחֲמֶיךָ: זְכָר־
Davar Le'avdecha Al Asher	דָּבָר לְעַבְדְּךָ עַל אֲשֶׁר
Yichaltanu. Zechor Al-Tafer	יִחַלְתָּנוּ. זְכֹר אַל־תָּפֵר
Beritcha Itanu: Chon Shotechim	בְּרִיתְךָ אִתָּנוּ: חֹן שׁוֹטְחִים
Eleicha Kapayim. Chanun	אֵלֶיךָ כַּפָּיִם. חַנּוּן
Verachum Adonai Erech	וְרַחוּם יְהֹוָה אֶרֶךְ
Apayim: Tuvecha Meyachalim	אַפָּיִם: טוּבְךָ מְיַחֲלִים
Lamo Techishenu. Tov	לָמוֹ תְּחִישֵׁנוּ. טוֹב
Adonai Lekovav Lenefesh	יְהֹוָה לְקֹוָו לְנֶפֶשׁ
Tidreshenu: Yasisu Veyismechu	תִּדְרְשֶׁנּוּ: יָשִׂישׂוּ וְיִשְׂמְחוּ
Becha Dallai Ve'evyonai. Yomru	בְּךָ דַּלַּי וְאֶבְיוֹנָי. יֹאמְרוּ
Tamid Yigdal Adonai: Konen	תָמִיד יִגְדַּל יְהֹוָה: כּוֹנֵן
Segulah Asher Leshimcha	סְגֻלָּה אֲשֶׁר לְשִׁמְךָ
Shatah. Ki-Tif'eret Uzamo	שָׁתָה. כִּי־תִפְאֶרֶת עֻזָּמוֹ
Atah: Mager Tzorerei Amecha	אַתָּה: מַגֵּר צוֹרְרֵי עַמֶּךָ
Asher Tamid Yeshimenu. Matzil	אֲשֶׁר תָּמִיד יְשִׂימֵנוּ. מַצִּיל
Ani Mechazak Mimenu:	עָנִי מֵחָזָק מִמֶּנּוּ:

Strengthen me, my God, at my appointed times and my festivals. Hear my words, Hashem, recognize my celebration: When I stand before You like a poor man asking to seek You. When I lift my hands to the Holy of Holies: Be the dwelling of those who inherit the Law and statutes. Great is the counsel and great in deeds: Your word establishes those who long for Your will. Generation after generation seeks Your face: The plea of those calling to You in the morning. My Lord, listen and act, do not delay: Their mouths cannot stop from the unity of your name. You, Lord, do not withhold your mercy: Remember your word to your servant, upon which you have made us hope. Remember, do not break your covenant with us: Show favor to those who spread their hands to you. Gracious and merciful Lord, slow to anger: Your goodness is what we long for, renew us. Good is the Lord to the strong, to the soul that seeks us: Let the poor and the needy rejoice and be glad in you. They will always say, "May the Lord be exalted": Establish a treasure that you have placed for your name. For you are the glory of their strength: Drive away the enemies of your people, who always make us suffer. Save the poor from the strong who oppress them:

Hosha'ana. Hosha'ana: הוֹשַׁעֲנָא. הוֹשַׁעֲנָא:

Please save us. Please save us:

Ana Hoshi'ah Na.   אָנָא הוֹשִׁיעָה נָא.

Ana Hoshi'ah Na: אָנָא הוֹשִׁיעָה נָא:

Please save us now. Please save us now:

Ana Yased Yesod Mikdashi.	אָנָא יַסֵּד יְסוֹד מִקְדָּשִׁי.
La'arov Bo Nichochei Ishi.	לַעֲרוֹב בּוֹ נִיחוֹחֵי אִשִּׁי.
Vetazriach Or Shimshi. Hayom	וְתַזְרִיחַ אוֹר שִׁמְשִׁי. הַיּוֹם
Beyom Shelishi. Hoshi'ah Na:	בְּיוֹם שְׁלִישִׁי. הוֹשִׁיעָה נָא:
Ana Hoshi'ah Na.	אָנָא הוֹשִׁיעָה נָא.
Ana Hoshi'ah Na:	אָנָא הוֹשִׁיעָה נָא:

Please establish the foundation of my Sanctuary, to mingle within it the fragrance of my fire offerings, and may the sun's light shine forth, today, on the third day, please save us: Please, save us now. Please, save us now.

Ana Secheh Na Mokeshi.	אָנָּא סְחֵה נָא מוֹקְשִׁי.
Veshovev Me'on Mikdashi.	וְשׁוֹבֵב מְעוֹן מִקְדָּשִׁי.
Pedeh Beshalom Nafshi. Hayom	פְּדֵה בְּשָׁלוֹם נַפְשִׁי. הַיּוֹם
Beyom Shelishi. Hoshi'ah Na:	בְּיוֹם שְׁלִישִׁי. הוֹשִׁיעָה נָּא:
Ana Hoshi'ah Na.	אָנָּא הוֹשִׁיעָה נָא.
Ana Hoshi'ah Na:	אָנָּא הוֹשִׁיעָה נָּא:

Please remove my snares, and restore the dwelling of my Sanctuary. Redeem my soul in peace. Today, on the third day, please save us: Please, save us now. Please, save us now.

Ani Vahu Hoshi'ah Na.	אֲנִי וָהוּ הוֹשִׁיעָה נָא.
Ani Vahu Hoshi'ah Na:	אֲנִי וָהוּ הוֹשִׁיעָה נָּא:

Ani VaHu, please save us now. Ani VaHu, please save us now:

Kehosha'ta Yedidim. Mikaf	כְּהוֹשַׁעְתָּ יְדִידִים. מִכַּף
Ma'avidim. Vatimchatz Ludim.	מַעֲבִידִים. וַתִּמְחַץ לוּדִים.
Ba'alot Lecha Rachshi: Segulah	בַּעֲלוֹת לְךָ רַחְשִׁי: סְגֻלָּה
Me'usheret. Asher Lecha	מְאֻשֶּׁרֶת. אֲשֶׁר לְךָ
Soveret. Potzachat Lecha Ateret.	סוֹבֶרֶת. פּוֹצַחַת לְךָ עֲטֶרֶת.
Nehalach Beyom Shelishi. Ken	נְהַלְלְךָ בְּיוֹם שְׁלִישִׁי. כֵּן
Hosha'ana. Ani Vahu Hoshi'ah	הוֹשַׁעֲנָא. אֲנִי וָהוּ הוֹשִׁיעָה
Na. Ani Vahu Hoshi'ah Na:	נָא. אֲנִי וָהוּ הוֹשִׁיעָה נָּא:

As you saved Your beloved from the grasp of the slave-drivers. And You crushed the evil-doers with the ascent of my prayer to You. A treasured possession, enriched, which You maintain. Breaking forth for you in supplication. We shall praise You on the third day, so save us. Ani Vahu, please save us now. Ani Vahu, please save us now:

Kehosha'ta Yefeh Nof.	כְּהוֹשַׁעְתָּ יְפֵה נוֹף.
Mimichle'ei Nof. Vate'enaf	מִמִּכְלְאֵי נוֹף. וַתֶּאֱנַף
Anof. Ad Tzeti Chafeshi: Seridei	אֲנוֹף. עַד צֵאתִי חָפְשִׁי: שְׂרִידֵי
Ha'eder. Me'aderim Eder. Petzot	הָעֵדֶר. מְאַדְּרִים אֶדֶר. פְּצוֹת
Lecha Hod Vaheder. Nehalach	לְךָ הוֹד וְהֶדֶר. נְהַלְּךָ
Beyom Shelishi: Ken	בְּיוֹם שְׁלִישִׁי: כֵּן
Hosha'ana. Ani Vahu Hoshi'ah	הוֹשַׁעֲנָא. אֲנִי וָהוּ הוֹשִׁיעָה
Na. Ani Vahu Hoshi'ah Na:	נָא. אֲנִי וָהוּ הוֹשִׁיעָה נָא:

As You saved the beautiful sight from the imprisonment of the land [Egypt], and You struck with anger until I went out free, the remnants of the flock. Adorning the flock, they burst forth to You with splendor and majesty. We shall praise You on the third day, so save us. Ani Vahu, please save us now. Ani Vahu, please save us now:

Meyachadim Shem Ha'el.	מְיַחֲדִים שֵׁם הָאֵל.
Hayom Beshirah Aruchah.	הַיּוֹם בְּשִׁירָה עֲרוּכָה.
Uvevi'at Hago'el. Ha'aleh Lanu	וּבְבִיאַת הַגּוֹאֵל. הַעֲלֵה לָנוּ
Aruchah. Meshorerim Ein Ka'el.	אֲרוּכָה. מְשׁוֹרְרִים אֵין כָּאֵל.
Am Lo Te'ot Meluchah. Yihyeh	עַם לוֹ תְּאַוֹת מְלוּכָה. יִהְיֶה
Leyisra'el. Shelishiyah	לְיִשְׂרָאֵל. שְׁלִישִׁיָּה
Berachah: Sovevei Te'udatecha.	בְּרָכָה: סוֹבְבֵי תְּעוּדָתֶךָ.
Ha'er Afelatam. Hayom	הָאֵר אֲפֵלָתָם. הַיּוֹם
Beveitecha. Takshiv Techinatam.	בְּבֵיתֶךָ. תַּקְשִׁיב תְּחִנָּתָם.
Ledin Beshivtecha. Ha'aver	לְדִין בְּשִׁבְתֶּךָ. הַעֲבֵר
Chatatam. Heshivem	חַטָּאתָם. הֲשִׁיבֵם
Lekadmutam. Ma'arachah Likrat	לְקַדְמוּתָם. מַעֲרָכָה לִקְרַאת
Ma'arachah:	מַעֲרָכָה:

Who unify the name of God. Today, in an arranged song and with the coming of the Redeemer, raise up for us a restoration. Singing, there is none like God. A nation to whom the desires of royalty belong. May it be for Yisrael a three-fold blessing: those who encircle Your Testimony. Illuminate their darkness. Today, in your house listen to their supplication. When sitting to judge, pass-over their sin. Return them to their former state, formation by formation.

Kehosha'ta Me'az Adatecha.	כְּהוֹשַׁעְתָּ מֵאָז עֲדָתֶךָ.
Ken Hoshi'ah Et-Amecha	כֵּן הוֹשַׁעֲנָא אֶת־עַמֶּךָ
Uvarech Et-Nachalatecha.	וּבָרֵךְ אֶת־נַחֲלָתֶךָ.
Nehalach Beyom Shelishi. Ken	נְהַלֵּךְ בְּיוֹם שְׁלִישִׁי. כֵּן
Hosha'ana:	הוֹשַׁעֲנָא:

As You have saved, from then, Your congregation, so save Your people and bless Your heritage. We will praise you on the third day. So, please save us:

Ani Vahu Hoshi'ah Na.	אֲנִי וָהוּ הוֹשִׁיעָה נָא.
Ani Vahu Hoshi'ah Na:	אֲנִי וָהוּ הוֹשִׁיעָה נָא:

Ani VaHu, please save us now. Ani VaHu, please save us now:

Kakatuv: Hoshi'ah Et-Amecha	כַּכָּתוּב: הוֹשִׁיעָה אֶת־עַמֶּךָ
Uvarech Et-Nachalatecha	וּבָרֵךְ אֶת־נַחֲלָתֶךָ
Ure'em Venase'em Ad-Ha'olam:	וּרְעֵם וְנַשְּׂאֵם עַד־הָעוֹלָם:
Vene'emar: Veyihyu Devarai Eleh	וְנֶאֱמַר: וְיִהְיוּ דְבָרַי אֵלֶּה
Asher Hitchananti Lifnei	אֲשֶׁר הִתְחַנַּנְתִּי לִפְנֵי
Adonai Kerovim El-Adonai	יְהֹוָה קְרֹבִים אֶל־יְהֹוָה
Eloheinu Yomam Valayelah	אֱלֹהֵינוּ יוֹמָם וָלָיְלָה
La'asot Mishpat Avdo Umishpat	לַעֲשׂוֹת מִשְׁפַּט עַבְדּוֹ וּמִשְׁפַּט

Amo Yisra'el Devar-Yom

Beyomo: Lema'an Da'at Kol-

Amei Ha'aretz Ki Adonai Hu

Ha'elohim Ein Od: Lo-Yamush

Sefer Hatorah Hazeh Mipicha

Vehagita Bo Yomam Valaylah

Lema'an Tishmor La'asot Kechol-

Hakatuv Bo Ki-Az Tatzliach Et-

Derachecha Ve'az Taskil: Halo

Tzivlticha Chazak Ve'ematz Al-

Ta'arotz Ve'al-Techat Ki Imecha

Adonai Eloheicha Bechol Asher

Telech:

עַמּוֹ יִשְׂרָאֵל דְּבַר־יוֹם
בְּיוֹמוֹ: לְמַעַן דַּעַת כָּל־
עַמֵּי הָאָרֶץ כִּי יְהֹוָה הוּא
הָאֱלֹהִים אֵין עוֹד: לֹא־יָמוּשׁ
סֵפֶר הַתּוֹרָה הַזֶּה מִפִּיךָ
וְהָגִיתָ בּוֹ יוֹמָם וָלַיְלָה
לְמַעַן תִּשְׁמֹר לַעֲשׂוֹת כְּכָל־
הַכָּתוּב בּוֹ כִּי־אָז תַּצְלִיחַ אֶת־
דְּרָכֶךָ וְאָז תַּשְׂכִּיל: הֲלוֹא
צִוִּיתִיךָ חֲזַק וֶאֱמָץ אַל־
תַּעֲרֹץ וְאַל־תֵּחָת כִּי עִמְּךָ
יְהֹוָה אֱלֹהֶיךָ בְּכֹל אֲשֶׁר
תֵּלֵךְ:

As it is written: Save Your people and bless Your inheritance, and shepherd them and exalt them forever. And says: May these words of my supplication before Hashem be close to Hashem our God, day and night, to do justice to His servant and justice to His people Yisrael, each matter day by day. So that all the peoples of the Earth may know that Hashem is God, there is no other. Do not let the Book of this Torah depart from your mouth, meditate on it day and night, in order that you may keep and do according to all that is written in it, for then you will succeed in your ways and then you will be wise. Have I not commanded you? Be strong and courageous, do not be afraid and do not be dismayed, for Hashem your God is with you wherever you go.

Hoshanot for the Fourth Day
הושענות ליום הרביעי

Erchatz Benikayon Kapai

אֶרְחַץ בְּנִקָּיוֹן כַּפָּי

Va'asovevah Et-Mizbachacha

וַאֲסֹבְבָה אֶת־מִזְבַּחֲךָ

Adonai: Lashmia' Bekol Todah

יְהוָה: לַשְׁמִעַ בְּקוֹל תּוֹדָה

Ulesaper Kol-Nifle'oteicha.

וּלְסַפֵּר כָּל־נִפְלְאוֹתֶיךָ:

I will wash my hands in innocence, and I will encircle your altar, Hashem. That I may make the voice of thanksgiving to be heard, and tell of all Your wondrous works. (Ps. 26:6-7)

Hosha'ana. Hosha'ana:

הוֹשַׁעֲנָא. הוֹשַׁעֲנָא:

Please save us. Please save us:

Lema'anach Eloheinu.

לְמַעַנְךָ אֱלֹהֵינוּ.

Lema'anach Bore'enu.

לְמַעַנְךָ בּוֹרְאֵנוּ.

Lema'anach Go'alenu.

לְמַעַנְךָ גּוֹאֲלֵנוּ.

Lema'anach Doreshenu:

לְמַעַנְךָ דּוֹרְשֵׁנוּ:

For Your sake, our God. For Your sake, our Creator. For Your sake, our Redeemer. For Your sake, our Seeker.

Lema'anach Adir Adirim.

לְמַעַנְךָ אַדִּיר אַדִּירִים.

Lema'anach Borei Ruach

לְמַעַנְךָ בּוֹרֵא רוּחַ

Veyotzer Harim.

וְיוֹצֵר הָרִים.

Lema'anach Gedol Ha'etzah

לְמַעַנְךָ גְּדוֹל הָעֵצָה

Mashpil Umerim.

מַשְׁפִּיל וּמֵרִים.

Lema'anach Dover Tzedek

לְמַעַנְךָ דּוֹבֵר צֶדֶק

Magid Meisharim. מַגִּיד מֵישָׁרִים.

Lema'anach Hayodea' Va'ed Im לְמַעַנְךָ הַיּוֹדֵעַ וָעֵד אִם

Yisater Ish Bemistarim. יִסָּתֵר אִישׁ בְּמִסְתָּרִים.

Lema'anach Vehu Be'echad Umi לְמַעַנְךָ וְהוּא בְּאֶחָד וּמִי

Yeshivenu Amarim. יְשִׁיבֵנוּ אֲמָרִים.

Lema'anach Zach Venaki לְמַעַנְךָ זַךְ וְנָקִי

Umitbarer Im Barim. וּמִתְבָּרֵר עִם בָּרִים.

Lema'anach Chofes Matzpun לְמַעַנְךָ חוֹפֵשׂ מַצְפּוּן

Vechoker Kol-Chadarim. וְחוֹקֵר כָּל־חֲדָרִים.

Lema'anach Tipechah Yemino לְמַעַנְךָ טִפְּחָה יְמִינוֹ

Shamayim Ve'asah Me'orim. שָׁמַיִם וְעָשָׂה מְאוֹרִים.

Lema'anach Yasad Eretz Batzurot לְמַעַנְךָ יָסַד אֶרֶץ בַּצּוּרוֹת

Bika Ye'orim. Lema'anach Kabir בִּקַּע יְאוֹרִים. לְמַעַנְךָ כַּבִּיר

Koach Mechubad Ba'urim. כֹּחַ מְכֻבָּד בָּאוּרִים.

Lema'anach Lo Yitamu Shenotav לְמַעַנְךָ לֹא יִתַּמּוּ שְׁנוֹתָיו

Ledor Dorim: לְדוֹר דּוֹרִים:

For Your sake, Mightiest of the mighty. For Your sake, Creator of the wind and the Former of mountains. For Your sake, Great in counsel, Who humbles and lifts high. For Your sake, Speaker of righteousness, declaring uprightness. For Your sake, Knower and Witness, whether a person hides in secret places. For Your sake, He Who is One, and Who will return us with utterances. For Your sake, Pure and Innocent and Who is pure with the pure. For Your sake, Liberator of the hidden and Searcher of all chambers. For Your sake, He Who spread out the sky with His right hand and made the luminaries. For Your sake, He Who founded the earth with its boundaries, carving the rivers in rocks. For Your sake, the Great in Power, honored with lights. For Your sake, His years will never end for generations of generations:

Hosha'ana. Hosha'ana:

הוֹשַׁעְנָא. הוֹשַׁעְנָא:

Please save us. Please save us:

Ana Haborei Olamo Bisodot — אָנָּא הַבּוֹרֵא עוֹלָמוֹ בִּיסוֹדוֹת

Arba'ah. Hanoten Noshe'ei — אַרְבָּעָה. הַנּוֹתֵן נוֹשְׂאֵי

Chis'o Chayot Arba'ah. — כִּסְאוֹ חַיּוֹת אַרְבָּעָה.

Hamatziv Pinot Arba'ah — הַמַּצִּיב פִּנּוֹת אַרְבָּעָה

Utekufot Arba'ah. Hoshi'anu — וּתְקוּפוֹת אַרְבָּעָה. הוֹשִׁיעֵנוּ

Bachagigat Yamim Arba'ah: — בַּחֲגִיגַת יָמִים אַרְבָּעָה:

Please, Who created His world with four foundations [elements]. Who gives lifters of His throne, four Chayot. Who established the four corners and the four seasons. Save us on the celebration of four days.

Ana Zechor Av He'ir Mimizrach — אָנָּא זְכֹר אָב הֵעִיר מִמִּזְרָח

Be'or Leyamim Arba'ah. Radaf — בְּאוֹר לְיָמִים אַרְבָּעָה. רָדַף

Vayechalek Al Melachim — וַיֵּחָלֵק עַל מְלָכִים אַרְבָּעָה.

Arba'ah. Bisarto Lashuv Zar'o — בִּשַּׂרְתוֹ לָשׁוּב זַרְעוֹ לְדוֹרוֹת

Ledorot Arba'ah. Hoshi'anu — אַרְבָּעָה.הוֹשִׁיעֵנוּ בַּחֲגִיגַת

Bachagigat Yamim Arba'ah: — יָמִים אַרְבָּעָה:

Please, remember the father [Avraham] from the city from the east with light like fourth day. He pursued and divided among four kings. In his announcement [given to him], his offspring would return after four generations. Save us on the celebration of four days.

Ana Zechor Ben Hugash	אָנָּא זְכֹר בֶּן הֻגַּשׁ
La'akedah Al Keranot Arba'ah.	לַעֲקֵדָה עַל קַרְנוֹת אַרְבָּעָה.
Chafar Bifleshet Borot Arba'ah.	חָפַר בִּפְלֶשֶׁת בּוֹרוֹת אַרְבָּעָה.
Vaya'tek Lechevron Kiryat	וַיַּעְתֵּק לְחֶבְרוֹן קִרְיַת
Arba'ah. Hoshi'anu Bachagigat	אַרְבָּעָה. הוֹשִׁיעֵנוּ בַּחֲגִיגַת
Yamim Arba'ah:	יָמִים אַרְבָּעָה:

Please, remember the son [Yitzchak] who was brought to the binding on four corners [of the alter]. He dug four wells in the land of the Philistines. And he moved to Chevron, the city of four. Save us on the celebration of four days.

Ana Zechor Tam Ne'ezar	אָנָּא זְכֹר תָּם נֶעֱזַר
Be'imahot Arba'ah. Chinen	בְּאִמָּהוֹת אַרְבָּעָה. חִנֵּן
Lehinatzel Mishpatim Arba'ah.	לְהִנָּצֵל מִשְׁפָּטִים אַרְבָּעָה.
Bitfilato Kilkalta Banav Bidvarim	בִּתְפִלָּתוֹ כִּלְכַּלְתָּ בָּנָיו בִּדְבָרִים
Arba'ah. Hoshi'anu Bachagigat	אַרְבָּעָה. הוֹשִׁיעֵנוּ בַּחֲגִיגַת
Yamim Arba'ah:	יָמִים אַרְבָּעָה:

Please, remember the perfect one [Ya'akov] who was helped by his four matriarchs. He pleaded to be saved from four judgements. In his prayer You sustained his sons with four things. Save us on the celebration of four days.

Ana Hamolichenu Bamidbar	אָנָּא הַמּוֹלִיכֵנוּ בַּמִּדְבָּר
Bidgalim Arba'ah. Tzivah	בִּדְגָלִים אַרְבָּעָה. צִוָּה
Lemalot Bachoshen Turim	לְמַלֹּאת בַּחֹשֶׁן טוּרִים
Arba'ah. Hametzavenu Lehalo	אַרְבָּעָה. הַמְצַוֵּנוּ לְהַלְּלוֹ
Bechag Beminim Arba'ah.	בְּחַג בְּמִינִים אַרְבָּעָה.
Hoshi'anu Bachagigat Yamim	הוֹשִׁיעֵנוּ בַּחֲגִיגַת יָמִים
Arba'ah:	אַרְבָּעָה:

Please, the One Who led us in the desert with four banners. Who commanded to fill the Choshen [breastplate] with four rows. Who commanded us to praise Him during the holiday with four species. Save us on the celebration of four days.

Hosha'ana. Hosha'ana:	הוֹשַׁעֲנָא. הוֹשַׁעֲנָא:

Please save us. Please save us:

El-Pitchach Yaron Seh Oved	אֵל־פִּתְחָךְ יָרוֹן שֶׂה אֹבֵד
Bahadomecha. Adonai Adoneinu	בַּהֲדוֹמֶךָ. יְהֹוָה אֲדֹנֵינוּ
Mah-Adir Shimcha: Baya'ar	מָה־אַדִּיר שְׁמֶךָ: בַּיַּעַר
Ba'aravah Bekol Ya'oz.	בָּעֲרָבָה בְּקוֹל יָעֹז.
Adonai Birtzonecha He'emadtah	יְהֹוָה בִּרְצוֹנְךָ הֶעֱמַדְתָּה
Lehari Oz: Game Tzame	לְהַרְרִי עֹז: גָּמֵא צָמֵא
Leyish'acha Po'er Piv	לְיִשְׁעֶךָ פּוֹעֵר פִּיו
Lemalkosho. Adonai Go'al	לְמַלְקוֹשׁוֹ. יְהֹוָה גָּאַל
Yisra'el Ukedosho: Diber Vayikra	יִשְׂרָאֵל וּקְדוֹשׁוֹ: דִּבֶּר וַיִּקְרָא
Eretz Deleh Asireicha	אֶרֶץ דְּלֵה אֲסִירֶיךָ
Mimetzarim. Adonai Dover	מִמְּצָרִים. יְהֹוָה דֹּבֵר
Tzedek Magid Meisharim: Havei	צֶדֶק מַגִּיד מֵישָׁרִים: הָבֵא
Shenat Shilumim La'asher	שְׁנַת שִׁלּוּמִים לַאֲשֶׁר
Badeshen Nidshanu. Adonai	בַּדֶּשֶׁן נִדְשָׁנוּ. יְהֹוָה
Hat-Shameicha Vetered Ga	הַט־שָׁמֶיךָ וְתֵרֵד גַּע
Beharim Veye'eshanu: Veharek	בֶּהָרִים וְיֶעֱשָׁנוּ: וְהָרֵק
Chanit Usegor Likrat Rodefei	חֲנִית וּסְגוֹר לִקְרָאת רֹדְפַי
Kemehim. Adonai Ve'ein Od	כְּמֵהִים. יְהֹוָה וְאֵין עוֹד
Zulati Ein Elohim: Zera Adam	זוּלָתִי אֵין אֱלֹהִים: זֶרַע אָדָם

Vezera Behemah Toshia' Vechish   וְזֶרַע בְּהֵמָה תּוֹשִׁיעַ וְחִישׁ

Fedut Legolat Ari'el.   פְּדוּת לְגוֹלַת אֲרִיאֵל.

Adonai Zecharanu Yevarech   יְהֹוָה זְכָרָנוּ יְבָרֵךְ

Yevarech Et-Beit Yisra'el: יְבָרֵךְ אֶת־בֵּית יִשְׂרָאֵל:

To Your door, will come rejoicing the lost sheep in Your world. Hashem our Lord, how majestic is Your name: in the forest, in the desert, with a mighty voice. Hashem, in Your favor, You have supported me with mountains of strength: quench the thirst of those who long for Your salvation, opening their mouths to the late rains. Hashem, Redeemer of Yisrael and it's Holy One: He spoke and called to the land of the weary, releasing Your captives from distress. Hashem, speaking righteousness, and declaring uprightness: Bring a time of wholeness to those who have been driven away. Hashem, stretch out the heavens and descend, touch the mountains, and they will smoke: Draw the spear and close in on the pursuers of those who yearn. Hashem, there is none besides You, there are no other gods: Save the seed of man and the seed of beasts, hasten the redemption from the exile of Ariel. Hashem, Who remembers us will bless. He will bless the house of Yisrael.

Hosha'ana. Hosha'ana: הוֹשַׁעְנָא. הוֹשַׁעְנָא:

Please save us. Please save us:

Ana Hoshi'ah Na.   אָנָּא הוֹשִׁיעָה נָּא.

Ana Hoshi'ah Na: אָנָּא הוֹשִׁיעָה נָּא:

Please save us now. Please save us now:

Ana Ye'erav Lecha Shav'i.	אָנָּא יֶעֱרַב לְךָ שַׁוְעִי.
Belulavi Bena'ne'i. Vekarev Na	בְּלוּלָבִי בְּנַעְנְעִי. וְקָרֵב נָא
Ketz Yish'i. Hayom Beyom	קֵץ יִשְׁעִי. הַיּוֹם בְּיוֹם
Revi'i. Hoshi'ah Na:	רְבִיעִי. הוֹשִׁיעָה נָא:
Ana Hoshi'ah Na.	אָנָּא הוֹשִׁיעָה נָא.
Ana Hoshi'ah Na:	אָנָּא הוֹשִׁיעָה נָא:

Please, let my cry be pleasing to You. With my lulav, I wave. And please bring the end of my salvation closer. Today, on the fourth day, please save us: Please, save us now. Please, save us now.

Ana Sov Na Lehargi'i. Vechonen	אָנָּא סוֹב נָא לְהַרְגִּיעִי. וְכוֹנֵן
Arechi Veriv'i. Pa'oli She'eh	אָרְחִי וְרִבְעִי. פָּעֳלִי שְׁעֵה
Behishta'she'i. Nahel Linveh	בְּהִשְׁתַּעְשְׁעִי. נַהֵל לִנְוֵה
Margo'i. Hayom Beyom Revi'i.	מַרְגּוֹעִי. הַיּוֹם בְּיוֹם רְבִיעִי.
Hoshi'ah Na: Ana Hoshi'ah Na.	הוֹשִׁיעָה נָא: אָנָּא הוֹשִׁיעָה
Ana Hoshi'ah Na:	נָא. אָנָּא הוֹשִׁיעָה נָא:

Please, now surround me for calm. Establish my path and my footing. Accept, my actions which I do in delight. Guide me to a place of rest. Today, on the fourth day, please save us: Please, save us now. Please, save us now.

Ani Vahu Hoshi'ah Na.	אֲנִי וָהוּ הוֹשִׁיעָה נָא.
Ani Vahu Hoshi'ah Na:	אֲנִי וָהוּ הוֹשִׁיעָה נָא:

Ani VaHu, please save us now. Ani VaHu, please save us now:

Kehosha'ta Yakir. Mishod	כְּהוֹשַׁעְתָּ יַקִּיר. מִשּׁוֹד
Mekarker Kir. Vatach Vata'akir.	מְקַרְקֵר קִיר. וַתָּךְ וַתַּעֲקִיר.
Shokek Sheku'i: Gam Attah	שׁוֹקֵק שְׁקוּעִי: גַּם עַתָּה
Chaletz. Alutz Mime'aletz.	חַלֵּץ. אַלּוּץ מִמְּאַלֵּץ.
Umadveh Lev Te'aletz.	וּמַדְוֵה לֵב תְּעַלֵּץ.
Nehalach Beyom Revi'i. Ken	נְהַלֶּךְ בְּיוֹם רְבִיעִי. כֵּן
Hosha'na. Ani Vahu Hoshi'ah	הוֹשַׁעְנָא. אֲנִי וָהוּ הוֹשִׁיעָה
Na. Ani Vahu Hoshi'ah Na:	נָא. אֲנִי וָהוּ הוֹשִׁיעָה נָא:

As You have saved, the precious one [Yisrael] from plunder and the destruction of the walls and struck and uprooted. Who desired my sinking: even now, deliver. A Champion against the oppressor. And Cheerer the heart of the afflicted. We praise You on the fourth day, so please save us. AniVaHu, please save us now. AniVaHu, please save us now.

Kehosha'ta Sorek. Mikaf Tzar	כְּהוֹשַׁעְתָּ שׂוֹרֵק. מִכַּף צַר
Shorek. Asher Shinav Chorek.	שׁוֹרֵק. אֲשֶׁר שִׁנָּיו חוֹרֵק.
Lekatzetz Et Giz'i: Peta Pit'om.	לְקַצֵּץ אֶת גִּזְעִי: פֶּתַע פִּתְאֹם.
Na'amta Na'om. Lehashbito	נָאַמְתָּ נָאוֹם. לְהַשְׁבִּיתוֹ
Mile'om. Nehalach Beyom	מִלְּאֹם. נְהַלֶּךְ בְּיוֹם
Revi'i. Ken Hosha'ana.	רְבִיעִי. כֵּן הוֹשַׁעֲנָא.
Ani Vahu Hoshi'ah Na.	אֲנִי וָהוּ הוֹשִׁיעָה נָא.
Ani Vahu Hoshi'ah Na:	אֲנִי וָהוּ הוֹשִׁיעָה נָא:

As You have saved the one who cries out from the grasp of the enemy, whose teeth are gnashing to cut off my stock: Suddenly, You expressed words to cease their oppression. We praise You on the fourth day. So please save us.AniVaHu, please save us now. AniVaHu, please save us now.

Yish'acha Har'eh Yah. Ha'el   יִשְׁעֲךָ הַרְאֵה יָהּ. הָאֵל

Gedol De'ah. Maher Ketz Pedut   גְּדוֹל דֵּעָה. מַהֵר קֵץ פְּדוּת

Le'om Nivashe'ah. Sovevei   לְאוֹם נְוָשֵׁעָה. סוֹבְבֵי

Toratecha Pe'amim Arba'ah: תוֹרָתְךָ פְּעָמִים אַרְבָּעָה:

Show Your salvation, Hashem, The great God of knowledge. Hasten the time of redemption for a people in need of salvation, who encircle Your Torah four times:

Go'el Yisra'el. Heyeh Na   גּוֹאֵל יִשְׂרָאֵל. הֱיֵה נָא

Moshi'am. Uve'itot Ka'el.   מוֹשִׁיעָם. וּבְעִתּוֹת כָּאֵל.

Heyeh Na Margo'am. Galeh   הֱיֵה נָא מַרְגּוֹעָם. גַּלֵּה

Ketz Yish'am. Ulecha Lishu'ah.   קֵץ יִשְׁעָם. וּלְךָ לִישׁוּעָה.

Sovevei Toratecha Pe'amim   סוֹבְבֵי תוֹרָתְךָ פְּעָמִים

Arba'ah: אַרְבָּעָה:

Redeemer of Yisrael, please be their Savior. And in times of distress, be their comfort. Reveal the time of their redemption and Your salvation. Those who encircle Your Torah four times:

Kehosha'ta Me'az Adatecha.   כְּהוֹשַׁעְתָּ מֵאָז עֲדָתֶךָ.

Ken Hoshi'ah Et-Amecha   כֵּן הוֹשִׁיעָה אֶת־עַמֶּךָ

Uvarech Et-Nachalatecha.   וּבָרֵךְ אֶת־נַחֲלָתֶךָ.

Nehalach Beyom Revi'i.   נְהַלֵּךְ בְּיוֹם רְבִיעִי.

Ken Hosha'ana: כֵּן הוֹשַׁעֲנָא:

As You have saved since the days of Your congregation, so save Your people and bless Your inheritance. We praise You on the fourth day, so please save us.

Ani Vahu Hoshi'ah Na.	אֲנִי וָהוּ הוֹשִׁיעָה נָּא.
Ani Vahu Hoshi'ah Na:	אֲנִי וָהוּ הוֹשִׁיעָה נָּא:

Ani VaHu. please save us now. Ani VaHu. please save us now:

Kakatuv: Hoshi'ah Et-Amecha	כַּכָּתוּב: הוֹשִׁיעָה אֶת־עַמֶּךָ
Uvarech Et-Nachalatecha	וּבָרֵךְ אֶת־נַחֲלָתֶךָ
Ure'em Venase'em Ad-Ha'olam:	וּרְעֵם וְנַשְּׂאֵם עַד־הָעוֹלָם:
Vene'emar: Veyihyu Devarai	וְנֶאֱמַר: וְיִהְיוּ דְבָרַי
Eleh Asher Hitchananti Lifnei	אֵלֶּה אֲשֶׁר הִתְחַנַּנְתִּי לִפְנֵי
Adonai Kerovim El-Adonai	יְהוָה קְרֹבִים אֶל־יְהוָה
Eloheinu Yomam Valayelah	אֱלֹהֵינוּ יוֹמָם וָלַיְלָה
La'asot Mishpat Avdo Umishpat	לַעֲשׂוֹת מִשְׁפַּט עַבְדּוֹ וּמִשְׁפַּט
Amo Yisra'el Devar-Yom	עַמּוֹ יִשְׂרָאֵל דְּבַר־יוֹם
Beyomo: Lema'an Da'at Kol-	בְּיוֹמוֹ: לְמַעַן דַּעַת כָּל־
Amei Ha'aretz Ki Adonai Hu	עַמֵּי הָאָרֶץ כִּי יְהוָה הוּא
Ha'elohim Ein Od: Lo-Yamush	הָאֱלֹהִים אֵין עוֹד: לֹא־יָמוּשׁ
Sefer Hatorah Hazeh Mipicha	סֵפֶר הַתּוֹרָה הַזֶּה מִפִּיךָ
Vehagita Bo Yomam Valaylah	וְהָגִיתָ בּוֹ יוֹמָם וָלַיְלָה
Lema'an Tishmor La'asot	לְמַעַן תִּשְׁמֹר לַעֲשׂוֹת
Kechol-Hakatuv Bo Ki-Az	כְּכָל־הַכָּתוּב בּוֹ כִּי־אָז
Tatzliach Et-Derachecha Ve'az	תַּצְלִיחַ אֶת־דְּרָכֶךָ וְאָז
Taskil: Halo Tziviticha Chazak	תַּשְׂכִּיל: הֲלוֹא צִוִּיתִיךָ חֲזַק
Ve'ematz Al-Ta'arotz Ve'al-	וֶאֱמָץ אַל־תַּעֲרֹץ וְאַל־
Techat Ki Imecha Adonai	תֵּחָת כִּי עִמְּךָ יְהוָה
Eloheicha Bechol Asher Telech:	אֱלֹהֶיךָ בְּכֹל אֲשֶׁר תֵּלֵךְ:

As it is written: Save Your people and bless Your inheritance, and shepherd them and exalt them forever. And says: May these words of my supplication before Hashem be close to Hashem our God, day and night, to do justice to His servant and justice to His people Yisrael, each matter day by day. So that all the peoples of the Earth may know that Hashem is God, there is no other. Do not let the Book of this Torah depart from your mouth, meditate on it day and night, in order that you may keep and do according to all that is written in it, for then you will succeed in your ways and then you will be wise. Have I not commanded you? Be strong and courageous, do not be afraid and do not be dismayed, for Hashem your God is with you wherever you go.

Hoshanot for the Fifth Day
הושענות ליום החמישי

Erchatz Benikayon Kapai   אֶרְחַץ בְּנִקָּיוֹן כַּפָּי

Va'asovevah Et-Mizbachacha   וַאֲסֹבְבָה אֶת־מִזְבַּחֲךָ

Adonai: Lashmia' Bekol Todah   יְהֹוָה: לַשְׁמִעַ בְּקוֹל תּוֹדָה

Ulesaper Kol-Nifle'oteicha.   וּלְסַפֵּר כָּל־נִפְלְאוֹתֶיךָ:

I will wash my hands in innocence, and I will encircle your altar, Hashem. That I may make the voice of thanksgiving to be heard, and tell of all Your wondrous works. (Ps. 26:6-7)

Hosha'ana. Hosha'ana: הוֹשַׁעֲנָא. הוֹשַׁעֲנָא:

Please save us. Please save us:

Lema'anach Eloheinu.   לְמַעַנְךָ אֱלֹהֵינוּ.

Lema'anach Bore'enu.   לְמַעַנְךָ בּוֹרְאֵנוּ.

Lema'anach Go'alenu.   לְמַעַנְךָ גּוֹאֲלֵנוּ.

Lema'anach Doreshenu: לְמַעַנְךָ דּוֹרְשֵׁנוּ:

For Your sake, our God. For Your sake, our Creator. For Your sake, our Redeemer. For Your sake, our Seeker.

Lema'anach Adir Adirim.   לְמַעַנְךָ אַדִּיר אַדִּירִים.

Lema'anach Boreiruach Veyotzer   לְמַעַנְךָ בּוֹרֵא רוּחַ וְיוֹצֵר

Harim. Lema'anach Gedol   הָרִים. לְמַעַנְךָ גְּדוֹל

Ha'etzah Mashpil Umerim.   הָעֵצָה מַשְׁפִּיל וּמֵרִים.

Lema'anach Dover Tzedek   לְמַעַנְךָ דּוֹבֵר צֶדֶק

Magid Meisharim.   מַגִּיד מֵישָׁרִים.

Lema'anach Hayodea' Va'ed Im   לְמַעֲנָךְ הַיּוֹדֵעַ וָעֵד אִם

Yisater Ish Bemistarim.   יִסָּתֵר אִישׁ בְּמִסְתָּרִים.

Lema'anach Vehu Be'echad Umi   לְמַעֲנָךְ וְהוּא בְּאֶחָד וּמִי

Yeshivenu Amarim.   יְשִׁיבֶנּוּ אֲמָרִים.

Lema'anach Zach Venaki   לְמַעֲנָךְ זַךְ וְנָקִי

Umitbarer Im Barim.   וּמִתְבָּרֵר עִם בָּרִים.

Lema'anach Chofes Matzpun   לְמַעֲנָךְ חוֹפֵשׂ מַצְפּוּן

Vechoker Kol-Chadarim.   וְחוֹקֵר כָּל־חֲדָרִים.

Lema'anach Tipechah Yemino   לְמַעֲנָךְ טִפְּחָה יְמִינוֹ

Shamayim Ve'asah Me'orim.   שָׁמַיִם וְעָשָׂה מְאוֹרִים.

Lema'anach Yasad Eretz Batzurot   לְמַעֲנָךְ יָסַד אֶרֶץ בַּצּוּרוֹת

Bika Ye'orim. Lema'anach Kabir   בִּקַּע יְאוֹרִים. לְמַעֲנָךְ כַּבִּיר

Koach Mechubad Ba'urim.   כֹּחַ מְכֻבָּד בָּאוּרִים.

Lema'anach Lo Yitamu Shenotav   לְמַעֲנָךְ לֹא יִתַּמּוּ שְׁנוֹתָיו

Ledor Dorim: לְדוֹר דּוֹרִים:

For Your sake, Mightiest of the mighty. For Your sake, Creator of the wind and the Former of mountains. For Your sake, Great in counsel, Who humbles and lifts high. For Your sake, Speaker of righteousness, declaring uprightness. For Your sake, Knower and Witness, whether a person hides in secret places. For Your sake, He Who is One, and Who will return us with utterances. For Your sake, Pure and Innocent and Who is pure with the pure. For Your sake, Liberator of the hidden and Searcher of all chambers. For Your sake, He Who spread out the sky with His right hand and made the luminaries. For Your sake, He Who founded the earth with its boundaries, carving the rivers in rocks. For Your sake, the Great in Power, honored with lights. For Your sake, His years will never end for generations of generations:

Hosha'ana. Hosha'ana:

הוֹשַׁעְנָא. הוֹשַׁעְנָא:

Please save us. Please save us:

Ana Hameyached Lichvodo	אָנָּא הַמְיַחֵד לִכְבוֹדוֹ שֵׁמוֹת
Shemot Chamishah. Hakoneh	חֲמִשָּׁה. הַקּוֹנֶה בְּעוֹלָמוֹ
Ve'olamo Kinyanim Chamishah.	קִנְיָנִים חֲמִשָּׁה. הַיּוֹצֵר
Hayotzer Bivriyotav Giborim	בִּבְרִיּוֹתָיו גִּבּוֹרִים
Chamishah. Hoshi'enu	חֲמִשָּׁה. הוֹשִׁיעֵנוּ בַּחֲגִיגַת
Bachagigat Yamim Chamishah:	יָמִים חֲמִשָּׁה:

Please, the One Who unifies for His glory five names. The One Who acquires in His world five acquisitions. The One Who forms in His creatures five mighty-ones. Save us on the festival of five days.

Ana Zechor Av Karat Berit	אָנָּא זְכֹר אָב כָּרַת בְּרִית
Bivtarim Chamishah. Veheshiv	בִּבְתָרִים חֲמִשָּׁה. וְהֵשִׁיב
Rechush Limlachim Chamishah.	רְכוּשׁ לִמְלָכִים חֲמִשָּׁה. וְחָנַן
Vechanan Al Hafichat Arim	עַל הֲפִיכַת עָרִים
Chamishah. Hoshi'enu	חֲמִשָּׁה. הוֹשִׁיעֵנוּ בַּחֲגִיגַת
Bachagigat Yamim Chamishah:	יָמִים חֲמִשָּׁה:

Please, remember the father [Avraham] who cut a covenant between pieces of five kinds. He returned the property to five kings. And pleaded against the destruction of five cities. Save us on the festival of five days.

Ana Zechor Hane'ekad Behar	אָנָּא זְכֹר הַנֶּעֱקַד בְּהַר
Mor She'arim Chamishah.	מוֹר שְׁעָרִים חֲמִשָּׁה.
Yarash Mehoro Berachot	יָרַשׁ מֵהוֹרוֹ בְּרָכוֹת
Chamishah. Vehishlim Nefesh	חֲמִשָּׁה. וְהִשְׁלִים נֶפֶשׁ
Nekuvah Beshemot	נְקוּבָה בְּשֵׁמוֹת
Chamishah. Hoshi'enu	חֲמִשָּׁה. הוֹשִׁיעֵנוּ
Bachagigat Yamim Chamishah:	בַּחֲגִיגַת יָמִים חֲמִשָּׁה:

Please, remember the one [Yitzchak] who was bound on Mount Moriah with five gates. Who inherited from his trail, five blessings. And completed his soul that was pierced with five names. Save us on the festival of five days.

Ana Zechor Tam Na'asu Lo	אָנָּא זְכֹר תָּם נַעֲשׂוּ לוֹ
Nisim Chamishah. Vayatzeg	נִסִּים חֲמִשָּׁה. וַיַּצֵּג
Mibanav Achim Chamishah.	מִבָּנָיו אַחִים חֲמִשָּׁה.
Kofro Shat Lenazir Hamachalif	כָּפְרוֹ שָׁת לְנָזִיר הַמַּחֲלִיף
Chamishah. Hoshi'enu	חֲמִשָּׁה. הוֹשִׁיעֵנוּ
Bachagigat Yamim Chamishah:	בַּחֲגִיגַת יָמִים חֲמִשָּׁה:

Please, remember the perfect one [Ya'akov] for whom five miracles were performed. And who presented from his sons, five brothers. A gift he gave to the pure one [Yosef] five exchanges of clothing. Save us on the festival of five days.

Ana Hamanchilenu Dat Sefarim	אָנָּא הַמַנְחִילֵנוּ דַּת סְפָרִים
Chamishah. Hamashmi'enu	חֲמִשָּׁה. הַמַּשְׁמִיעֵנוּ
Diberotav Bekolot Chamishah.	דִּבְּרוֹתָיו בְּקוֹלוֹת חֲמִשָּׁה.
Haketuvim Al Haluchot	הַכְּתוּבִים עַל הַלֻּחוֹת

Chamishah Chamishah.	חֲמִשָּׁה חֲמִשָּׁה.
Hoshi'enu Bachagigat	הוֹשִׁיעֵנוּ בַּחֲגִיגַת
Yamim Chamishah:	יָמִים חֲמִשָּׁה:

Please, the One Who gave us a Law of five books. The One who related to us His sayings in five voices. The writings on the tablets were five and five. Save us on the festival of five days.

Hosha'ana. Hosha'ana:	הוֹשַׁעֲנָא. הוֹשַׁעֲנָא:

Please, save us. Please, save us.

Emuneicha Mitchanenim	אֱמוּנֶיךָ מִתְחַנְּנִים
Lachavosh Machtzam Keme'az	לַחֲבוֹשׁ מַחְצָם כְּמֵאָז
Chavasheta. Adonai Elohai	חָבַשְׁתָּ. יְהֹוָה אֱלֹהַי
Gadalta Me'od Hod Vehadar	גָּדַלְתָּ מְאֹד הוֹד וְהָדָר
Lavasheta: Nahaleni	לָבַשְׁתָּ: נַהֲלֵנִי
Bechukoteicha Lema'an	בְּחֻקֹּתֶיךָ לְמַעַן
Sheloshet Horai. Adonai	שְׁלֹשֶׁת הוֹרַי. יְהֹוָה
Necheni Vetzidkatecha Lema'an	נְחֵנִי בְּצִדְקָתֶךָ לְמַעַן
Shorerai: Yeriveicha Yovedu	שׁוֹרְרָי: יְרִיבֶיךָ יֹאבֵדוּ
Asher Betigratam Sigartanu.	אֲשֶׁר בְּתִגְרָתָם סִגַּרְתָּנוּ.
Adonai Ha'er Paneicha	יְהֹוָה הָאֵר פָּנֶיךָ
Itanu: Yah Asher Ein Lo Cheker	אִתָּנוּ: יָהּ אֲשֶׁר אֵין לוֹ חֵקֶר
Shelach Mevaser Tzur Eilom.	שְׁלַח מְבַשֵּׂר צוּר עֵילוֹם.
Adonai Oz Le'amo Yiten Adonai	יְהֹוָה עֹז לְעַמּוֹ יִתֵּן יְהֹוָה
Yevarech Et-Amo Vashalom:	יְבָרֵךְ אֶת־עַמּוֹ בַשָּׁלוֹם:
Tzefeh Galuti Ve'aneyi El	צְפֵה גָלוּתִי וְעָנְיִי אֵל

Nidrash Lechol-Sho'el.

נִדְרָשׁ לְכָל־שׁוֹאֵל.

Adonai Tzeva'ot Elohei

יְהוָה צְבָאוֹת אֱלֹהֵי

Yisra'el: Chanun Hamerachem

יִשְׂרָאֵל: חַנּוּן הַמְרַחֵם

Mi-Hikshah Elav Vayishlam.

מִי־הִקְשָׁה אֵלָיו וַיִּשְׁלָם.

Adonai Chasdecha Le'olam:

יְהוָה חַסְדְּךָ לְעוֹלָם:

Kabel Shav'i. Malki Vego'ali.

קַבֵּל שַׁוְעִי. מַלְכִּי וְגוֹאֲלִי.

Adonai Keraticha Chushah Li:

יְהוָה קְרָאתִיךָ חוּשָׁה לִּי:

Your faithful-ones are pleading to bind their wounds as You have bound before. Hashem, my God, You are very great; You are clothed with honor and majesty. Guide me in Your statutes for the sake of my three forefathers. Hashem, lead me in Your righteousness because of my enemies. Your adversaries will be lost, those who confined us in their conflict. Hashem, illuminate Your face upon us. Hashem, Who is beyond comprehension, send the messenger, Eternal Rock. Hashem, may He give strength to His people, may the Hashem bless His people with peace. Observe my exile and my poverty, God is answers all who ask. Hashem, God of Hosts, God of Yisrael, the Merciful One Who shows mercy, Who has hardened against Him and remained whole? Hashem, Your kindness is eternal. Accept my cry, my King and my Redeemer. Hashem, I have called You, hasten to me.

Hosha'ana. Hosha'ana:

הוֹשַׁעְנָא. הוֹשַׁעְנָא:

Please, save us. Please, save us.

Ana Hoshi'ah Na.

אָנָּא הוֹשִׁיעָה נָּא.

Ana Hoshi'ah Na:

אָנָּא הוֹשִׁיעָה נָּא:

Please, save us now. Please, save us now.

Ana Yotzeri Ukedoshi. She'eh

Lachshi Verachshi. Umecheh

Veha'aver Yokeshi. Hayom

Beyom Chamishi.

Hoshi'ah Na: Ana Hoshi'ah Na.

Ana Hoshi'ah Na:

אָנָּא יוֹצְרִי וּקְדוֹשִׁי. שְׁעֵה
לַחְשִׁי וְרַחְשִׁי. וּמְחֵה
וְהַעֲבֵר יוֹקְשִׁי. הַיּוֹם
בְּיוֹם חֲמִישִׁי.
הוֹשִׁיעָה נָּא: אָנָּא הוֹשִׁיעָה
נָא. אָנָּא הוֹשִׁיעָה נָּא:

Please, my Creator and my Holy One, listen to my whisper and my
thought. Erase and remove my snare. Today, on the fifth day:
please, save us now. Please, save us now. Please, save us now.

Ana Secheh Na Mokeshi. Ve'al-

Tizkor Aneshi. Peneh Elai

Doreshi. Hayom Beyom

Chamishi. Hoshi'ah Na:

Ana Hoshi'ah Na.

Ana Hoshi'ah Na:

אָנָּא סְחֵה נָא מוֹקְשִׁי. וְאַל־
תִּזְכֹּר עָנְשִׁי. פְּנֵה אֵלַי
דּוֹרְשִׁי. הַיּוֹם בְּיוֹם
חֲמִישִׁי. הוֹשִׁיעָה נָּא:
אָנָּא הוֹשִׁיעָה נָא.
אָנָּא הוֹשִׁיעָה נָּא:

Please, remove my snares and do not remember my punishment.
Turn to me, my Seeker, today, on the fifth day: please, save us now.
Please, save us now. Please, save us now.

Ani Vahu Hoshi'ah Na.

Ani Vahu Hoshi'ah Na:

אֲנִי וָהוּ הוֹשִׁיעָה נָא.
אֲנִי וָהוּ הוֹשִׁיעָה נָּא:

Ani VaHu, please save us now. Ani VaHu, please save us now.

Kehosha'ta Yekushei Malben.

Merimsat Hateven. Uchehidush

Matben. Dishashta Dosheshi:

Sifurei Eser. Yatze'u Mima'asar.

Petzem Na Mechoser. Nehalach

Beyom Chamishi. Ken

Hosha'ana. Ani Vahu Hoshi'ah

Na. Ani Vahu Hoshi'ah Na:

כְּהוֹשַׁעְתָּ יְקוּשֵׁי מַלְבֵּן.

מֵרְמִסַת הַתֶּבֶן. וּכְהִדּוּשׁ

מַתְבֵּן. דִּשַׁשְׁתָּ דוֹשְׁשִׁי:

סִפּוּרֵי עֶשֶׂר. יָצְאוּ מִמַּאֲסָר.

פְּצֶם נָא מֵחוֹסֶר. נְהַלֶּלְךָ

בְּיוֹם חֲמִישִׁי. כֵּן

הוֹשַׁעֲנָא. אֲנִי וָהוּ הוֹשִׁיעָה

נָא. אֲנִי וָהוּ הוֹשִׁיעָה נָא:

As You saved the ones surrounded by brick, from the crushing of the straw, and as if treading the straw. You have treaded those who crush me: the ones counted ten times came out from imprisonment. Save them, please, from their lack. We will praise You on the fifth day, so please save us. Ani VaHu, please save us now. Ani VaHu, please save us now.

Kehosha'ta Yeshurun. Migoy

Yetzirun. Ulecha Yeshorerun. El

Merim Roshi: Siftei Renanot.

Patzu Lecha Neginot. Betodah

Uvitchinot. Nehalach Beyom

Chamishi. Ken Hosha'ana.

Ani Vahu Hoshi'ah Na.

Ani Vahu Hoshi'ah Na:

כְּהוֹשַׁעְתָּ יְשֻׁרוּן. מִגּוֹי

יְצִירוּן. וּלְךָ יְשׁוֹרְרוּן. אֵל

מֵרִים רֹאשִׁי: שִׂפְתֵּי רְנָנוֹת.

פָּצוּ לְךָ נְגִינוֹת. בְּתוֹדָה

וּבִתְחִנוֹת. נְהַלֶּלְךָ בְּיוֹם

חֲמִישִׁי. כֵּן הוֹשַׁעֲנָא.

אֲנִי וָהוּ הוֹשִׁיעָה נָא.

אֲנִי וָהוּ הוֹשִׁיעָה נָא:

As you saved Yeshurun [Yisrael] from a nation, it's Craftsman and to You, they sing praises. God Who raises my head: lips full of joyous songs. They have opened for you melodies with gratitude and supplications. We will praise You on the fifth day: so, please save us. Ani VaHu, please save us now. Ani VaHu, please save us now.

Marom Shochen Ad. Na'aratz	מָרוֹם שׁוֹכֵן עַד. נַעֲרָץ
Bikdushah. Titbarach La'ad.	בִּקְדֻשָׁה. תִּתְבָּרַךְ לָעַד.
Shem El Ram Venisa.	שֵׁם אֵל רָם וְנִשָּׂא.
Meshorerim Umehalim.	מְשׁוֹרְרִים וּמְהַלְלִים.
Beshirah Chadashah. Sovevei	בְּשִׁירָה חֲדָשָׁה. סוֹבְבֵי
Toratecha Pe'amim Chamishah:	תוֹרָתְךָ פְּעָמִים חֲמִשָּׁה:

The Most High, dwelling forever, revered in holiness, be blessed forever. The name of God is raised and exalted. They sing and praise with a new song, those who encircle Your Torah five times.

Hoshi'ah Serideicha. El Shomer	הוֹשִׁיעָה שְׂרִידֶיךָ. אֵל שׁוֹמֵר
Emunim. Rachum Na	אֱמוּנִים. רַחוּם נָא
Chasadeicha. Chish Le'eitanim.	חֲסָדֶיךָ. חִישׁ לְאֵיתָנִים.
Uzechor Et-Beritecha. Lanu	וּזְכֹר אֶת־בְּרִיתְךָ. לָנוּ
Velivnei Vanim. Lehoshi'ah	וְלִבְנֵי בָנִים. לְהוֹשִׁיעָה
Lehargi'ah. Even Haroshah.	לְהַרְגִּיעָה. אֶבֶן הָרֹאשָׁה.
Sovevei Toratecha Pe'amim	סוֹבְבֵי תוֹרָתֶךָ פְּעָמִים
Chamishah:	חֲמִשָּׁה:

Save Your remnants, God, the Keeper of the faithful. Merciful one, please, hasten Your kindness to the mighty-ones. And remember Your covenant, for us and for our children's children. To save her, to calm her, the cornerstone. Those who encircle Your Torah five times.

Kehosha'ta Me'az Adatecha. Ken	כְּהוֹשַׁעְתָּ מֵאָז עֲדָתְךָ. כֵּן
Hoshi'ah Et-Amecha Uvarech	הוֹשִׁיעָה אֶת־עַמְּךָ וּבָרֵךְ
Et-Nachalatecha. Nehalach	אֶת־נַחֲלָתֶךָ. נְהַלֵּךְ

Beyom Chamishi. Ken	בְּיוֹם חֲמִישִׁי. כֵּן
Hosha'ana:	הוֹשַׁעֲנָא:

As You saved Your congregation from the beginning. So save Your people and bless Your inheritance. We will praise You on the fifth day, so please save us.

Ani Vahu Hoshi'ah Na.	אֲנִי וָהוּ הוֹשִׁיעָה נָּא.
Ani Vahu Hoshi'ah Na:	אֲנִי וָהוּ הוֹשִׁיעָה נָּא:

Ani VaHu, please save us now. Ani VaHu, please save us now.

Kakatuv: Hoshi'ah Et-Amecha	כַּכָּתוּב: הוֹשִׁיעָה אֶת־עַמֶּךָ
Uvarech Et-Nachalatecha	וּבָרֵךְ אֶת־נַחֲלָתֶךָ
Ure'em Venase'em Ad-Ha'olam:	וּרְעֵם וְנַשְּׂאֵם עַד־הָעוֹלָם:
Vene'emar: Veyihyu Devarai Eleh	וְנֶאֱמַר: וְיִהְיוּ דְבָרַי אֵלֶּה
Asher Hitchananti Lifnei	אֲשֶׁר הִתְחַנַּנְתִּי לִפְנֵי
Adonai Kerovim El-Adonai	יְהוָה קְרֹבִים אֶל־יְהוָה
Eloheinu Yomam Valayelah	אֱלֹהֵינוּ יוֹמָם וָלָיְלָה
La'asot Mishpat Avdo Umishpat	לַעֲשׂוֹת מִשְׁפַּט עַבְדּוֹ וּמִשְׁפַּט
Amo Yisra'el Devar-Yom	עַמּוֹ יִשְׂרָאֵל דְּבַר־יוֹם
Beyomo: Lema'an Da'at Kol-	בְּיוֹמוֹ: לְמַעַן דַּעַת כָּל־
Amei Ha'aretz Ki Adonai Hu	עַמֵּי הָאָרֶץ כִּי יְהוָה הוּא
Ha'elohim Ein Od: Lo-Yamush	הָאֱלֹהִים אֵין עוֹד: לֹא־יָמוּשׁ
Sefer Hatorah Hazeh Mipicha	סֵפֶר הַתּוֹרָה הַזֶּה מִפִּיךָ
Vehagita Bo Yomam Valaylah	וְהָגִיתָ בּוֹ יוֹמָם וָלָיְלָה
Lema'an Tishmor La'asot Kechol-	לְמַעַן תִּשְׁמֹר לַעֲשׂוֹת כְּכָל־
Hakatuv Bo Ki-Az Tatzliach Et-	הַכָּתוּב בּוֹ כִּי־אָז תַּצְלִיחַ אֶת־

Derachecha Ve'az Taskil: Halo
Tziviticha Chazak Ve'ematz Al-
Ta'arotz Ve'al-Techat Ki Imecha
Adonai Eloheicha Bechol Asher
Telech:

דְּרָכֶךָ וְאָז תַּשְׂכִּיל: הֲלוֹא
צִוִּיתִיךָ חֲזַק וֶאֱמָץ אַל־
תַּעֲרֹץ וְאַל־תֵּחָת כִּי עִמְּךָ
יְהֹוָה אֱלֹהֶיךָ בְּכֹל אֲשֶׁר
תֵּלֵךְ:

As it is written: Save Your people and bless Your inheritance, and shepherd them and exalt them forever. And says: May these words of my supplication before Hashem be close to Hashem our God, day and night, to do justice to His servant and justice to His people Yisrael, each matter day by day. So that all the peoples of the Earth may know that Hashem is God, there is no other. Do not let the Book of this Torah depart from your mouth, meditate on it day and night, in order that you may keep and do according to all that is written in it, for then you will succeed in your ways and then you will be wise. Have I not commanded you? Be strong and courageous, do not be afraid and do not be dismayed, for Hashem your God is with you wherever you go.

Hoshanot for the Sixth Day
הושענות ליום הששי

Erchatz Benikayon Kapai

אֶרְחַץ בְּנִקָיוֹן כַּפָּי

Va'asovevah Et-Mizbachacha

וַאֲסֹבְבָה אֶת־מִזְבַּחֲךָ

Adonai: Lashmia' Bekol Todah

יְהֹוָה: לַשְׁמִעַ בְּקוֹל תּוֹדָה

Ulesaper Kol-Nifle'oteicha.

וּלְסַפֵּר כָּל־נִפְלְאוֹתֶיךָ:

I will wash my hands in innocence, and I will encircle your altar, Hashem. That I may make the voice of thanksgiving to be heard, and tell of all Your wondrous works. (Ps. 26:6-7)

Hosha'ana. Hosha'ana:

הוֹשַׁעֲנָא. הוֹשַׁעֲנָא:

Please save us. Please save us:

Lema'anach Eloheinu.

לְמַעֲנָךְ אֱלֹהֵינוּ.

Lema'anach Bore'enu.

לְמַעֲנָךְ בּוֹרְאֵנוּ.

Lema'anach Go'alenu.

לְמַעֲנָךְ גּוֹאֲלֵנוּ.

Lema'anach Doreshenu:

לְמַעֲנָךְ דּוֹרְשֵׁנוּ:

For Your sake, our God. For Your sake, our Creator. For Your sake, our Redeemer. For Your sake, our Seeker.

Lema'anach Adir Adirim.

לְמַעֲנָךְ אַדִּיר אַדִּירִים.

Lema'anach Boreiruach Veyotzer

לְמַעֲנָךְ בּוֹרֵא רוּחַ וְיוֹצֵר

Harim. Lema'anach Gedol

הָרִים. לְמַעֲנָךְ גְּדוֹל

Ha'etzah Mashpil Umerim.

הָעֵצָה מַשְׁפִּיל וּמֵרִים.

Lema'anach Dover Tzedek

לְמַעֲנָךְ דּוֹבֵר צֶדֶק

Magid Meisharim.

מַגִּיד מֵישָׁרִים.

Lema'anach Hayodea' Va'ed Im	לְמַעֲנָךְ הַיּוֹדֵעַ וָעֵד אִם
Yisater Ish Bemistarim.	יִסָּתֵר אִישׁ בְּמִסְתָּרִים.
Lema'anach Vehu Be'echad Umi	לְמַעֲנָךְ וְהוּא בְּאֶחָד וּמִי
Yeshivenu Amarim.	יְשִׁיבֶנּוּ אֲמָרִים.
Lema'anach Zach Venaki	לְמַעֲנָךְ זַךְ וְנָקִי
Umitbarer Im Barim.	וּמִתְבָּרֵר עִם בָּרִים.
Lema'anach Chofes Matzpun	לְמַעֲנָךְ חוֹפֵשׂ מַצְפּוּן
Vechoker Kol-Chadarim.	וְחוֹקֵר כָּל־חֲדָרִים.
Lema'anach Tipechah Yemino	לְמַעֲנָךְ טִפְּחָה יְמִינוֹ
Shamayim Ve'asah Me'orim.	שָׁמַיִם וְעָשָׂה מְאוֹרִים.
Lema'anach Yasad Eretz Batzurot	לְמַעֲנָךְ יָסַד אֶרֶץ בַּצּוּרוֹת
Bika Ye'orim. Lema'anach Kabir	בִּקַּע יְאוֹרִים. לְמַעֲנָךְ כַּבִּיר
Koach Mechubad Ba'urim.	כֹּחַ מְכֻבָּד בָּאוּרִים.
Lema'anach Lo Yitamu Shenotav	לְמַעֲנָךְ לֹא יִתַּמּוּ שְׁנוֹתָיו
Ledor Dorim:	לְדוֹר דוֹרִים:

For Your sake, Mightiest of the mighty. For Your sake, Creator of the wind and the Former of mountains. For Your sake, Great in counsel, Who humbles and lifts high. For Your sake, Speaker of righteousness, declaring uprightness. For Your sake, Knower and Witness, whether a person hides in secret places. For Your sake, He Who is One, and Who will return us with utterances. For Your sake, Pure and Innocent and Who is pure with the pure. For Your sake, Liberator of the hidden and Searcher of all chambers. For Your sake, He Who spread out the sky with His right hand and made the luminaries. For Your sake, He Who founded the earth with its boundaries, carving the rivers in rocks. For Your sake, the Great in Power, honored with lights. For Your sake, His years will never end for generations of generations:

Hosha'ana. Hosha'ana: הוֹשַׁעְנָא. הוֹשַׁעְנָא:

Please save us. Please save us:

Ana Haborei Olamo Beyamim
Shishah. Haboneh Shesh
Tzela'ot Litzdadim Shishah.
Hayotzer Serafim Bichnafayim
Shishah. Hoshi'enu Bachagigat
Yamim Shishah:

אָנָּא הַבּוֹרֵא עוֹלָמוֹ בְּיָמִים
שִׁשָּׁה. הַבּוֹנֶה שֵׁשׁ
צְלָעוֹת לִצְדָדִים שִׁשָּׁה.
הַיוֹצֵר שְׂרָפִים בִּכְנָפַיִם
שִׁשָּׁה. הוֹשִׁיעֵנוּ בַּחֲגִיגַת
יָמִים שִׁשָּׁה:

Please, Creator of His world in six days. Who builds six sides, to the six sides. Who forms seraphs with six wings. Save us on the celebration of six days.

Ana Zechor Av Zanach To'evot
Shishah. Acharei Zikunav
Noledu Lo Banim Shishah. Nata
Eshel Uvorach Beketz Shanim
Shishah. Hoshi'enu Bachagigat
Yamim Shishah:

אָנָּא זְכֹר אָב זָנַח תּוֹעֵבוֹת
שִׁשָּׁה. אַחֲרֵי זְקֻנָיו
נוֹלְדוּ לוֹ בָנִים שִׁשָּׁה. נָטַע
אֵשֶׁל וּבֹרַךְ בְּקֵץ שָׁנִים
שִׁשָּׁה. הוֹשִׁיעֵנוּ בַּחֲגִיגַת
יָמִים שִׁשָּׁה:

Please, remember the father [Avraham] who abandoned six abominations. After his old age, six sons were born to him. He planted an Eshel [tree] and was blessed at the end of six years. Save us on the celebration of six days.

Ana Zechor Hane'ekad Bimkom	אָנָּא זְכֹר הַנֶּעֱקַד בִּמְקוֹם
Ma'arachot Shishah. Gonanto	מַעֲרְכוֹת שִׁשָּׁה. גּוֹנַנְתּוֹ
Umilato Mitzarot Shishah.	וּמִלַּטְתּוֹ מִצָּרוֹת שִׁשָּׁה.
Karah Mikva'ot Ledoreshei Vam	כָּרָה מִקְוָאוֹת לְדוֹרְשֵׁי בָם
Ma'alot Shishah. Hoshi'enu	מַעֲלוֹת שִׁשָּׁה. הוֹשִׁיעֵנוּ
Bachagigat Yamim Shishah:	בַּחֲגִיגַת יָמִים שִׁשָּׁה:

Please, remember the bound one [Yitzchak] in his sacrificial place of six levels. He groaned and escaped from six troubles. He dug wells for those seeking them, six levels. Save us on the celebration of six days.

Ana Zechor Tam Holid Min	אָנָּא זְכֹר תָּם הוֹלִיד מִן
Habechirah Shishah. Vetzivah	הַבְּכִירָה שִׁשָּׁה. וְצִוָּה
Kachat Minchah Miminim	קַחַת מִנְחָה מִמִּינִים
Shishah. Vehigbir Avi Shishah	שִׁשָּׁה. וְהִגְבִּיר אֲבִי שִׁשָּׁה
Hamevorachim Beshishah.	הַמְבוֹרָכִים בְּשִׁשָּׁה.
Hoshi'enu Bachagigat	הוֹשִׁיעֵנוּ בַּחֲגִיגַת
Yamim Shishah:	יָמִים שִׁשָּׁה:

Please, remember the innocent [Ya'akov] who begot from the firstborn [Leah] six [sons]. He commanded to take an offering [to Yosef] of six types. And strengthened the father of six who were blessed six [times]. Save us on the celebration of six days.

Ena Hamechaber La'efod	אָנָּא הַמְחַבֵּר לָאֵפוֹד
Shemot Shishah. Hamatzil	שְׁמוֹת שִׁשָּׁה. הַמַּצִּיל
Nefashot Be'arei Miklat Shishah.	נְפָשׁוֹת בְּעָרֵי מִקְלָט שִׁשָּׁה.
Hamorishenu Chachemat	הַמּוֹרִישֵׁנוּ חָכְמַת

Sedarim Shishah. Hoshi'enu   סְדָרִים שִׁשָׁה. הוֹשִׁיעֵנוּ

Bachagigat Yamim Shishah: בַּחֲגִיגַת יָמִים שִׁשָׁה:

Please, the One Who [commanded to] attached to the ephod six names. The One Who saves souls in six refuge cities. The One Who gives us wisdom [the Mishnah] of six orders. Save us on the celebration of six days.

Hosha'ana. Hosha'ana: הוֹשַׁעְנָא. הוֹשַׁעְנָא:

Please, save us. Please, save us.

Lema'an Av Atz Lavo Beyichud   לְמַעַן אָב אָץ לָבֹא בְּיִחוּד

Hashem Udevar Hamelech   הַשֵׁם וּדְבַר הַמֶּלֶךְ

Hayah Nachutz. Bo Beruch   הָיָה נָחוּץ. בֹּא בָּרוּךְ

Adonai Lamah Ta'amod Bachutz: יְהֹוָה לָמָה תַעֲמֹד בַּחוּץ:

Lema'an Ga'ah Limrirut   לְמַעַן גָּעָה לִמְרִירוּת

Matbeach Uvusar Be'ehyeh   מַטְבֵּחַ וּבָשַׂר בְּאֶהְיֶה

Asher Ehyeh. Devar   אֲשֶׁר אֶהְיֶה. דִּבֶּר

Adonai Shalom Yihyeh: Lema'an   יְהֹוָה שָׁלוֹם יִהְיֶה: לְמַעַן

Asher Haberit Karat Le'ish Tam   אֲשֶׁר הַבְּרִית כָּרַת לְאִישׁ תָּם

Yoshev Ohalav. Vehineh   יוֹשֵׁב אֹהָלָיו. וְהִנֵּה

Adonai Nitzav Alav: Lema'an   יְהֹוָה נִצָּב עָלָיו: לְמַעַן

Zach Nir'eita Lo Baser   זַךְ נִרְאֵיתָ לוֹ בָּשֵׂר

Lahamonai. Chizku Veya'ametz   לַהֲמוֹנַי. חִזְקוּ וְיַאֲמֵץ

Levavchem Kol-Hameyachalim   לְבַבְכֶם כָּל־הַמְיַחֲלִים

L'Adonai. Lema'an Kore'eicha   לַיהֹוָה: לְמַעַן קֹרְאֶיךָ

Be'asor Anashim Venashim   בֶּעָשׂוֹר אֲנָשִׁים וְנָשִׁים

Vataf. Re'evim Gam-Tzeme'im   וָטָף. רְעֵבִים גַּם־צְמֵאִים

Nafsham Bahem Tit'ataf:	נַפְשָׁם בָּהֶם תִּתְעַטָּף:
Lema'an Shem Kodshecha	לְמַעַן שֵׁם קָדְשֶׁךָ
She'on Yamim Tashbiach.	שְׁאוֹן יַמִּים תַּשְׁבִּיחַ.
Tiftach-Eretz Veyifru-Yesha	תִּפְתַּח־אֶרֶץ וְיִפְרוּ־יֶשַׁע
Utzedakah Tatzmiach:	וּצְדָקָה תַצְמִיחַ:

For the sake of the father [Avraham], who desired to come into unity with God, and the King's word was immediate. Come, blessed of Hashem, why do you stand outside? For the sake of [Yitzchak] who cried out for the bitterness of the altar, and was proclaimed 'I will be what I will be.' The word of Hashem, is that peace will be: for the sake of the covenant He made with the perfect on who would dwell in his tents. And behold, Hashem stands over him: for the sake of Your pure one [Moshe] to proclaim to the masses. Strengthen and let your hearts take courage, all who hope in Hashem. For the sake of those who call to You on the tenth [Yom Kippur]: men, women, and children. Hungry, and also thirsty, their souls faint within them. For the sake of Your holy name, the roar of the seas will praise You. The earth will open up and salvation will bud, and righteousness will spring up.

Hosha'ana. Hosha'ana:	הוֹשַׁעֲנָא. הוֹשַׁעֲנָא:

Please, save us. Please, save us.

Ana Hoshi'ah Na.	אָנָּא הוֹשִׁיעָה נָּא.
Ana Hoshi'ah Na:	אָנָּא הוֹשִׁיעָה נָּא:

Please, save us now. Please, save us now.

Ana Hayeshar Ma'aravi.

Vehayeshar Mahalachi.

Vechonenah Et Darki. Lalechet

El Har Kadeshi: Ukera Na

Deror. Lirvuyei Mamror.

Vesicham Ye'erav Kemo Mar-

Deror. Hayom Beyom Shishi.

Hoshi'ah Na: Ana Hoshi'ah

Na. Ana Hoshi'ah Na:

אָנָּא הַיְשַׁר מַעֲרָבִי.

וְהַיְשַׁר מַהֲלָכִי.

וְכוֹנְנָה אֶת דַּרְכִּי. לָלֶכֶת

אֶל הַר קָדְשִׁי: וּקְרָא נָא

דְרוֹר. לִרְוֵויֵי מַמְרוֹר.

וְשִׂיחָם יֶעֱרַב כְּמוֹ מָר־

דְּרוֹר. הַיּוֹם בְּיוֹם שִׁשִּׁי.

הוֹשִׁיעָה נָּא: אָנָּא הוֹשִׁיעָה

נָּא. אָנָּא הוֹשִׁיעָה נָּא:

Please, make my plan straight and straighten my progress, and prepare my way, to go to my holy mountain. And please proclaim freedom, for those filled with bitterness. Their conversation will be sweet like pure myrrh . Today, on the sixth day, save us now. Please, save us now. Please, save us now.

Ana Sagel Segulatecha.

Vekabetz Kehilatecha. Lehar

Nachalatecha. Mekom

Mikdashi: Pezurim Tekabetz.

Linveh Marbetz. Vetalbishem

Tashbetz. Hayom Beyom Shishi.

Hoshi'ah Na: Ana Hoshi'ah

Na. Ana Hoshi'ah Na:

אָנָּא סַגֵּל סְגֻלָּתֶךָ.

וְקַבֵּץ קְהִלָּתֶךָ. לְהַר

נַחֲלָתֶךָ. מְקוֹם

מִקְדָּשִׁי: פְּזוּרִים תְּקַבֵּץ.

לִנְוֵה מַרְבֵּץ. וְתַלְבִּישֵׁם

תַּשְׁבֵּץ. הַיּוֹם בְּיוֹם שִׁשִּׁי.

הוֹשִׁיעָה נָּא: אָנָּא הוֹשִׁיעָה

נָּא. אָנָּא הוֹשִׁיעָה נָּא:

Please, treasure Your treasured one [Yisrael] and gather Your assembly, to the mountain of Your inheritance, the place of my sanctuary. You will gather the scattered, to their land of rest, and dress them elegantly. Today, on the sixth day, save us now. Please, save us now. Please, save us now.

Ani Vahu Hoshi'ah Na.   אֲנִי וָהוּ הוֹשִׁיעָה נָּא.

Ani Vahu Hoshi'ah Na: אֲנִי וָהוּ הוֹשִׁיעָה נָּא:

Ani VaHu, please save us now. Ani VaHu, please save us now.

Kehosha'ta Yelidei Ahav. Me'ur   כְּהוֹשַׁעְתָּ יְלִידֵי אָהַב. מְאוֹר

Halahav. Umachatzta Rahav.   הַלַּהַב. וּמָחַצְתָּ רָהַב.

Lechalot Am Kadeshi: Selul   לְכַלּוֹת עַם קָדְשִׁי: סָלוּל

Umaslul. Pitachta Bematzlul.   וּמַסְלוּל. פִּתַּחְתָּ בְּמַצְלוּל.

La'avor Am Kalul. Nehalach   לַעֲבוֹר עַם כָּלוּל. נְהַלְּלָךְ

Beyom Shishi. Ken   בְּיוֹם שִׁשִּׁי. כֵּן

Hosha'ana. Ani Vahu Hoshi'ah   הוֹשַׁעֲנָא. אֲנִי וָהוּ הוֹשִׁיעָה

Na. Ani Vahu Hoshi'ah Na: נָּא. אֲנִי וָהוּ הוֹשִׁיעָה נָּא:

As You saved the children of the beloved [Avraham], from the flame's burning, and You crushed Mitzrayim, to complete my holy people. You made a path and trail, You opened in the depts, to pass a people whole. We will praise You on the sixth day, so please save us. Ani VaHu, please save us now. Ani VaHu, please save us now.

Kehosha'ta Yechilei Tor.   כְּהוֹשַׁעְתָּ יְחִילֵי תוֹר.

Me'eretz Kaftor. Vatasem Mistor.   מֵאֶרֶץ כַּפְתּוֹר. וַתָּשֶׂם מִסְתּוֹר.

Aleimo Kedoshi: Segafta Put.   עָלֵימוֹ קְדוֹשִׁי: סָגַפְתָּ פוּט.

Bishchin Nafut. Lechaletz Am   בִּשְׁחִין נָפוּט. לְחַלֵּץ עַם

Shafut. Nehalach Beyom   שָׁפוּט. נְהַלְּלָךְ בְּיוֹם

Shishi.Ken Hosha'ana. Ani Vahu   שִׁשִּׁי. כֵּן הוֹשַׁעֲנָא. אֲנִי וָהוּ

Hoshi'ah Na. Ani Vahu   הוֹשִׁיעָה נָּא. אֲנִי וָהוּ

Hoshi'ah Na: הוֹשִׁיעָה נָּא:

As You saved those who feared, from the land of Caphtor [Mitzrayim], And You placed in refuge, His people, my holy-ones: You afflicted Put [Mitzrayim] with boils that burned to save a condemned people. Let us praise You on the sixth day, so please save us. Ani VaHu, please save us now. Ani VaHu, please save us now.

She'eh Elyon Lachshi. Na'aratz	שְׁעֵה עֶלְיוֹן לַחֲשִׁי. נַעֲרָץ
Bikdushah. Hayom Lecha	בִּקְדֻשָּׁה. הַיּוֹם לְךָ
Bedareshi. Beshirah Chadashah.	בְּדָרְשִׁי. בְּשִׁירָה חֲדָשָׁה.
Uchevosh Na Et Koveshi. Refa	וּכְבוֹשׁ נָא אֶת כּוֹבְשִׁי. רְפָא
Makah Anushah. Sovevei	מַכָּה אֲנוּשָׁה. סוֹבְבֵי
Toratecha Zot Hapa'am Shishah:	תוֹרָתְךָ זֹאת הַפַּעַם שִׁשָּׁה:

Attend, Most High, to my whisper. Revered in holiness. Today when I seek You with a new song. And conquer, please, my conquerors, heal the human wound. Who encircle Your Torah, this sixth time.

Hakshev Na Kol Evyon. Bekor'o	הַקְשֵׁב נָא קוֹל אֶבְיוֹן. בְּקָרְאוֹ
Min-Metzarim. Am Homeh	מִן־מְצָרִים. עַם הוֹמֶה
Betzayon. Bidei Amim Vetzarim.	בְּצָיוֹן. בִּידֵי עַמִּים וְצָרִים.
Vechish Yesha Ufidyon. Le'am	וְחִישׁ יֵשַׁע וּפִדְיוֹן. לְעַם
Belo Hon Nimkarim. Ushevut	בְּלֹא הוֹן נִמְכָּרִים. וּשְׁבוּת
Ge'ulatam Temaher Tachishah.	גְּאֻלָּתָם תְּמַהֵר תָּחִישָׁה.
Sovevei Toratecha Zot Hapa'am	סוֹבְבֵי תוֹרָתְךָ זֹאת הַפַּעַם
Shishah:	שִׁשָּׁה:

Please listen to the voice of the poor, when he calls from distress. A nation murmuring in desolation, in the hands of nations and enemies, hasten salvation and redemption. To a nation sold for no wealth. Hasten their redemption and return them speedily. The ones who encircle Your Torah, this sixth time.

Kehosha'ta Me'az Adatecha.	כְּהוֹשַׁעְתָּ מֵאָז עֲדָתֶךָ.
Ken Hoshi'ah Et-Amecha	כֵּן הוֹשִׁיעָה אֶת־עַמֶּךָ
Uvarech Et-Nachalatecha.	וּבָרֵךְ אֶת־נַחֲלָתֶךָ.
Nehalach Beyom Shishi. Ken	נְהַלֵּךְ בְּיוֹם שִׁשָּׁה. כֵּן
Hosha'ana:	הוֹשַׁעְנָא:

As You have saved Your congregation from the beginning, so save Your people now and bless Your inheritance. We praise you on the sixth day, so please save us.

Ani Vahu Hoshi'ah Na.	אֲנִי וָהוּ הוֹשִׁיעָה נָּא.
Ani Vahu Hoshi'ah Na:	אֲנִי וָהוּ הוֹשִׁיעָה נָּא:

Ani VaHu, please save us now. Ani VaHu, please save us now.

Kakatuv: Hoshi'ah Et-Amecha	כַּכָּתוּב: הוֹשִׁיעָה אֶת־עַמֶּךָ
Uvarech Et-Nachalatecha	וּבָרֵךְ אֶת־נַחֲלָתֶךָ
Ure'em Venase'em Ad-Ha'olam:	וּרְעֵם וְנַשְּׂאֵם עַד־הָעוֹלָם:
Vene'emar: Veyihyu Devarai Eleh	וְנֶאֱמַר: וְיִהְיוּ דְבָרַי אֵלֶּה
Asher Hitchananti Lifnei	אֲשֶׁר הִתְחַנַּנְתִּי לִפְנֵי
Adonai Kerovim El-Adonai	יְהֹוָה קְרֹבִים אֶל־יְהֹוָה
Eloheinu Yomam Valayelah	אֱלֹהֵינוּ יוֹמָם וָלָיְלָה
La'asot Mishpat Avdo Umishpat	לַעֲשׂוֹת מִשְׁפַּט עַבְדּוֹ וּמִשְׁפַּט
Amo Yisra'el Devar-Yom	עַמּוֹ יִשְׂרָאֵל דְּבַר־יוֹם
Beyomo: Lema'an Da'at Kol-	בְּיוֹמוֹ: לְמַעַן דַּעַת כָּל־
Amei Ha'aretz Ki Adonai Hu	עַמֵּי הָאָרֶץ כִּי יְהֹוָה הוּא
Ha'elohim Ein Od: Lo-Yamush	הָאֱלֹהִים אֵין עוֹד: לֹא־יָמוּשׁ
Sefer Hatorah Hazeh Mipicha	סֵפֶר הַתּוֹרָה הַזֶּה מִפִּיךָ

Vehagita Bo Yomam Valaylah

Lema'an Tishmor La'asot Kechol-

Hakatuv Bo Ki-Az Tatzliach Et-

Derachecha Ve'az Taskil:

Halo Tziviticha Chazak Ve'ematz

Al-Ta'arotz Ve'al-Techat Ki

Imecha Adonai Eloheicha Bechol

Asher Telech:

וְהָגִיתָ בּוֹ יוֹמָם וָלַיְלָה
לְמַעַן תִּשְׁמֹר לַעֲשׂוֹת כְּכָל־
הַכָּתוּב בּוֹ כִּי־אָז תַּצְלִיחַ
אֶת־דְּרָכֶךָ וְאָז תַּשְׂכִּיל:
הֲלוֹא צִוִּיתִיךָ חֲזַק וֶאֱמָץ
אַל־תַּעֲרֹץ וְאַל־תֵּחָת כִּי
עִמְּךָ יְהוָה אֱלֹהֶיךָ בְּכֹל
אֲשֶׁר תֵּלֵךְ:

As it is written: Save Your people and bless Your inheritance, and shepherd them and exalt them forever. And says: May these words of my supplication before Hashem be close to Hashem our God, day and night, to do justice to His servant and justice to His people Yisrael, each matter day by day. So that all the peoples of the Earth may know that Hashem is God, there is no other. Do not let the Book of this Torah depart from your mouth, meditate on it day and night, in order that you may keep and do according to all that is written in it, for then you will succeed in your ways and then you will be wise. Have I not commanded you? Be strong and courageous, do not be afraid and do not be dismayed, for Hashem your God is with you wherever you go.

The Order of Hoshanah Rabbah

סדר הושענה רבה

Hoshanah Rabbah: First Hakafah

Erchatz Benikayon Kapai	אֶרְחַץ בְּנִקָיוֹן כַּפָּי
Va'asovevah Et-Mizbachacha	וַאֲסֹבְבָה אֶת־מִזְבַּחֲךָ
Adonai: Lashmia' Bekol Todah	יְהוָה: לַשְׁמִעַ בְּקוֹל תּוֹדָה
Ulesaper Kol-Nifle'oteicha.	וּלְסַפֵּר כָּל־נִפְלְאוֹתֶיךָ:

I will wash my hands in innocence, and I will encircle your altar, Hashem. That I may make the voice of thanksgiving to be heard, and tell of all Your wondrous works. (Ps. 26:6-7)

Hosha'ana. Hosha'ana:	הוֹשַׁעֲנָא. הוֹשַׁעֲנָא:

Please save us. Please save us:

Lema'anach Eloheinu.	לְמַעַנְךָ אֱלֹהֵינוּ.
Lema'anach Bore'enu.	לְמַעַנְךָ בּוֹרְאֵנוּ.
Lema'anach Go'alenu.	לְמַעַנְךָ גּוֹאֲלֵנוּ.
Lema'anach Doreshenu:	לְמַעַנְךָ דּוֹרְשֵׁנוּ:

For Your sake, our God. For Your sake, our Creator. For Your sake, our Redeemer. For Your sake, our Seeker.

Lema'anach Adir Adirim.	לְמַעַנְךָ אַדִּיר אַדִּירִים.
Lema'anach Boreiruach Veyotzer	לְמַעַנְךָ בּוֹרֵא רוּחַ וְיוֹצֵר
Harim. Lema'anach Gedol	הָרִים. לְמַעַנְךָ גְּדוֹל

Ha'etzah Mashpil Umerim. הָעֵצָה מַשְׁפִּיל וּמֵרִים.

Lema'anach Dover Tzedek לְמַעַנְךָ דּוֹבֵר צֶדֶק

Magid Meisharim. מַגִּיד מֵישָׁרִים.

Lema'anach Hayodea' Va'ed Im לְמַעַנְךָ הַיּוֹדֵעַ וָעֵד אִם

Yisater Ish Bemistarim. יִסָּתֵר אִישׁ בְּמִסְתָּרִים.

Lema'anach Vehu Be'echad Umi לְמַעַנְךָ וְהוּא בְּאֶחָד וּמִי

Yeshivenu Amarim. יְשִׁיבֵנוּ אֲמָרִים.

Lema'anach Zach Venaki לְמַעַנְךָ זַךְ וְנָקִי

Umitbarer Im Barim. וּמִתְבָּרֵר עִם בָּרִים.

Lema'anach Chofes Matzpun לְמַעַנְךָ חוֹפֵשׂ מַצְפּוּן

Vechoker Kol-Chadarim. וְחוֹקֵר כָּל־חֲדָרִים.

Lema'anach Tipechah Yemino לְמַעַנְךָ טִפְּחָה יְמִינוֹ

Shamayim Ve'asah Me'orim. שָׁמַיִם וְעָשָׂה מְאוֹרִים.

Lema'anach Yasad Eretz Batzurot לְמַעַנְךָ יָסַד אֶרֶץ בַּצּוּרוֹת

Bika Ye'orim. Lema'anach Kabir בִּקַּע יְאוֹרִים. לְמַעַנְךָ כַּבִּיר

Koach Mechubad Ba'urim. כֹּחַ מְכֻבָּד בָּאוּרִים.

Lema'anach Lo Yitamu Shenotav לְמַעַנְךָ לֹא יִתַּמּוּ שְׁנוֹתָיו

Ledor Dorim: לְדוֹר דּוֹרִים:

For Your sake, Mightiest of the mighty. For Your sake, Creator of the wind and the Former of mountains. For Your sake, Great in counsel, Who humbles and lifts high. For Your sake, Speaker of righteousness, declaring uprightness. For Your sake, Knower and Witness, whether a person hides in secret places. For Your sake, He Who is One, and Who will return us with utterances. For Your sake, Pure and Innocent and Who is pure with the pure. For Your sake, Liberator of the hidden and Searcher of all chambers. For Your sake, He Who spread out the sky with His right hand and made the luminaries. For Your sake, He Who founded the earth with its boundaries, carving the rivers in rocks. For Your sake, the Great in

Power, honored with lights. For Your sake, His years will never end for generations of generations:

Hosha'ana. Hosha'ana:	הוֹשַׁעְנָא. הוֹשַׁעְנָא:

Please, save us. Please, save us:

Ana El Echad Ushemo Echad.	אָנָּא אֵל אֶחָד וּשְׁמוֹ אֶחָד.
Umi Yeshivenu Vehu Ve'echad.	וּמִי יְשִׁיבֵנוּ וְהוּא בְאֶחָד.
Kara Shamayim Va'aretz	קָרָא שָׁמַיִם וָאָרֶץ
Vaya'amdu	וַיַּעֲמֹדוּ
Che'echad. Hoshi'enu	כְּאֶחָד. הוֹשִׁיעֵנוּ
Behakafat Pa'am Echat:	בְּהַקָּפַת פַּעַם אֶחָת:

Please, God, Who is One and His name is One. And Who will return us, He is One. He called heaven and earth, and they stood as one. Save us in this first hakafah:

Ana Zechor Av Yarash Et-	אָנָּא זְכֹר אָב יָרַשׁ אֶת־
Ha'aretz Vehayah Echad.	הָאָרֶץ וְהָיָה אֶחָד.
Hechin Lamoredim Lev Echad	הֵכִין לַמּוֹרְדִים לֵב אֶחָד
Vederech Echad. Likro Chulam	וְדֶרֶךְ אֶחָד. לִקְרֹא כֻלָּם
Beshem Adonai Ule'ovdo	בְּשֵׁם יְהוָה וּלְעָבְדוֹ
Shechem Echad. Hoshi'enu	שְׁכֶם אֶחָד. הוֹשִׁיעֵנוּ
Behakafat Pa'am Echat:	בְּהַקָּפַת פַּעַם אֶחָת:

Please remember, a father [Avraham] inherited who inherited the land and was one man. Who prepared for the rebels one heart and one way. To they would all call in the name of Hashem, and to serve Him, shoulder to shoulder, as one. Save us in this first hakafah:

Ana Zechor Ben Yachid Hayah	אָנָּא זְכֹר בֵּן יָחִיד הָיָה
Lifnei Aviv Echad. Sheneihem	לִפְנֵי אָבִיו אֶחָד. שְׁנֵיהֶם
Benisayon Halechu Che'echad.	בְּנִסָּיוֹן הָלְכוּ כְאֶחָד.
Natata Kofer Tachtav Ayil	נָתַתָּ כֹּפֶר תַּחְתָּיו אַיִל
Echad. Hoshi'enu Behakafat	אֶחָד. הוֹשִׁיעֵנוּ בְּהַקָּפַת
Pa'am Echat:	פַּעַם אֶחָת:

Please remember, the only son [Yitzchak] who was before his father as one. Both of them went through the test as one. You provided a ram as a substitute, one ram. Save us in this first hakafah:

Ana Zechor Av Hosif Chelek	אָנָּא זְכֹר אָב הוֹסִיף חֵלֶק
Shechem Echad. Kivah Lehaflit	שְׁכֶם אֶחָד. קִוָּה לְהַפְלִיט
Hamachaneh Ha'echad. Asaf	הַמַּחֲנֶה הָאֶחָד. אָסַף
Banav Lekabel Malchut	בָּנָיו לְקַבֵּל מַלְכוּת
Shamayim Peh	שָׁמַיִם פֶּה
Echad. Hoshi'enu Behakafat	אֶחָד. הוֹשִׁיעֵנוּ בְּהַקָּפַת
Pa'am Echat:	פַּעַם אֶחָת:

Please remember a father [Ya'akov], who added one more portion [to Yosef]. Who hoped to save one of the camps, and gathered his sons to accept the kingship of heaven with one voice. Save us in this first hakafah:

Ana Hamashmi'enu Shetayim	אָנָּא הַמַּשְׁמִיעֵנוּ שְׁתַּיִם
Bekolot Uverakim Ke'echad.	בְּקוֹלוֹת וּבְרָקִים כְּאֶחָד.
Hamanchilenu Torah Achat	הַמַּנְחִילֵנוּ תּוֹרָה אַחַת
Umishpat Echad. Hoshi'enu	וּמִשְׁפָּט אֶחָד. הוֹשִׁיעֵנוּ
Behakafat Pa'am Echat:	בְּהַקָּפַת פַּעַם אֶחָת:

Please, Who let us hear two [mitzvot] in thunder and lightning as if one. Who endowed us with one Torah and one Law. Save us in this first hakafah:

Hosha'ana. Hosha'ana:	הוֹשַׁעְנָא. הוֹשַׁעְנָא:

Please, save us. Please, save us:

Yah Ayom. Zechor Hayom. Berit	יָהּ אָיֹם. זְכֹר הַיּוֹם. בְּרִית
Shiv'at Temimeicha. Berit	שִׁבְעַת תְּמִימֶיךָ. בְּרִית
Ezrach. Asher Arach. Bechukot	אֶזְרָח. אֲשֶׁר אָרַח. בְּחֻקּוֹת
Dat Ne'umeicha. Av Rachman.	דָּת נְאוּמֶיךָ. אָב רַחְמָן.
Karev Zeman. Pedutenu	קָרֵב זְמַן. פְּדוּתֵנוּ
Berachameicha. Zacherenu	בְּרַחֲמֶיךָ. זָכְרֵנוּ
Adonai Birtzon Amecha:	יְהוָה בִּרְצוֹן עַמֶּךָ:

Awesome God, remember today, the covenant of Your seven perfect ones. The covenant of the Ezrachi [Avraham], who followed in the Law of Your proclamation. Compassionate Father, bring near the time of our redemption in Your mercy. Remember us, Hashem, in favoring Your people.

Mecholel Kol. Vechol Yachol.	מְחוֹלֵל כֹּל. וְכֹל יָכֹל.
Heyeh Nidrash Ledoresheicha.	הֱיֵה נִדְרָשׁ לְדוֹרְשֶׁיךָ.
Vehimatze. Vehitratzeh. Le'am	וְהִמָּצֵא. וְהִתְרַצֵּה. לְעַם
Dofekei Delateicha. Behazkiram.	דּוֹפְקֵי דְלָתֶיךָ. בְּהַזְכִּירָם.
Zechut Avraham. Vetzidkat Kol-	זְכוּת אַבְרָהָם. וְצִדְקַת כָּל־
Chasideicha. She'eh Nivam.	חֲסִידֶיךָ. שְׁעֵה נִיבָם.
Behitkorvam. Belulavam	בְּהִתְקָרְבָם. בְּלוּלָבָם

Leshachareicha. Zacherenu   לְשַׁחֲרֶיךָ. זָכְרֵנוּ

Adonai Birtzon Amecha: יְהֹוָה בִּרְצוֹן עַמֶּךָ:

Creator of all, and of everything, be accessible to those who seek You. Be present and gracious to the people knocking on Your doors. When they recall the merit of Avraham and the righteousness of all Your pious ones, receive their words as they draw near with their lulavim to seek You. Remember us, Hashem, in favoring Your people.

Rachamana Idkar Lan Keyameh   רַחֲמָנָא אִדְכַּר לָן קְיָמֵהּ

De'avraham Rechima: דְּאַבְרָהָם רְחִימָא:

Merciful One, remember for us the merit of Avraham, Your beloved.

Rachamana Areim Areim   רַחֲמָנָא אָרֵים אָרֵים

Yeminach Ve'atzmach   יְמִינָךְ וְאַצְמַח

Purkanach: פֻּרְקָנָךְ:

Merciful One, raise Your right hand and bring forth Your salvation.

Rachamana Chatminan Besifra   רַחֲמָנָא חַתְמִנָן בְּסִפְרָא

Dechayei: דְּחַיֵּי:

Merciful One, inscribe us in the Book of Life.

Rachamana Chatminan Besifra   רַחֲמָנָא חַתְמִנָן בְּסִפְרָא

Derachamei: דְּרַחֲמֵי:

Merciful One, inscribe us in the Book of Mercy.

Rachamana Chatminan Besifra   רַחֲמָנָא חַתְמִנָן בְּסִפְרָא

Detzadikei Vachasidei: דְּצַדִּיקֵי וַחֲסִידֵי:

Merciful One, inscribe us in the Book of the Righteous and the Pious.

Rachamana Chatminan Besifra
Disharei Utemimei:

רַחֲמָנָא חַתְמִנָן בְּסִפְרָא
דִישָׁרֵי וּתְמִימֵי:

Merciful One, inscribe us in the Book of the Upright and the Perfect.

Rachamana Chatminan Besifra
Defarnasata Tavta Umezonei
Tavei:

רַחֲמָנָא חַתְמִנָן בְּסִפְרָא
דְּפַרְנָסָתָא טַבְתָא וּמְזוֹנֵי
טָבֵי:

Merciful One, inscribe us in the Book of Good Livelihood and Good Sustenance.

Rachamana Petach Shemaya
Litzlotin:

רַחֲמָנָא פְּתַח שְׁמַיָא
לִצְלוֹתִין:

Merciful One, open the heavens to our prayers.

Rachamana Tuv Merugzach:

רַחֲמָנָא תּוּב מֵרֻגְזָךְ:

Merciful One, turn back from Your anger.

Rachamana Vela Nehdar
Reikam Min-Kamach:

רַחֲמָנָא וְלָא נֶהְדָּר
רֵיקָם מִן־קַמָּךְ:

Merciful One, let us not return empty handed from before You.

Shema Yisra'el Adonai Eloheinu
Adonai Echad.

שְׁמַע יִשְׂרָאֵל יְהֹוָה אֱלֹהֵינוּ
יְהֹוָה אֶחָד:

Hear, O Yisrael: Hashem is our God, Hashem is One.

Adonai Hu Ha'elohim

Adonai Hu Ha'elohim. (say two times)

Hashem, He is God. Hashem, He is God. (say two times)

יְהוָֹה הוּא הָאֱלֹהִים
יְהוָֹה הוּא הָאֱלֹהִים: (שתי פעמים)

Adonai Melech.

Adonai Malach.

Adonai Yimloch Le'olam Va'ed. (say two times)

Hashem reigns, Hashem has reigned, Hashem will reign forever and ever. (say two times)

יְהוָֹה מֶלֶךְ.
יְהוָֹה מָלָךְ.
יְהוָֹה יִמְלֹךְ לְעֹלָם וָעֶד: (שתי פעמים)

Eloheinu Shebashamayim

Shema Kolenu Vekabel

Tefilatenu Beratzon:

Our God in Heaven, hear our voice and accept our prayers with favor.

אֱלֹהֵינוּ שֶׁבַּשָּׁמַיִם
שְׁמַע קוֹלֵנוּ וְקַבֵּל
תְּפִלָּתֵנוּ בְּרָצוֹן:

Eloheinu Shebashamayim Al-

Te'abedenu Be'orech Galutenu:

Our God in Heaven, do not abandon us in our long exile.

אֱלֹהֵינוּ שֶׁבַּשָּׁמַיִם אַל־
תְּאַבְּדֵנוּ בְּאֹרֶךְ גָּלוּתֵנוּ:

Abed Kol-Hakamim Aleinu

Lera'ah:

Destroy all who rise against us for evil.

אַבֵּד כָּל־הַקָּמִים עָלֵינוּ
לְרָעָה:

Eloheinu Shebashamayim

Chatemenu Besefer Chayim

Tovim:

Our God in Heaven, inscribe us in the Book of Good Life.

אֱלֹהֵינוּ שֶׁבַּשָּׁמַיִם
חָתְמֵנוּ בְּסֵפֶר חַיִּים
טוֹבִים:

Chatemenu Besefer Tzadikim
Vachasidim: חָתְמֵנוּ בְּסֵפֶר צַדִּיקִים וַחֲסִידִים:

Inscribe us in the Book of the Righteous and the Pious.

Chatemenu Besefer Yesharim
Utemimim: חָתְמֵנוּ בְּסֵפֶר יְשָׁרִים וּתְמִימִים:

Inscribe us in the Book of the Upright and the Perfect.

Chatemenu Besefer Mezonot
Ufarnasah Tovah: חָתְמֵנוּ בְּסֵפֶר מְזוֹנוֹת וּפַרְנָסָה טוֹבָה:

Inscribe us in the Book of Sustenance and Good Livelihood.

Eloheinu Shebashamayim
Karevenu La'avodatecha: אֱלֹהֵינוּ שֶׁבַּשָּׁמַיִם קָרְבֵנוּ לַעֲבוֹדָתֶךָ:

Our God in Heaven, draw us near to Your service.

Eloheinu Shebashamayim Refa
Kol-Cholei Amecha Yisra'el: אֱלֹהֵינוּ שֶׁבַּשָּׁמַיִם רְפָא כָּל־חוֹלֵי עַמְּךָ יִשְׂרָאֵל:

Our God in Heaven, heal all of the sick of Your people Yisrael.

Anenu Elohei Avraham Anenu: עֲנֵנוּ אֱלֹהֵי אַבְרָהָם עֲנֵנוּ:

Anenu Ha'oneh Be'et Ratzon   עֲנֵנוּ הָעוֹנֶה בְּעֵת רָצוֹן

Anenu: Anenu Rachum   עֲנֵנוּ: עֲנֵנוּ רַחוּם

Vechanun Anenu: וְחַנּוּן עֲנֵנוּ:

Answer us, God of Avraham, answer us; Answer us, He who answers at a favorable time, answer us; Answer us, Merciful and Gracious One, answer us.

Adonai Chonenu

Vahakimenu. Uvesefer Chayim

Zacherenu Vechatemenu:

יְהֹוָה חָנֵּנוּ
וַהֲקִימֵנוּ. וּבְסֵפֶר חַיִּים
זָכְרֵנוּ וְחָתְמֵנוּ:

Hashem, be gracious to us and lift us up. And in the Book of Life, remember us and inscribe us.

Adonai Or Paneicha Hayom

Nesah Aleinu. Uvesefer Chayim

Zacherenu Vechatemenu:

יְהֹוָה אוֹר פָּנֶיךָ הַיּוֹם
נְסָה עָלֵינוּ. וּבְסֵפֶר חַיִּים
זָכְרֵנוּ וְחָתְמֵנוּ:

Hashem, let the light of Your face shine upon us today. And in the Book of Life, remember us and inscribe us.

Adonai Aseh Lema'an

Shemecha. Vechusah Al Yisra'el

Amecha:

יְהֹוָה עֲשֵׂה לְמַעַן
שְׁמֶךָ. וְחוּסָה עַל יִשְׂרָאֵל
עַמֶּךָ:

Hashem, do it for the sake of Your name, and have compassion on Yisrael, Your people.

Adonai Aseh Lema'an Avraham

Ezrach Temimecha. Vechusah Al

Yisra'el Amecha:

יְהֹוָה עֲשֵׂה לְמַעַן אַבְרָהָם
אֶזְרַח תְּמִימֶךָ. וְחוּסָה עַל
יִשְׂרָאֵל עַמֶּךָ:

Hashem, do it for the sake of Avraham, Your perfect citizen, and have compassion on Yisrael, Your people.

Adonai Aseh Lema'an Harugim

Userufim Al Yichud Kedushat

Shemecha. Vechusah Al Yisra'el

Amecha:

יְהֹוָה עֲשֵׂה לְמַעַן הַרוּגִים
וּשְׂרוּפִים עַל יִחוּד קְדֻשַּׁת
שְׁמֶךָ. וְחוּסָה עַל יִשְׂרָאֵל
עַמֶּךָ:

Hashem, do it for the sake of those who were killed and burned for the sanctification of Your name, and have compassion on Yisrael, Your people.

De'anei Le'avraham Avinu
Behar Hamoriyah. Aneinan:

דְּעָנֵי לְאַבְרָהָם אָבִינוּ
בְּהַר הַמּוֹרִיָּה. עֲנֵינָן:

He who answered our father Avraham on Mount Moriah, answer us.

De'anei Letzadikei Vachasidei
Utemimei Di Bechol-Dor
Vedor. Aneinan:

דְּעָנֵי לְצַדִּיקֵי וַחֲסִידֵי
וּתְמִימֵי דִּי בְּכָל־דָּר
וָדָר. עֲנֵינָן:

He who answers the righteous, the pious, and the perfect in every generation, answer us.

Todi'eni Orach Chayim Sova
Semachot Et-Paneicha Ne'imot
Bimincha Netzach.

תּוֹדִיעֵנִי אֹרַח חַיִּים שֹׂבַע
שְׂמָחוֹת אֶת־פָּנֶיךָ נְעִמוֹת
בִּימִינְךָ נֶצַח:

You make known to me the path of life; in Your presence is fullness of joy; at Your right hand are pleasures forevermore.

Ana Bechoach. Gedulat
Yeminecha. Tatir Tzerurah:

אָנָּא בְּכֹחַ. גְּדוּלַת
יְמִינְךָ. תַּתִּיר צְרוּרָה:

Please, with the power of Your great right hand, release the bound.

Continue on the next page with the Second Hakafah.

Hoshanah Rabbah: Second Hakafah

Hosha'ana. Hosha'ana: הוֹשַׁעְנָא. הוֹשַׁעְנָא:

Please, save us. Please, save us:

Ana El Echad Umevayesh	אָנָּא אֵל אֶחָד וּמְבַיֵּשׁ
Omerim Shenayim. Bachatzi	אוֹמְרִים שְׁנַיִם. בַּחֲצִי
Hashem Bara Olamot Be'otiyot	הַשֵּׁם בָּרָא עוֹלָמוֹת בְּאוֹתִיּוֹת
Shenayim. Yatzar Hakol Ba'avur	שְׁנַיִם. יָצַר הַכֹּל בַּעֲבוּר
Adam Ve'ezro Shenayim.	אָדָם וְעֶזְרוֹ שְׁנַיִם.
Hoshi'enu Behakafat Pe'amim	הוֹשִׁיעֵנוּ בְּהַקָּפַת פְּעָמִים
Shenayim:	שְׁנַיִם:

Please, God, Who is One and Who humiliates those who say two.
With half of the Name, He created worlds with two letters. He
formed everything for the sake of man and his help, two. Save us in
this second hakafah:

Ana Zechor Av Banah Beveit-El	אָנָּא זְכֹר אָב בָּנָה בְּבֵית־אֵל
Mizbechot Shenayim.	מִזְבְּחוֹת שְׁנַיִם.
Benisayon Halach Im Ne'arim	בְּנִסָּיוֹן הָלַךְ עִם נְעָרִים
Shenayim. Ukerato Min	שְׁנַיִם. וּקְרָאתוֹ מִן־
Hashamayim Pe'amim	הַשָּׁמַיִם פְּעָמִים
Shenayim. Hoshi'enu Behakafat	שְׁנַיִם. הוֹשִׁיעֵנוּ בְּהַקָּפַת
Pe'amim Shenayim:	פְּעָמִים שְׁנַיִם:

Please remember the father [Avraham] who built two altars in Beit-El. He went through trials with two youths. And You called him from heaven two times. Save us in this second hakafah:

Ana Zechor Ben Hichmir	אָנָּא זְכֹר בֵּן הִכְמִיר
Rachamei Av Ba'amirot	רַחֲמֵי אָב בַּאֲמִירוֹת
Shenayim. Chananto Goyim	שְׁנַיִם. חֲנַנְתּוֹ גוֹיִם
Shenayim Ule'umim Shenayim.	שְׁנַיִם וּלְאֻמִּים שְׁנַיִם.
Vayvarech Heveh Gevir	וַיְבָרֶךְ הֱוֵה גְבִיר
Pe'amim Shenayim. Hoshi'enu	פְּעָמִים שְׁנַיִם. הוֹשִׁיעֵנוּ
Behakafat Pe'amim Shenayim:	בְּהַקָּפַת פְּעָמִים שְׁנַיִם:

Please remember the son who aroused the mercy of his father with two utterances. You favored him with two nations and two peoples. And he [Ya'akov] blessed him "to be a lord [over his brother]' two times. Save us in this second hakafah:

Ana Zechor Hayah Tza'ir	אָנָּא זְכֹר הָיָה צָעִיר
Venachal Pi Shenayim. Ve'asah	וְנָחַל פִּי שְׁנַיִם. וְעָשָׂה
Mat'amim Gedayim Shenayim.	מַטְעַמִּים גְּדָיִים שְׁנַיִם.
Avar Bemaklo Et-Hayarden	עָבַר בְּמַקְלוֹ אֶת־הַיַּרְדֵּן
Vehayah Lemachanot	וְהָיָה לְמַחֲנוֹת
Shenayim. Hoshi'enu Behakafat	שְׁנַיִם. הוֹשִׁיעֵנוּ בְּהַקָּפַת
Pe'amim Shenayim:	פְּעָמִים שְׁנַיִם:

Please remember [Ya'akov] who was younger and inherited twice. And he made great delicacies from young goats, two. He crossed the Yarden with his staff and was two camps. Save us in this second hakafah:

Ana Hamashmi'enu Torah	אָנָּא הַמַּשְׁמִיעֵנוּ תוֹרָה
Al-Yedei Ro'im Shenayim.	עַל־יְדֵי רוֹעִים שְׁנַיִם.
Hamanchilenu Aseret Devarim	הַמַּנְחִילֵנוּ עֲשֶׂרֶת דְּבָרִים
Al Luchot Shenayim. Hama'azin	עַל לֻחוֹת שְׁנַיִם. הַמַּאֲזִין
Ume'id Banu Edim	וּמֵעִיד בָּנוּ עֵדִים
Shenayim. Hoshi'enu Behakafat	שְׁנַיִם. הוֹשִׁיעֵנוּ בְּהַקָּפַת
Pe'amim Shenayim:	פְּעָמִים שְׁנַיִם:

Please, the One Who made us hear the Torah through two shepherds. Who bequeathed to us the Ten Commandments on two tablets. Who listens and bears witness for us with two witnesses. Save us in this second hakafah:

| Hosha'ana. Hosha'ana: | הוֹשַׁעֲנָא. הוֹשַׁעֲנָא: |

Please, save us. Please, save us:

Berit Nifkad. Asher Ne'ekad.	בְּרִית נִפְקַד. אֲשֶׁר נֶעֱקַד.
Leha'alot Lefaneicha. Keseh	לְהַעֲלוֹת לְפָנֶיךָ. כְּשֶׂה
Ne'esar. Vegam Nimsar. Asot	נֶאֱסַר. וְגַם נִמְסָר. עֲשׂוֹת
Hatov Be'eineicha. Retzeh	הַטּוֹב בְּעֵינֶיךָ. רְצֵה
Giz'o. Vechon Zar'o. Be'et	גִּזְעוֹ. וְחוֹן זַרְעוֹ. בְּעֵת
Bo'am Lefaneicha. Ve'im	בּוֹאָם לְפָנֶיךָ. וְאִם
Chovam. Anah Vam. Aseh Na	חוֹבָם. עֲנָה בָם. עֲשֵׂה נָא
Lema'an Shemecha. Zacherenu	לְמַעַן שְׁמֶךָ. זָכְרֵנוּ
Adonai Birtzon Amecha:	יְהֹוָה בִּרְצוֹן עַמֶּךָ:

The covenant remembered, of the appointed one who was bound, to be offered before You. Like a lamb that was tied up and also delivered, doing what was good in Your eyes. Favor his offspring, and have mercy on his seed, when they come before You. And if their sin responds against them, please act for the sake of Your name. Remember us, Hashem, in favoring Your people:

Zechut Yitzchak. Bashachak.	זְכוּת יִצְחָק. בַּשַּׁחַק.
Chatum Bemidat Hagevurah.	חָתוּם בְּמִדַּת הַגְּבוּרָה.
Tizkor Eli. Tzur Go'ali. Le'am	תִּזְכֹּר אֵלִי. צוּר גּוֹאֲלִי. לְעַם
Sho'el Mimach Ezrah. Akdato.	שׁוֹאֵל מִמָּךְ עֶזְרָה. עֲקֵדָתוֹ.
Vetzidkato. Meshoch Le'am	וְצִדְקָתוֹ. מְשׁוֹךְ לְעַם
Bishmach Nikra. Chatemem	בְּשִׁמְךָ נִקְרָא. חָתְמֵם
Letovah. Bindavah. El Ne'ezar	לְטוֹבָה. בִּנְדָבָה. אֵל נֶאְזָר
Bigvurah. Minachalatecha.	בִּגְבוּרָה. מִנַּחֲלָתְךָ.
Usegulatecha. Lo Tichla	וּסְגֻלָּתְךָ. לֹא תִכְלָא
Rachameicha. Zacherenu	רַחֲמֶיךָ. זָכְרֵנוּ
Adonai Birtzon Amecha:	יְהֹוָה בִּרְצוֹן עַמֶּךָ:

The merit of Yitzchak, in the heavens, is sealed with the attribute of Gevurah (might). Remember, my God, Rock, my Redeemer, the people asking for Your help. His binding and his righteousness, extend to the people called by Your name. Seal them for good, willingly, God endowed with might. From Your inheritance, and Your treasured possession, do not withhold Your mercy. Remember us, Hashem, in favoring Your people:

Rachamana Idkar Lan Keyameh	רַחֲמָנָא אִדְכַּר לָן קְיָמֵהּ
Deyitzchak Akeida:	דְּיִצְחָק עֲקֵידָא:

Merciful One, remember for us the merit of the binding of Yitzchak:

Rachamana Bechisufei Apin　　רַחֲמָנָא בְּכִסּוּפֵי אַפִּין

Ateina Lemikrei Kamach　　אָתֵינָא לְמִקְרֵי קַמָּךְ

Rachem Alan:　　רַחֵם עֲלָן:

Merciful One, with longing faces, we come to call upon You, have mercy on us:

Rachamana Chatminan　　רַחֲמָנָא חָתְמִנָּן

Besifra Dechayei:　　בְּסִפְרָא דְחַיֵּי:

Merciful One, inscribe us in the Book of Life.

Rachamana Chatminan Besifra　　רַחֲמָנָא חָתְמִנָּן בְּסִפְרָא

Derachamei:　　דְרַחֲמֵי:

Merciful One, inscribe us in the Book of Mercy.

Rachamana Chatminan Besifra　　רַחֲמָנָא חָתְמִנָּן בְּסִפְרָא

Detzadikei Vachasidei:　　דְצַדִּיקֵי וַחֲסִידֵי:

Merciful One, inscribe us in the Book of the Righteous and the Pious.

Rachamana Chatminan Besifra　　רַחֲמָנָא חָתְמִנָּן בְּסִפְרָא

Disharei Utemimei:　　דִישָׁרֵי וּתְמִימֵי:

Merciful One, inscribe us in the Book of the Upright and the Perfect.

Rachamana Chatminan Besifra　　רַחֲמָנָא חָתְמִנָּן בְּסִפְרָא

Defarnasata Tavta Umezonei　　דְפַרְנָסָתָא טַבְתָא וּמְזוֹנֵי

Tavei:　　טָבֵי:

Merciful One, inscribe us in the Book of Good Livelihood and Good Sustenance.

Rachamana Petach Shemaya
Litzlotin:

רַחֲמָנָא פְּתַח שְׁמַיָּא לִצְלוֹתִין:

Merciful One, open the heavens to our prayers.

Rachamana Tuv Merugzach:

רַחֲמָנָא תּוּב מֵרֻגְזָךְ:

Merciful One, turn back from Your anger.

Rachamana Vela Nehdar
Reikam Min-Kamach:

רַחֲמָנָא וְלָא נֶהְדַּר רֵיקָם מִן־קַמָּךְ:

Merciful One, let us not return empty handed from before You.

Shema Yisra'el Adonai Eloheinu
Adonai Echad.

שְׁמַע יִשְׂרָאֵל יְהֹוָה אֱלֹהֵינוּ יְהֹוָה אֶחָד:

Hear, O Yisrael: Hashem is our God, Hashem is One.

Adonai Hu Ha'elohim
Adonai Hu Ha'elohim. (say two times)

יְהֹוָה הוּא הָאֱלֹהִים יְהֹוָה הוּא הָאֱלֹהִים: (שתי פעמים)

Hashem, He is God. Hashem, He is God. (say two times)

Adonai Melech.
Adonai Malach.
Adonai Yimloch Le'olam Va'ed. (say two times)

יְהֹוָה מֶלֶךְ. יְהֹוָה מָלָךְ. יְהֹוָה יִמְלֹךְ לְעֹלָם וָעֶד: (שתי פעמים)

Hashem reigns, Hashem has reigned, Hashem will reign forever and ever. (say two times)

Eloheinu Shebashamayim
Shema Kolenu Vekabel
Tefilatenu Beratzon:

אֱלֹהֵינוּ שֶׁבַּשָּׁמַיִם
שְׁמַע קוֹלֵנוּ וְקַבֵּל
תְּפִלָּתֵנוּ בְּרָצוֹן:

Our God in Heaven, hear our voice and accept our prayers with favor.

Eloheinu Shebashamayim
Beritcha Zechor Ve'al-
Tishkachenu:

אֱלֹהֵינוּ שֶׁבַּשָּׁמַיִם
בְּרִיתְךָ זְכֹר וְאַל־
תִּשְׁכָּחֵנוּ:

Our God in Heaven, remember Your covenant and do not forget us.

Barech Et Lachmenu Ve'et
Meimeinu:

בָּרֵךְ אֶת לַחְמֵנוּ וְאֶת
מֵימֵינוּ:

Bless our bread and our water.

Eloheinu Shebashamayim
Chatemenu Besefer Chayim
Tovim:

אֱלֹהֵינוּ שֶׁבַּשָּׁמַיִם
חָתְמֵנוּ בְּסֵפֶר חַיִּים
טוֹבִים:

Our God in Heaven, inscribe us in the Book of Good Life.

Chatemenu Besefer Tzadikim
Vachasidim:

חָתְמֵנוּ בְּסֵפֶר צַדִּיקִים
וַחֲסִידִים:

Inscribe us in the Book of the Righteous and the Pious.

Chatemenu Besefer Yesharim
Utemimim:

חָתְמֵנוּ בְּסֵפֶר יְשָׁרִים
וּתְמִימִים:

Inscribe us in the Book of the Upright and the Perfect.

Chatemenu Besefer Mezonot

Ufarnasah Tovah:

חָתְמֵנוּ בְּסֵפֶר מְזוֹנוֹת

וּפַרְנָסָה טוֹבָה:

Inscribe us in the Book of Sustenance and Good Livelihood.

Eloheinu Shebashamayim

Karevenu La'avodatecha:

אֱלֹהֵינוּ שֶׁבַּשָּׁמַיִם

קָרְבֵנוּ לַעֲבוֹדָתֶךָ:

Our God in Heaven, draw us near to Your service.

Eloheinu Shebashamayim Refa

Kol-Cholei Amecha Yisra'el:

אֱלֹהֵינוּ שֶׁבַּשָּׁמַיִם רְפָא

כָּל־חוֹלֵי עַמְּךָ יִשְׂרָאֵל:

Our God in Heaven, heal all of the sick of Your people Yisrael.

Anenu Ufachad Yitzchak Anenu:

Anenu Ha'oneh Be'et Tzarah

Anenu: Anenu Rachum

Vechanun Anenu:

עֲנֵנוּ וּפַחַד יִצְחָק עֲנֵנוּ:

עֲנֵנוּ הָעוֹנֶה בְּעֵת צָרָה

עֲנֵנוּ: עֲנֵנוּ רַחוּם

וְחַנּוּן עֲנֵנוּ:

Answer us, Fear of Yitzchak, answer us: Answer us, the One who responds in times of trouble, answer us: Answer us, Merciful and Gracious One, answer us:

Adonai Chonenu

Vahakimenu. Uvesefer Chayim

Zacherenu Vechatemenu:

יְהֹוָה חָנֵּנוּ

וַהֲקִימֵנוּ. וּבְסֵפֶר חַיִּים

זָכְרֵנוּ וְחָתְמֵנוּ:

Hashem, be gracious to us and lift us up. And in the Book of Life, remember us and inscribe us.

Adonai Beyom Yeshu'atah

Basrenu Verachamenu. Uvesefer

Chayim Zacherenu

Vechatemenu:

יְהֹוָה בְּיוֹם יְשׁוּעָתָה
בַּשְּׂרֵנוּ וְרַחֲמֵנוּ. וּבְסֵפֶּר
חַיִּים זָכְרֵנוּ
וְחָתְמֵנוּ:

Hashem, on the day of Your salvation, bring us good news and have mercy on us. And in the Book of Life, remember and inscribe us:

Adonai Aseh Lema'an

Shemecha. Vechusah Al Yisra'el

Amecha:

יְהֹוָה עֲשֵׂה לְמַעַן
שְׁמֶךָ. וְחוּסָה עַל יִשְׂרָאֵל
עַמֶּךָ:

Hashem, do it for the sake of Your name, and have compassion on Yisrael, Your people.

Adonai Aseh Lema'an Yitzchak

Ne'ekad Be'ulamecha.

Vechusah Al Yisra'el Amecha:

יְהֹוָה עֲשֵׂה לְמַעַן יִצְחָק
נֶעֱקַד בְּאוּלָמֶךָ.
וְחוּסָה עַל יִשְׂרָאֵל עַמֶּךָ:

Hashem, act for the sake of Yitzchak, who was bound on Your altar, and have mercy on Yisrael, Your people:

Adonai Aseh Lema'an Harugim

Userufim Al Yichud Kedushat

Shemecha. Vechusah Al Yisra'el

Amecha:

יְהֹוָה עֲשֵׂה לְמַעַן הַרוּגִים
וּשְׂרוּפִים עַל יִחוּד קְדֻשַּׁת
שְׁמֶךָ. וְחוּסָה עַל יִשְׂרָאֵל
עַמֶּךָ:

Hashem, do it for the sake of those who were killed and burned for the sanctification of Your name, and have compassion on Yisrael, Your people.

De'anei Leyitzchak Al Gabei-
Madbecha. Aneinan:

דְּעָנֵי לְיִצְחָק עַל גַּבֵּי־
מַדְבְּחָא. עֲנֵינָן:

The One who answered Yitzchak on the altar, answer us:

De'anei Letzadikei Vachasidei
Utemimei Di Bechol-Dor
Vedor. Aneinan:

דְּעָנֵי לְצַדִּיקֵי וַחֲסִידֵי
וּתְמִימֵי דִּי בְּכָל־דָּר
וָדָר. עֲנֵינָן:

He who answers the righteous, the pious, and the perfect in every generation, answer us.

Todi'eni Orach Chayim Sova
Semachot Et-Paneicha Ne'imot
Bimincha Netzach.

תּוֹדִיעֵנִי אֹרַח חַיִּים שֹׂבַע
שְׂמָחוֹת אֶת־פָּנֶיךָ נְעִמוֹת
בִּימִינְךָ נֶצַח:

You make known to me the path of life; in Your presence is fullness of joy; at Your right hand are pleasures forevermore.

Kabel Rinat. Amecha Sagveinu.
Tahareinu Nora.

קַבֵּל רִנַּת. עַמְּךָ שַׂגְּבֵנוּ.
טַהֲרֵנוּ נוֹרָא:

God of awe, accept Your people's prayer; strengthen us, cleanse us.

Continue on the next page with the Third Hakafah.

Hoshanah Rabbah: Third Hakafah

Hosha'ana. Hosha'ana: הוֹשַׁעֲנָא. הוֹשַׁעֲנָא:

Please, save us. Please, save us:

Ana Ha'el Hanikdash Bikdushot	אָנָּא הָאֵל הַנִּקְדָּשׁ בִּקְדֻשּׁוֹת
Sheloshah. Bara Bema'aseh	שְׁלֹשָׁה. בָּרָא בְּמַעֲשֵׂה
Vereshit Bechol-Yom Sheloshah.	בְרֵאשִׁית בְּכָל־יוֹם שְׁלֹשָׁה.
Uvashishi Uvashevi'i Sheloshah	וּבַשִּׁשִּׁי וּבַשְּׁבִיעִי שְׁלֹשָׁה
Sheloshah. Hoshi'enu Behakafat	שְׁלֹשָׁה. הוֹשִׁיעֵנוּ בְּהַקָּפַת
Pe'amim Sheloshah:	פְּעָמִים שְׁלֹשָׁה:

Please, God, Who is sanctified with three sanctifications. Who created in the acts of creation each day with three. And on the sixth and seventh, three and three. Save us in this third hakafah:

Ana Zechor Av Ra'ah Mal'achim	אָנָּא זְכֹר אָב רָאָה מַלְאָכִים
Sheloshah. Vaymaher	שְׁלֹשָׁה. וַיְמַהֵר
Lehas'idam Se'im Sheloshah.	לְהַסְעִידָם סְאִים שְׁלֹשָׁה.
Halechu Ito Ba'alei Verit	הָלְכוּ אִתּוֹ בַּעֲלֵי בְרִית
Sheloshah. Hoshi'enu Behakafat	שְׁלֹשָׁה. הוֹשִׁיעֵנוּ בְּהַקָּפַת
Pe'amim Sheloshah:	פְּעָמִים שְׁלֹשָׁה:

Please, remember the father [Avraham] who saw three angels. And he hurried to prepare for them three semi [measures]. Save us in this third hakafah:

Ana Zechor Ben Huchan   אָנָּא זְכֹר בֵּן הוּכַן

La'akedah Leyamim Sheloshah.   לַעֲקֵדָה לְיָמִים שְׁלֹשָׁה.

Karat Berit Im Melech   כָּרַת בְּרִית עִם מֶלֶךְ

Umere'ehu Veshar Tzeva'o   וּמֵרֵעֵהוּ וְשַׂר צְבָאוֹ

Sheloshah. Bizchuto Nachalu   שְׁלֹשָׁה. בִּזְכוּתוֹ נָחֲלוּ

Vanav Ketarim. Sheloshah.   בָנָיו כְּתָרִים. שְׁלֹשָׁה.

Hoshi'enu Behakafat Pe'amim   הוֹשִׁיעֵנוּ בְּהַקָּפַת פְּעָמִים

Sheloshah: שְׁלֹשָׁה:

Please, remember the son [Yitzchak] who was prepared for the binding for three days. He made a covenant with the king, and his friend, and the army chief, three. By his merit, his sons inherited three crowns. Save us in this third hakafah:

Ana Zechor Av Chazah Sulam   אָנָּא זְכֹר אָב חָזָה סֻלָּם

Be'olim Veyoredim Sheloshah.   בְּעוֹלִים וְיוֹרְדִים שְׁלֹשָׁה.

Ufitzel Barehatim Maklot   וּפִצֵּל בָּרְהָטִים מַקְלוֹת

Sheloshah. Vayeshalach Banav   שְׁלֹשָׁה. וַיִּשְׁלַח בָּנָיו

Letzo'an Pe'amim Sheloshah.   לְצוֹעַן פְּעָמִים שְׁלֹשָׁה.

Hoshi'enu Behakafat Pe'amim   הוֹשִׁיעֵנוּ בְּהַקָּפַת פְּעָמִים

Sheloshah: שְׁלֹשָׁה:

Please, remember the father [Ya'akov] who saw a ladder with ascending and descending, three [angels]. And he carved with a chisel three sticks. And he sent his sons to Zoan three times. Save us in this third hakafah:

Ana Hago'alenu Al-Yedei Achim   אָנָּא הַגּוֹאֲלֵנוּ עַל־יְדֵי אַחִים

Sheloshah. Hassam Banu   שְׁלֹשָׁה. הַשָּׂם בָּנוּ

Ma'alot Kohanim Leviyim   מַעֲלוֹת כֹּהֲנִים לְוִים

Veyisra'el Sheloshah.	וְיִשְׂרָאֵל שְׁלֹשָׁה.
Hamanchilenu Torah Nevi'im	הַמַּנְחִילֵנוּ תּוֹרָה נְבִיאִים
Uchetuvim Sheloshah.	וּכְתוּבִים שְׁלֹשָׁה.
Hoshi'enu Behakafat Pe'amim	הוֹשִׁיעֵנוּ בְּהַקָּפַת פְּעָמִים
Sheloshah:	שְׁלֹשָׁה:

Please, our Redeemer, through brothers who were three. He placed among us three levels: Kohanim, Levi'im, and Yisrael. He gave to us the Torah, Nevi'im, and Ketuvim, three. Save us in this third hakafah:

Hosha'ana. Hosha'ana:	הוֹשַׁעֲנָא. הוֹשַׁעֲנָא:

Please, save us. Please, save us:

Limudach. Vegam Yedidach.	לִמּוּדָךְ. וְגַם יְדִידָךְ.
Yisra'el Lach Mekora. Asher	יִשְׂרָאֵל לָךְ מִקְרָא. אֲשֶׁר
Chalam. Vehen Sulam.	חָלַם. וְהֵן סֻלָּם.
Bamarom Lo Mora. El Echad.	בַּמָּרוֹם לוֹ מוֹרָא. אֵל אֶחָד.
Lecha Pachad. Vayomer Mah-	לְךָ פָּחַד. וַיֹּאמֶר מַה־
Norah. Zechor Tzidko. Vegam	נּוֹרָה. זְכֹר צִדְקוֹ. וְגַם
Na'ako. Lish'erit Nish'arah	נַאֲקוֹ. לִשְׁאֵרִית נִשְׁאָרָה
Nahala'ah. Asher Nashe'ah. Zeh	נַחֲלָאָה. אֲשֶׁר נָשָׁאָה. זֶה
Kameh Eimecha. Zacherenu	כַּמֶּה אֵימֶךָ. זָכְרֵנוּ
Adonai Birtzon Amecha:	יְהוָה בִּרְצוֹן עַמֶּךָ:

Your disciple and also Your beloved, Yisrael is called by You. Who dreamed, and behold, a ladder in the heights to him was awesome. God, Who is One, he feared You, and he said, "How awesome!" Remember his righteousness and also his cry, for the remaining remnant. The weary who have borne this, Your fear, so much. Remember us, Hashem, in favoring Your people:

Zechor Achuz. Vegam Shavutz.	זְכֹר אָחוּז. וְגַם שָׁבוּץ.
Chatum Bemidat Tif'eret. Medat	חָתוּם בְּמִדַּת תִּפְאֶרֶת. מִדַּת
Emet. Be'emet. Yerushah Lo	אֱמֶת. בֶּאֱמֶת. יְרֻשָׁה לוֹ
Vechoteret. Tif'arto. Betumato.	וְכוֹתֶרֶת. תִּפְאַרְתּוֹ. בְּתֻמָּתוֹ.
Tamid Bo Niksheret. Udemuto.	תָּמִיד בּוֹ נִקְשֶׁרֶת. וּדְמוּתוֹ.
Vetzurato. Chakukah Ba'ateret.	וְצוּרָתוֹ. חֲקוּקָה בַּעֲטֶרֶת.
Hu Ish Tam. Bishmach	הוּא אִישׁ תָּם. בְּשִׁמְךָ
Nechtam. Samto Al Kes	נֶחְתָּם. שַׂמְתּוֹ עַל כֵּס
Rachameicha. Zacherenu	רַחֲמֶיךָ. זָכְרֵנוּ
Adonai Birtzon Amecha:	יְהֹוָה בִּרְצוֹן עַמֶּךָ:

Remember the one who was grasped and also engraved, sealed with the attribute of Tiferet (beauty), the attribute of truth. Truly, an inheritance for him and crown. His beauty in his perfection is always bound to him. His likeness and form are engraved on the crown. He is a perfect man, sealed with Your name. You have placed him on the throne of Your mercy. Remember us, Hashem, in favoring Your people:

Rachamana Idkar Lan Keyameh	רַחֲמָנָא אִדְכַּר לָן קְיָמֵהּ
Deya'akov Sheleima:	דְּיַעֲקֹב שְׁלֵימָא:

Merciful One, remember for us the merit of Ya'akov, the perfect one:

Rachamana Gallei Gevurtach	רַחֲמָנָא גַּלֵּי גְבוּרְתָּךְ
Uferok Lan:	וּפְרֹק לָן:

Merciful One, reveal Your strength and redeem us:

Rachamana Chatminan Besifra Dechayei:

רַחֲמָנָא חַתְמִנָן בְּסִפְרָא דְחַיֵּי:

Merciful One, inscribe us in the Book of Life.

Rachamana Chatminan Besifra Derachamei:

רַחֲמָנָא חַתְמִנָן בְּסִפְרָא דְרַחֲמֵי:

Merciful One, inscribe us in the Book of Mercy.

Rachamana Chatminan Besifra Detzadikei Vachasidei:

רַחֲמָנָא חַתְמִנָן בְּסִפְרָא דְצַדִּיקֵי וַחֲסִידֵי:

Merciful One, inscribe us in the Book of the Righteous and the Pious.

Rachamana Chatminan Besifra Disharei Utemimei:

רַחֲמָנָא חַתְמִנָן בְּסִפְרָא דִישָׁרֵי וּתְמִימֵי:

Merciful One, inscribe us in the Book of the Upright and the Perfect.

Rachamana Chatminan Besifra Defarnasata Tavta Umezonei Tavei:

רַחֲמָנָא חַתְמִנָן בְּסִפְרָא דְפַרְנָסָתָא טַבְתָּא וּמְזוֹנֵי טָבֵי:

Merciful One, inscribe us in the Book of Good Livelihood and Good Sustenance.

Rachamana Petach Shemaya Litzlotin:

רַחֲמָנָא פְּתַח שְׁמַיָּא לִצְלוֹתִין:

Merciful One, open the heavens to our prayers.

Rachamana Tuv Merugzach:

רַחֲמָנָא תּוּב מֵרָגְזָךְ:

Merciful One, turn back from Your anger.

Rachamana Vela Nehdar   רַחֲמָנָא וְלָא נֶהְדַּר

Reikam Min-Kamach: רֵיקָם מִן־קַמָּךְ:

Merciful One, let us not return empty handed from before You.

Shema Yisra'el Adonai Eloheinu   שְׁמַע יִשְׂרָאֵל יְהֹוָה אֱלֹהֵינוּ

Adonai Echad.   יְהֹוָה אֶחָד:

Hear, O Yisrael: Hashem is our God, Hashem is One.

Adonai Hu Ha'elohim   יְהֹוָה הוּא הָאֱלֹהִים

Adonai Hu Ha'elohim. (say two   יְהֹוָה הוּא הָאֱלֹהִים: (שתי פעמים)

times)

Hashem, He is God. Hashem, He is God. (say two times)

Adonai Melech.   יְהֹוָה מֶלֶךְ.

Adonai Malach.   יְהֹוָה מָלָךְ.

Adonai Yimloch Le'olam Va'ed.   יְהֹוָה יִמְלֹךְ לְעֹלָם וָעֶד: (שתי

(say two times)   פעמים)

Hashem reigns, Hashem has reigned, Hashem will reign forever and ever. (say two times)

Eloheinu Shebashamayim   אֱלֹהֵינוּ שֶׁבַּשָּׁמַיִם

Shema Kolenu Vekabel   שְׁמַע קוֹלֵנוּ וְקַבֵּל

Tefilatenu Beratzon: תְּפִלָּתֵנוּ בְּרָצוֹן:

Our God in Heaven, hear our voice and accept our prayers with favor.

Eloheinu Shebashamayim Galeh	אֱלֹהֵינוּ שֶׁבַּשָּׁמַיִם גַּלֵּה
Kevod Malchutecha Aleinu	כְּבוֹד מַלְכוּתְךָ עָלֵינוּ
Meherah:	מְהֵרָה:

Our God in heaven, reveal the glory of Your kingdom upon us quickly:

Eloheinu Shebashamayim	אֱלֹהֵינוּ שֶׁבַּשָּׁמַיִם
Chatemenu Besefer Chayim	חָתְמֵנוּ בְּסֵפֶר חַיִּים
Tovim:	טוֹבִים:

Our God in Heaven, inscribe us in the Book of Good Life.

Chatemenu Besefer Tzadikim	חָתְמֵנוּ בְּסֵפֶר צַדִּיקִים
Vachasidim:	וַחֲסִידִים:

Inscribe us in the Book of the Righteous and the Pious.

Chatemenu Besefer Yesharim	חָתְמֵנוּ בְּסֵפֶר יְשָׁרִים
Utemimim:	וּתְמִימִים:

Inscribe us in the Book of the Upright and the Perfect.

Chatemenu Besefer Mezonot	חָתְמֵנוּ בְּסֵפֶר מְזוֹנוֹת
Ufarnasah Tovah:	וּפַרְנָסָה טוֹבָה:

Inscribe us in the Book of Sustenance and Good Livelihood.

Eloheinu Shebashamayim	אֱלֹהֵינוּ שֶׁבַּשָּׁמַיִם
Karevenu La'avodatecha:	קָרְבֵנוּ לַעֲבוֹדָתֶךָ:

Our God in Heaven, draw us near to Your service.

Eloheinu Shebashamayim Refa אֱלֹהֵינוּ שֶׁבַּשָּׁמַיִם רְפָא

Kol-Cholei Amecha Yisra'el: כָּל־חוֹלֵי עַמְּךָ יִשְׂרָאֵל:

Our God in Heaven, heal all of the sick of Your people Yisrael.

Anenu Avir Ya'akov Anenu: עֲנֵנוּ אֲבִיר יַעֲקֹב עֲנֵנוּ:

Anenu Ha'oneh Be'et עֲנֵנוּ הָעוֹנֶה בְּעֵת

Rachamim Anenu: Anenu רַחֲמִים עֲנֵנוּ: עֲנֵנוּ

Rachum Vechanun Anenu: רַחוּם וְחַנּוּן עֲנֵנוּ:

Answer us, Mighty One of Ya'akov, answer us; Answer us, You Who responds in a time of mercy, answer us; Answer us, Merciful and Gracious One, answer us.

Adonai Chonenu יְהֹוָה חָנֵּנוּ

Vahakimenu. Uvesefer Chayim וַהֲקִימֵנוּ. וּבְסֵפֶר חַיִּים

Zacherenu Vechatemenu: זָכְרֵנוּ וְחָתְמֵנוּ:

Hashem, be gracious to us and lift us up. And in the Book of Life, remember us and inscribe us.

Adonai Galgel Hamon יְהֹוָה גַּלְגֵּל הֲמוֹן

Rachameicha Aleinu. Uvesefer רַחֲמֶיךָ עָלֵינוּ. וּבְסֵפֶר

Chayim Zacherenu חַיִּים זָכְרֵנוּ

Vechatemenu: וְחָתְמֵנוּ:

Hashem, let Your abundant mercy come upon us. And in the Book of Life, remember us and inscribe us.

Adonai Aseh Lema'an
Shemecha. Vechusah Al Yisra'el
Amecha:

יְהֹוָה עֲשֵׂה לְמַעַן
שְׁמֶךָ. וְחוּסָה עַל יִשְׂרָאֵל
עַמֶּךָ:

Hashem, do it for the sake of Your name, and have compassion on Yisrael, Your people.

Adonai Aseh Lema'an Ya'akov
Ne'enah Vesulam
Mimeromeicha. Vechusah Al
Yisra'el Amecha:

יְהֹוָה עֲשֵׂה לְמַעַן יַעֲקֹב
נֶעֱנָה בְּסֻלָּם
מִמְּרוֹמֶיךָ. וְחוּסָה עַל
יִשְׂרָאֵל עַמֶּךָ:

Hashem, act for the sake of Ya'akov, who was answered with a ladder from Your heights, and have mercy on Yisrael, Your people:

Adonai Aseh Lema'an Harugim
Userufim Al Yichud Kedushat
Shemecha. Vechusah Al Yisra'el
Amecha:

יְהֹוָה עֲשֵׂה לְמַעַן הֲרוּגִים
וּשְׂרוּפִים עַל יִחוּד קְדֻשַּׁת
שְׁמֶךָ. וְחוּסָה עַל יִשְׂרָאֵל
עַמֶּךָ:

Hashem, do it for the sake of those who were killed and burned for the sanctification of Your name, and have compassion on Yisrael, Your people.

De'anei Leya'akov Beveit
El. Aneinan:

דְּעָנֵי לְיַעֲקֹב בְּבֵית
אֵל. עֲנֵינָן:

The One who answered Ya'akov at Beit-El, answer us:

De'anei Letzadikei Vachasidei

Utemimei Di Bechol-Dor

Vedor. Aneinan:

דְּעָנֵי לְצַדִּיקֵי וַחֲסִידֵי

וּתְמִימֵי דִי בְּכָל־דָּר

וְדָר. עֲנֵינָן:

He who answers the righteous, the pious, and the perfect in every generation, answer us.

Todi'eni Orach Chayim Sova

Semachot Et-Paneicha Ne'imot

Bimincha Netzach.

תּוֹדִיעֵנִי אֹרַח חַיִּים שֹׂבַע

שְׂמָחוֹת אֶת־פָּנֶיךָ נְעִמוֹת

בִּימִינְךָ נֶצַח:

You make known to me the path of life; in Your presence is fullness of joy; at Your right hand are pleasures forevermore.

Na Gibor. Doreshei Yichudecha.

Kevavat Shamerem.

נָא גִבּוֹר. דּוֹרְשֵׁי יְחוּדְךָ.

כְּבָבַת שָׁמְרֵם:

Almighty God, guard as the apple of the eye those who seek You.

Continue on the next page with the Fourth Hakafah.

Hoshanah Rabbah: Fourth Hakafah

Hosha'ana. Hosha'ana: הוֹשַׁעֲנָא. הוֹשַׁעֲנָא:

Please, save us. Please, save us:

Ana Haborei Olamo Bisodot	אָנָּא הַבּוֹרֵא עוֹלָמוֹ בִּיסוֹדוֹת
Arba'ah. Hanoten Nose'ei	אַרְבָּעָה. הַנּוֹתֵן נוֹשְׂאֵי
Chis'o Chayot Arba'ah.	כִסְאוֹ חַיּוֹת אַרְבָּעָה.
Hamatziv Pinot Arba'ah	הַמַּצִּיב פִּנּוֹת אַרְבָּעָה
Utekufot Arba'ah. Hoshi'enu	וּתְקוּפוֹת אַרְבָּעָה. הוֹשִׁיעֵנוּ
Behakafat Pe'amim Arba'ah:	בְּהַקָּפַת פְּעָמִים אַרְבָּעָה:

Please, Who created His world with four foundations [elements].
Who gives lifters of His throne, four Chayot. Who established the
four corners and the four seasons. Save us in this fourth hakafah:

Ana Zechor Av He'ir Mimizrach	אָנָּא זְכֹר אָב הֵעִיר מִמִּזְרָח
Be'or Leyamim Arba'ah. Radaf	בְּאוֹר לְיָמִים אַרְבָּעָה. רָדַף
Vayechalek Al Melachim	וַיֵּחָלֵק עַל מְלָכִים
Arba'ah. Bisarto Lashuv Zar'o	אַרְבָּעָה. בִּשַּׂרְתּוֹ לָשׁוּב זַרְעוֹ
Ledorot Arba'ah. Hoshi'enu	לְדוֹרוֹת אַרְבָּעָה. הוֹשִׁיעֵנוּ
Behakafat Pe'amim Arba'ah:	בְּהַקָּפַת פְּעָמִים אַרְבָּעָה:

Please, remember the father [Avraham] from the city from the east
with light like fourth day. He pursued and divided among four kings.
In his announcement [given to him], his offspring would return after
four generations. Save us in this fourth hakafah:

Ana Zechor Ben Hugash   אָנָּא זְכֹר בֶּן הֻגַּשׁ

La'akedah Al Keranot Arba'ah.   לַעֲקֵדָה עַל קַרְנוֹת אַרְבָּעָה.

Chafar Bifleshet Borot Arba'ah.   חָפַר בִּפְלֶשֶׁת בּוֹרוֹת אַרְבָּעָה.

Vaya'tek Lechevron Kiryat   וַיַּעְתֵּק לְחֶבְרוֹן קִרְיַת

Arba'ah. Hoshi'enu Behakafat   אַרְבָּעָה. הוֹשִׁיעֵנוּ בְּהַקָּפַת

Pe'amim Arba'ah: פְּעָמִים אַרְבָּעָה:

Please, remember the son [Yitzchak] who was brought to the binding on four corners [of the alter]. He dug four wells in the land of the Philistines. And he moved to Chevron, the city of four. Save us in this fourth hakafah:

Ana Zechor Tam Ne'ezar   אָנָּא זְכֹר תָּם נֶעֱזַר

Be'imahot Arba'ah. Chinen   בְּאִמָּהוֹת אַרְבָּעָה. חִנֵּן

Lehinatzel Mishefatim Arba'ah.   לְהִנָּצֵל מִשְׁפָּטִים אַרְבָּעָה.

Bitfilato Kilkalta Banav Bidvarim   בִּתְפִלָּתוֹ כִּלְכַּלְתָּ בָּנָיו בִּדְבָרִים

Arba'ah. Hoshi'enu Behakafat   אַרְבָּעָה. הוֹשִׁיעֵנוּ בְּהַקָּפַת

Pe'amim Arba'ah: פְּעָמִים אַרְבָּעָה:

Please, remember the perfect one [Ya'akov] who was helped by his four matriarchs. He pleaded to be saved from four judgements. In his prayer You sustained his sons with four things. Save us in this fourth hakafah:

Ana Hamolichenu Bamidbar   אָנָּא הַמּוֹלִיכֵנוּ בַּמִּדְבָּר

Bidgalim Arba'ah. Tzivah   בִּדְגָלִים אַרְבָּעָה. צִוָּה

Lemalot Bachoshen Turim   לְמַלֹּאת בַּחֹשֶׁן טוּרִים

Arba'ah. Hametzavenu Lehalo   אַרְבָּעָה. הַמְצַוֵּנוּ לְהַלֵּלוֹ

Bechag Beminim   בְּחַג בְּמִינִים

Arba'ah. Hoshi'enu Behakafat
Pe'amim Arba'ah:

אַרְבָּעָה. הוֹשִׁיעֵנוּ בְּהַקָּפַת פְּעָמִים אַרְבָּעָה:

Please, the One Who led us in the desert with four banners. Who commanded to fill the Choshen [breastplate] with four rows. Who commanded us to praise Him during the holiday with four species. Save us in this fourth hakafah:

Hosha'ana. Hosha'ana:

הוֹשַׁעְנָא. הוֹשַׁעְנָא:

Please, save us. Please, save us:

Zechut Mosheh. Al-Tinsheh.
Chatum Bemidat Hanetzach.
Bizchuto. Ve'anvato. Oyeveinu
Tenatzeach. Uvehar Hamor. Shir
Mizmor. Nashir
Velamenatzeach. El Netzach.
Lanetzach. Rachem Am
Romemecha. Zacherenu
Adonai Birtzon Amecha:

זְכוּת מֹשֶׁה. אַל־תִּנְשֶׁה.
חָתוּם בְּמִדַּת הַנֶּצַח.
בִּזְכוּתוֹ. וְעַנְוָתוֹ. אוֹיְבֵינוּ
תְּנַצֵּחַ. וּבְהַר הַמּוֹר. שִׁיר
מִזְמוֹר. נָשִׁיר
וְלַמְנַצֵּחַ. אֵל נֶצַח.
לָנֶצַח. רַחֵם עַם
רוֹמְמֶךָ. זָכְרֵנוּ
יְהֹוָה בִּרְצוֹן עַמֶּךָ:

The merit of Moshe, do not forget. Sealed with the attribute of Netzach (eternity). In his merit and in his humility, overcome our enemies. And on Mount Moriah, a song of praise we will sing and "for the conductor", God of eternity, forever, have mercy on the people who exalt You. Remember us, Hashem, in favoring Your people:

Torah Temimah. Une'imah.	תּוֹרָה תְמִימָה. וּנְעִימָה.
Yarash Anav Behar Sinai. Im El	יָרַשׁ עָנָו בְּהַר סִינַי. עִם אֵל
Ayom. Arba'im Yom. Amad	אָיוֹם. אַרְבָּעִים יוֹם. עָמַד
Sham Im Adonai. Lekabel Torah.	שָׁם עִם יְהוָה. לְקַבֵּל תּוֹרָה.
Zakah Uvarah. Mishemei	זַכָּה וּבָרָה. מִשְּׁמֵי
Me'onai. El Emet. Torat Emet.	מְעוֹנַי. אֵל אֱמֶת. תּוֹרַת אֱמֶת.
Hinchil Le'am Ne'emanai.	הִנְחִיל לְעַם נֶאֱמָנַי.
Tzidkato. Vetorato. Zechor-Na	צִדְקָתוֹ. וְתוֹרָתוֹ. זְכָר־נָא
Mishameicha. Zacherenu	מִשָּׁמֶיךָ. זָכְרֵנוּ
Adonai Birtzon Amecha:	יְהוָה בִּרְצוֹן עַמֶּךָ:

A perfect and pleasant Torah was inherited by the humble one [Moshe] on Mount Sinai. With the Awesome God, for forty days, he stood there with Hashem. To receive the Torah, pure and clear, from the heavenly abode. God of truth, Torah of truth, He gave to my faithful people. His righteousness and his Torah, please remember from Your heavens. Remember us, Hashem, in favoring Your people:

Rachamana Idkar Lan Keyameh	רַחֲמָנָא אִדְכַּר לָן קְיָמֵהּ
Demosheh Nevi'ah:	דְּמֹשֶׁה נְבִיאָה:

Merciful One, remember for us the merit of Moshe, the prophet:

Rachamana Dinan Apeik	רַחֲמָנָא דִּינָן אַפֵּיק
Linhora:	לִנְהוֹרָא:

Merciful One, bring our judgement to light:

Rachamana Chatminan Besifra	רַחֲמָנָא חַתְמִנָן בְּסִפְרָא
Dechayei:	דְּחַיֵּי:

Merciful One, inscribe us in the Book of Life.

Rachamana Chatminan Besifra
Derachamei:

רַחֲמָנָא חַתְמִנָן בְּסִפְרָא
דְּרַחֲמֵי:

Merciful One, inscribe us in the Book of Mercy.

Rachamana Chatminan Besifra
Detzadikei Vachasidei:

רַחֲמָנָא חַתְמִנָן בְּסִפְרָא
דְּצַדִּיקֵי וַחֲסִידֵי:

Merciful One, inscribe us in the Book of the Righteous and the Pious.

Rachamana Chatminan Besifra
Disharei Utemimei:

רַחֲמָנָא חַתְמִנָן בְּסִפְרָא
דִּישָׁרֵי וּתְמִימֵי:

Merciful One, inscribe us in the Book of the Upright and the Perfect.

Rachamana Chatminan Besifra
Defarnasata Tavta Umezonei
Tavei:

רַחֲמָנָא חַתְמִנָן בְּסִפְרָא
דְּפַרְנָסָתָא טָבְתָא וּמְזוֹנֵי
טָבֵי:

Merciful One, inscribe us in the Book of Good Livelihood and Good Sustenance.

Rachamana Petach Shemaya
Litzlotin:

רַחֲמָנָא פְּתַח שְׁמַיָּא
לִצְלוֹתִין:

Merciful One, open the heavens to our prayers.

Rachamana Tuv Merugzach:

רַחֲמָנָא תּוּב מֵרֻגְזָךְ:

Merciful One, turn back from Your anger.

Rachamana Vela Nehdar

Reikam Min-Kamach:

רַחֲמָנָא וְלָא נֶהְדַּר
רֵיקָם מִן־קַמָּךְ:

Merciful One, let us not return empty handed from before You.

Shema Yisra'el Adonai Eloheinu

Adonai Echad.

שְׁמַע יִשְׂרָאֵל יְהֹוָה אֱלֹהֵינוּ
יְהֹוָה אֶחָד:

Hear, O Yisrael: Hashem is our God, Hashem is One.

Adonai Hu Ha'elohim

Adonai Hu Ha'elohim. (say two
times)

יְהֹוָה הוּא הָאֱלֹהִים
יְהֹוָה הוּא הָאֱלֹהִים: (שתי פעמים)

Hashem, He is God. Hashem, He is God. (say two times)

Adonai Melech.

Adonai Malach.

Adonai Yimloch Le'olam Va'ed.
(say two times)

יְהֹוָה מֶלֶךְ.
יְהֹוָה מָלָךְ.
יְהֹוָה יִמְלֹךְ לְעֹלָם וָעֶד: (שתי
פעמים)

**Hashem reigns, Hashem has reigned, Hashem will reign forever and
ever. (say two times)**

Eloheinu Shebashamayim

Shema Kolenu Vekabel

Tefilatenu Beratzon:

אֱלֹהֵינוּ שֶׁבַּשָּׁמַיִם
שְׁמַע קוֹלֵנוּ וְקַבֵּל
תְּפִלָּתֵנוּ בְּרָצוֹן:

**Our God in Heaven, hear our voice and accept our prayers with
favor.**

Eloheinu Shebashamayim
Derashnucha Himatze Lanu:

אֱלֹהֵינוּ שֶׁבַּשָּׁמַיִם
דְּרַשְׁנוּךָ הִמָּצֵא לָנוּ:

Our God in Heaven, when we seek You, be present for us.

Eloheinu Shebashamayim

Chatemenu Besefer Chayim

Tovim:

אֱלֹהֵינוּ שֶׁבַּשָּׁמַיִם
חָתְמֵנוּ בְּסֵפֶר חַיִּים
טוֹבִים:

Our God in Heaven, inscribe us in the Book of Good Life.

Chatemenu Besefer Tzadikim

Vachasidim:

חָתְמֵנוּ בְּסֵפֶר צַדִּיקִים
וַחֲסִידִים:

Inscribe us in the Book of the Righteous and the Pious.

Chatemenu Besefer Yesharim

Utemimim:

חָתְמֵנוּ בְּסֵפֶר יְשָׁרִים
וּתְמִימִים:

Inscribe us in the Book of the Upright and the Perfect.

Chatemenu Besefer Mezonot

Ufarnasah Tovah:

חָתְמֵנוּ בְּסֵפֶר מְזוֹנוֹת
וּפַרְנָסָה טוֹבָה:

Inscribe us in the Book of Sustenance and Good Livelihood.

Eloheinu Shebashamayim

Karevenu La'avodatecha:

אֱלֹהֵינוּ שֶׁבַּשָּׁמַיִם
קָרְבֵנוּ לַעֲבוֹדָתֶךָ:

Our God in Heaven, draw us near to Your service.

Eloheinu Shebashamayim Refa   אֱלֹהֵינוּ שֶׁבַּשָּׁמַיִם רְפָא

Kol-Cholei Amecha Yisra'el: כָּל־חוֹלֵי עַמְּךָ יִשְׂרָאֵל:

Our God in Heaven, heal all of the sick of Your people Yisrael.

Anenu Ha'oneh Be'et Ratzon   עֲנֵנוּ הָעוֹנֶה בְּעֵת רָצוֹן

Anenu: Anenu Rachum   עֲנֵנוּ: עֲנֵנוּ רַחוּם

Vechanun Anenu: וְחַנּוּן עֲנֵנוּ:

Answer us, You Who responds in a time of favor, answer us; Answer us, Merciful and Gracious One, answer us.

Adonai Chonenu   יְהֹוָה חָנֵּנוּ

Vahakimenu. Uvesefer Chayim   וַהֲקִימֵנוּ. וּבְסֵפֶר חַיִּים

Zacherenu Vechatemenu: זָכְרֵנוּ וְחָתְמֵנוּ:

Hashem, be gracious to us and lift us up. And in the Book of Life, remember us and inscribe us.

Adonai Chasadeicha   יְהֹוָה חֲסָדֶיךָ

Yekademunu   יְקַדְּמוּנוּ

Verachamenu. Uvesefer Chayim   וְרַחֲמֵנוּ. וּבְסֵפֶר חַיִּים

Zacherenu Vechatemenu: זָכְרֵנוּ וְחָתְמֵנוּ:

Hashem, let Your kindness precede us and have mercy on us. And in the Book of Life, remember us and inscribe us.

Adonai Aseh Lema'an
Shemecha. Vechusah Al Yisra'el
Amecha:

יְהֹוָה עֲשֵׂה לְמַעַן שְׁמֶךָ. וְחוּסָה עַל יִשְׂרָאֵל עַמֶּךָ:

Hashem, do it for the sake of Your name, and have compassion on Yisrael, Your people.

Adonai Aseh Lema'an Mosheh
Ne'eman Bechol-Beitecha.
Vechusah Al Yisra'el Amecha:

יְהֹוָה עֲשֵׂה לְמַעַן מֹשֶׁה נֶאֱמָן בְּכָל־בֵּיתֶךָ. וְחוּסָה עַל יִשְׂרָאֵל עַמֶּךָ:

Hashem, act for the sake of Moshe, who was faithful in all Your house. And have compassion on Yisrael, Your people.

Adonai Aseh Lema'an Harugim
Userufim Al Yichud Kedushat
Shemecha. Vechusah Al Yisra'el
Amecha:

יְהֹוָה עֲשֵׂה לְמַעַן הֲרוּגִים וּשְׂרוּפִים עַל יִחוּד קְדֻשַּׁת שְׁמֶךָ. וְחוּסָה עַל יִשְׂרָאֵל עַמֶּךָ:

Hashem, do it for the sake of those who were killed and burned for the sanctification of Your name, and have compassion on Yisrael, Your people.

De'anei Lemosheh Va'avoteinu
Al Yam-Suf. Aneinan:

דְּעָנֵי לְמֹשֶׁה וַאֲבוֹתֵינוּ עַל יַם־סוּף. עֲנֵינָן:

The One who answered Moshe and our ancestors at the Red Sea, answer us:

De'anei Letzadikei Vachasidei דְּעָנֵי לְצַדִּיקֵי וַחֲסִידֵי

Utemimei Di Bechol-Dor וּתְמִימֵי דִּי בְּכָל־דָּר

Vedor. Aneinan: וָדָר. עֲנֵינָן:

He who answers the righteous, the pious, and the perfect in every generation, answer us.

Todi'eni Orach Chayim Sova תּוֹדִיעֵנִי אֹרַח חַיִּים שׂבַע

Semachot Et-Paneicha Ne'imot שְׂמָחוֹת אֶת־פָּנֶיךָ נְעִמוֹת

Bimincha Netzach. בִּימִינְךָ נֶצַח:

You make known to me the path of life; in Your presence is fullness of joy; at Your right hand are pleasures forevermore.

Barechem Taharem. Rachamei בָּרְכֵם טַהֲרֵם. רַחֲמֵי

Tzidkatecha. Tamid Gamelem. צִדְקָתֶךָ. תָּמִיד גָּמְלֵם:

Bless them, cleanse them, pity them; forever grant them Your truth.

Continue on the next page with the Fifth Hakafah.

Hoshanah Rabbah: Fifth Hakafah

Hosha'ana. Hosha'ana: הוֹשַׁעְנָא. הוֹשַׁעְנָא:

Please, save us. Please, save us:

Ana Hameyached Lichvodo	אָנָּא הַמְיַחֵד לִכְבוֹדוֹ
Shemot Chamishah. Hakoneh	שֵׁמוֹת חֲמִשָּׁה. הַקוֹנֶה
Ve'olamo Kinyanim Chamishah.	בְּעוֹלָמוֹ קִנְיָנִים חֲמִשָּׁה.
Hayotzer Bivriyotav Giborim	הַיּוֹצֵר בִּבְרִיּוֹתָיו גִבּוֹרִים
Chamishah. Hoshi'enu	חֲמִשָּׁה. הוֹשִׁיעֵנוּ
Behakafat Pe'amim Chamishah:	בְּהַקָּפַת פְּעָמִים חֲמִשָּׁה:

Please, the One Who unifies for His glory five names. The One Who acquires in His world five acquisitions. The One Who forms in His creatures five mighty-ones. Save us in this fifth hakafah:

Ana Zechor Av Karat Berit	אָנָּא זְכֹר אָב כָּרַת בְּרִית
Bivtarim Chamishah. Veheshiv	בִּבְתָרִים חֲמִשָּׁה. וְהֵשִׁיב
Rechush Limlachim Chamishah.	רְכוּשׁ לִמְלָכִים חֲמִשָּׁה.
Vechanan Al Hafichat Arim	וְחָנַן עַל הֲפִיכַת עָרִים
Chamishah. Hoshi'enu	חֲמִשָּׁה. הוֹשִׁיעֵנוּ
Behakafat Pe'amim Chamishah:	בְּהַקָּפַת פְּעָמִים חֲמִשָּׁה:

Please, remember the father [Avraham] who cut a covenant between pieces of five kinds. He returned the property to five kings. And pleaded against the destruction of five cities. Save us in this fifth hakafah:

Ana Zechor Hane'ekad Behar	אָנָּא זְכֹר הַנֶּעֱקַד בְּהַר
Mor She'arim Chamishah.	מוֹר שְׁעָרִים חֲמִשָּׁה.
Yarash Mehoro Berachot	יָרַשׁ מֵהוֹרוֹ בְּרָכוֹת
Chamishah. Vehishlim Nefesh	חֲמִשָּׁה. וְהִשְׁלִים נֶפֶשׁ
Nekuvah Beshemot	נְקוּבָה בְּשֵׁמוֹת
Chamishah. Hoshi'enu	חֲמִשָּׁה. הוֹשִׁיעֵנוּ
Behakafat Pe'amim Chamishah:	בְּהַקָּפַת פְּעָמִים חֲמִשָּׁה:

Please, remember the one [Yitzchak] who was bound on Mount Moriah with five gates. Who inherited from his trail, five blessings. And completed his soul that was pierced with five names. Save us in this fifth hakafah:

Ana Zechor Tam Na'asu Lo	אָנָּא זְכֹר תָּם נַעֲשׂוּ לוֹ
Nisim Chamishah. Vayatzeg	נִסִּים חֲמִשָּׁה. וַיַּצֵּג
Mibanav Achim Chamishah.	מִבָּנָיו אַחִים חֲמִשָּׁה.
Kofro Shat Lenazir Hamachalif	כָּפְרוֹ שָׁת לְנָזִיר הַמַּחֲלִיף
Chamishah. Hoshi'enu	חֲמִשָּׁה. הוֹשִׁיעֵנוּ
Behakafat Pe'amim Chamishah:	בְּהַקָּפַת פְּעָמִים חֲמִשָּׁה:

Please, remember the perfect one [Ya'akov] for whom five miracles were performed. And who presented from his sons, five brothers. A gift he gave to the pure one [Yosef] five exchanges of clothing. Save us in this fifth hakafah:

Ana Hamanchilenu Dat Sefarim	אָנָּא הַמַּנְחִילֵנוּ דָּת סְפָרִים
Chamishah. Hamashmi'enu	חֲמִשָּׁה. הַמַּשְׁמִיעֵנוּ
Diberotav Bekolot Chamishah.	דִּבְּרוֹתָיו בְּקוֹלוֹת חֲמִשָּׁה.
Haketuvim Al Haluchot	הַכְּתוּבִים עַל הַלֻּחוֹת

Chamishah Chamishah.	חֲמִשָּׁה חֲמִשָּׁה.
Hoshi'enu Behakafat	הוֹשִׁיעֵנוּ בְּהַקָּפַת
Pe'amim Chamishah:	פְּעָמִים חֲמִשָּׁה:

Please, the One Who gave us a Law of five books. The One who related to us His sayings in five voices. The writings on the tablets were five and five.

Hosha'ana. Hosha'ana:	הוֹשַׁעְנָא. הוֹשַׁעְנָא:

Please, save us. Please, save us:

Bizchut Aharon. Ron Yaron.	בִּזְכוּת אַהֲרֹן. רֹן יָרֹן.
Amach Be'omram Hosha'na.	עַמָּךְ בְּאָמְרָם הוֹשַׁעְנָא.
Nechtam Bechavod.	נֶחְתָּם בְּכָבוֹד.
Bemitznefet Na'ah. Leshamesh	בְּמִצְנֶפֶת נָאָה. לְשַׁמֵּשׁ
Bichunah. Bigdei Fe'er. Lefa'er.	בִּכְהֻנָּה. בִּגְדֵי פְאֵר. לְפָאֵר.
Shimcha Lavash Be'emunah.	שִׁמְךָ לָבַשׁ בֶּאֱמוּנָה.
Hodo Har'eh. Le'am Nich'eh.	הוֹדוֹ הַרְאֵה. לְעַם נִכְאֶה.
Ram Shochen Bim'onah.	רָם שׁוֹכֵן בִּמְעוֹנָה.
Uvizchuto. Utefilato. Toshia'	וּבִזְכוּתוֹ. וּתְפִלָּתוֹ. תּוֹשִׁיעַ
Liz'umecha. Zacherenu	לִזְעוּמֶךָ. זָכְרֵנוּ
Adonai Birtzon Amecha:	יְהֹוָה בִּרְצוֹן עַמֶּךָ:

In the merit of Aharon, joy will come to Your people when they say Hoshana (save us). Sealed with honor, with a beautiful turban, to serve in the priesthood. Garments of splendor, to adorn. He wore Your name faithfully. Show his glory to the afflicted people, Exalted One who dwells in His abode. In his merit and his prayer, save Your afflicted ones. Remember us, Hashem, in favoring Your people:

Bigdei Kodesh. Lakach   בִּגְדֵי קֹדֶשׁ. לָקַח

Lekadesh. Lesharet Bam Lifnim   לְקַדֵּשׁ. לְשָׁרֵת בָּם לִפְנִים

Lifnai. Ulevasham. Bevo'o   לִפְנַי. וּלְבָשָׁם. בְּבֹאוֹ

Sham. Kekadosh Kemal'ach   שָׁם. כְּקָדוֹשׁ כְּמַלְאַךְ

Adonai. Bekarebenotav.   יְהוָה. בְּקׇרְבְּנוֹתָיו.

Ve'olotav. Hayah Mechaper Al   וְעוֹלוֹתָיו. הָיָה מְכַפֵּר עַל

Avonai. Tefilotav. Utechinotav.   עֲוֹנָי. תְּפִלּוֹתָיו. וּתְחִנּוֹתָיו.

Zechor Hayom Le'am Emunai.   זְכֹר הַיּוֹם לְעַם אֱמוּנָי.

Vetita'em. Vetargi'em.   וְתִטָּעֵם. וְתַרְגִּיעֵם.

Bemikdash   בְּמִקְדַּשׁ

Hadomecha. Zacherenu   הֲדוֹמֶךָ. זָכְרֵנוּ

Adonai Birtzon Amecha: יְהוָה בִּרְצוֹן עַמֶּךָ:

He took holy garments to sanctify and to serve within the innermost sanctuary. And he wore them when he entered there, as a holy one, like an angel of Hashem. With his offerings and burnt offerings, he would atone for my sins. His prayers and supplications, remember today for my faithful people. And plant them and calm them in Your glorious sanctuary. Remember us, Hashem, in favoring Your people:

Rachamana Idkar Lan Keyameh   רַחֲמָנָא אִדְכַּר לָן קְיָמֵהּ

De'aharon Kahana: דְּאַהֲרֹן כַּהֲנָא:

Merciful One, remember for us the merit of Aharon the priest.

Rachamana Hadrach Shavi   רַחֲמָנָא הַדְרָךְ שַׁוִּי

Alan: עֲלָן:

Merciful One, rest your splendor upon us.

Rachamana Chatminan Besifra
Dechayei:

רַחֲמָנָא חַתְמִנָן בְּסִפְרָא
דְחַיֵּי:

Merciful One, inscribe us in the Book of Life.

Rachamana Chatminan Besifra
Derachamei:

רַחֲמָנָא חַתְמִנָן בְּסִפְרָא
דְרַחֲמֵי:

Merciful One, inscribe us in the Book of Mercy.

Rachamana Chatminan Besifra
Detzadikei Vachasidei:

רַחֲמָנָא חַתְמִנָן בְּסִפְרָא
דְצַדִּיקֵי וַחֲסִידֵי:

Merciful One, inscribe us in the Book of the Righteous and the Pious.

Rachamana Chatminan Besifra
Disharei Utemimei:

רַחֲמָנָא חַתְמִנָן בְּסִפְרָא
דִישָׁרֵי וּתְמִימֵי:

Merciful One, inscribe us in the Book of the Upright and the Perfect.

Rachamana Chatminan Besifra
Defarnasata Tavta Umezonei
Tavei:

רַחֲמָנָא חַתְמִנָן בְּסִפְרָא
דְפַרְנָסָתָא טַבְתָּא וּמְזוֹנֵי
טָבֵי:

Merciful One, inscribe us in the Book of Good Livelihood and Good Sustenance.

Rachamana Petach Shemaya
Litzlotin:

רַחֲמָנָא פְּתַח שְׁמַיָא
לִצְלוֹתִין:

Merciful One, open the heavens to our prayers.

Rachamana Tuv Merugzach:

רַחֲמָנָא תּוּב מֵרְגְזָךְ:

Merciful One, turn back from Your anger.

Rachamana Vela Nehdar
Reikam Min-Kamach:

רַחֲמָנָא וְלָא נֶהְדָּר
רֵיקָם מִן־קַמָּךְ:

Merciful One, let us not return empty handed from before You.

Shema Yisra'el Adonai Eloheinu
Adonai Echad.

שְׁמַע יִשְׂרָאֵל יְהֹוָה אֱלֹהֵינוּ
יְהֹוָה אֶחָד:

Hear, O Yisrael: Hashem is our God, Hashem is One.

Adonai Hu Ha'elohim
Adonai Hu Ha'elohim. (say two times)

יְהֹוָה הוּא הָאֱלֹהִים
יְהֹוָה הוּא הָאֱלֹהִים: (שתי פעמים)

Hashem, He is God. Hashem, He is God. (say two times)

Adonai Melech.
Adonai Malach.
Adonai Yimloch Le'olam Va'ed. (say two times)

יְהֹוָה מֶלֶךְ.
יְהֹוָה מָלָךְ.
יְהֹוָה יִמְלֹךְ לְעֹלָם וָעֶד: (שתי פעמים)

Hashem reigns, Hashem has reigned, Hashem will reign forever and ever. (say two times)

Eloheinu Shebashamayim
Shema Kolenu Vekabel
Tefilatenu Beratzon:

אֱלֹהֵינוּ שֶׁבַּשָּׁמַיִם
שְׁמַע קוֹלֵנוּ וְקַבֵּל
תְּפִלָּתֵנוּ בְּרָצוֹן:

Our God in Heaven, hear our voice and accept our prayers with favor.

Eloheinu Shebashamayim
He'ater-Lanu Hayom Uvechol-
Yom Vayom Bitfilatenu:

אֱלֹהֵינוּ שֶׁבַּשָּׁמַיִם
הֵעָתֶר־לָנוּ הַיּוֹם וּבְכָל־
יוֹם וָיוֹם בִּתְפִלָּתֵנוּ:

Our God in heaven, accept us today and every day in our prayers.

Eloheinu Shebashamayim
Chatemenu Besefer Chayim
Tovim:

אֱלֹהֵינוּ שֶׁבַּשָּׁמַיִם
חָתְמֵנוּ בְּסֵפֶר חַיִּים
טוֹבִים:

God in Heaven, inscribe us in the Book of Good Life.

Chatemenu Besefer Tzadikim
Vachasidim:

חָתְמֵנוּ בְּסֵפֶר צַדִּיקִים
וַחֲסִידִים:

Inscribe us in the Book of the Righteous and the Pious.

Chatemenu Besefer Yesharim
Utemimim:

חָתְמֵנוּ בְּסֵפֶר יְשָׁרִים
וּתְמִימִים:

Inscribe us in the Book of the Upright and the Perfect.

Chatemenu Besefer Mezonot
Ufarnasah Tovah:

חָתְמֵנוּ בְּסֵפֶר מְזוֹנוֹת
וּפַרְנָסָה טוֹבָה:

Inscribe us in the Book of Sustenance and Good Livelihood.

Eloheinu Shebashamayim

Karevenu La'avodatecha:

אֱלֹהֵינוּ שֶׁבַּשָּׁמַיִם

קָרְבֵנוּ לַעֲבוֹדָתֶךָ:

Our God in Heaven, draw us near to Your service.

Eloheinu Shebashamayim Refa

Kol-Cholei Amecha Yisra'el:

אֱלֹהֵינוּ שֶׁבַּשָּׁמַיִם רְפָא

כָּל־חוֹלֵי עַמְּךָ יִשְׂרָאֵל:

Our God in Heaven, heal all of the sick of Your people Yisrael.

Anenu Ha'oneh Be'et Tzarah

Anenu: Anenu Rachum

Vechanun Anenu:

עֲנֵנוּ הָעוֹנֶה בְּעֵת צָרָה

עֲנֵנוּ: עֲנֵנוּ רַחוּם

וְחַנּוּן עֲנֵנוּ:

Answer us, the One Who responds in times of trouble, answer us:
Answer us, Merciful and Gracious One, answer us.

Adonai Chonenu

Vahakimenu. Uvesefer Chayim

Zacherenu Vechatemenu:

יְהֹוָה חָנֵּנוּ

וַהֲקִימֵנוּ. וּבְסֵפֶר חַיִּים

זָכְרֵנוּ וְחָתְמֵנוּ:

Hashem, be gracious to us and lift us up. And in the Book of Life,
remember us and inscribe us.

Adonai Yehemu Na

Rachameicha Aleinu. Uvesefer

Chayim Zacherenu

Vechatemenu:

יְהֹוָה יֶהֱמוּ נָא

רַחֲמֶיךָ עָלֵינוּ. וּבְסֵפֶר

חַיִּים זָכְרֵנוּ

וְחָתְמֵנוּ:

Hashem, let Your mercy stir for us. And in the Book of Life,
remember us and inscribe us.

Adonai Aseh Lema'an
Shemecha. Vechusah Al Yisra'el
Amecha:

יְהֹוָה עֲשֵׂה לְמַעַן שְׁמֶךָ. וְחוּסָה עַל יִשְׂרָאֵל עַמֶּךָ:

Hashem, act for the sake of Your name, and have compassion on Yisrael, Your people:

Adonai Aseh Lema'an Aharon
Kihen Be'ureicha
Vetumeicha. Vechusah Al
Yisra'el Amecha:

יְהֹוָה עֲשֵׂה לְמַעַן אַהֲרֹן כֹּהֵן בְּאוּרֶיךָ וְתֻמֶּיךָ. וְחוּסָה עַל יִשְׂרָאֵל עַמֶּךָ:

Hashem, act for the sake of Aharon, the priest with Your Urim and Tumim, and have compassion on Yisrael, Your people:

Adonai Aseh Lema'an Harugim
Userufim Al Yichud Kedushat
Shemecha. Vechusah Al Yisra'el
Amecha:

יְהֹוָה עֲשֵׂה לְמַעַן הַרוּגִים וּשְׂרוּפִים עַל יִחוּד קְדֻשַּׁת שְׁמֶךָ. וְחוּסָה עַל יִשְׂרָאֵל עַמֶּךָ:

Hashem, act for the sake of those who were killed and burned for the sanctification of Your holy name, and have compassion on Yisrael, Your people:

De'anei Le'aharon
Bamachta. Aneinan:

דְּעָנֵי לְאַהֲרֹן בַּמַּחְתָּא. עֲנֵינָן:

He who answered Aharon with the censer, answer us:

De'anei Letzadikei Vachasidei
Utemimei Di Bechol-Dor
Vedor. Aneinan:

דְּעָנֵי לְצַדִּיקֵי וַחֲסִידֵי
וּתְמִימֵי דִי בְּכָל־דָּר
וָדָר. עֲנֵינָן:

He who answers the righteous, the pious, and the perfect in every generation, answer us.

Todi'eni Orach Chayim Sova
Semachot Et-Paneicha Ne'imot
Bimincha Netzach.

תּוֹדִיעֵנִי אֹרַח חַיִּים שֹׂבַע
שְׂמָחוֹת אֶת־פָּנֶיךָ נְעִמוֹת
בִּימִינְךָ נֶצַח:

You make known to me the path of life; in Your presence is fullness of joy; at Your right hand are pleasures forevermore.

Chasin Kadosh. Berov Tuvecha.
Nahel Adatecha.

חֲסִין קָדוֹשׁ. בְּרֹב טוּבְךָ.
נַהֵל עֲדָתֶךָ:

Almighty and holy, in Your abundant goodness, guide Your people.

Continue on the next page with the Sixth Hakafah.

Hoshanah Rabbah: Sixth Hakafah

Hosha'ana. Hosha'ana: הוֹשַׁעֲנָא. הוֹשַׁעֲנָא:

Please, save us. Please, save us:

Ana Haborei Olamo Beyamim   אָנָּא הַבּוֹרֵא עוֹלָמוֹ בְּיָמִים

Shishah. Haboneh Shesh   שִׁשָּׁה. הַבּוֹנֶה שֵׁשׁ

Tzela'ot Litzdadim Shishah.   צְלָעוֹת לְצְדָדִים שִׁשָּׁה.

Hayotzer Serafim Bichnafayim   הַיּוֹצֵר שְׂרָפִים בִּכְנָפַיִם

Shishah. Hoshi'enu Behakafat   שִׁשָּׁה. הוֹשִׁיעֵנוּ בְּהַקָּפַת

Pe'amim Shishah: פְּעָמִים שִׁשָּׁה:

Please, Creator of His world in six days. Who builds six sides, to the six sides. Who forms seraphs with six wings. Save us in this sixth hakafah:

Ana Zechor Av Zanach To'evot   אָנָּא זְכֹר אָב זָנַח תּוֹעֵבוֹת

Shishah. Acharei Zekunav   שִׁשָּׁה. אַחֲרֵי זְקֻנָיו

Noledu Lo Banim Shishah. Nata   נוֹלְדוּ לוֹ בָּנִים שִׁשָּׁה. נָטַע

Eshel Uvorach Beketz Shanim   אֶשֶׁל וּבֹרַךְ בְּקֵץ שָׁנִים

Shishah. Hoshi'enu Behakafat   שִׁשָּׁה. הוֹשִׁיעֵנוּ בְּהַקָּפַת

Pe'amim Shishah: פְּעָמִים שִׁשָּׁה:

Please, remember the father [Avraham] who abandoned six abominations. After his old age, six sons were born to him. He planted an Eshel [tree] and was blessed at the end of six years. Save us in this sixth hakafah:

Ana Zechor Hane'ekad Bimkom	אָנָּא זְכֹר הַנֶּעֱקַד בִּמְקוֹם
Ma'arachot Shishah. Gonanto	מַעֲרָכוֹת שִׁשָּׁה. גּוֹנַנְתּוֹ
Umilato Mitzarot Shishah.	וּמִלַּטְתּוֹ מִצָּרוֹת שִׁשָּׁה.
Karah Mikva'ot Ledoreshei Vam	כָּרָה מִקְוָאוֹת לְדוֹרְשֵׁי בָם
Ma'alot Shishah. Hoshi'enu	מַעֲלוֹת שִׁשָּׁה. הוֹשִׁיעֵנוּ
Behakafat Pe'amim Shishah:	בְּהַקָּפַת פְּעָמִים שִׁשָּׁה:

Please, remember the bound one [Yitzchak] in his sacrificial place of six levels. He groaned and escaped from six troubles. He dug wells for those seeking them, six levels. Save us in this sixth hakafah:

Ana Zechor Tam Holid Min	אָנָּא זְכֹר תָּם הוֹלִיד מִן
Habechirah Shishah. Vetzivah	הַבְּכִירָה שִׁשָּׁה. וְצִוָּה
Kachat Minchah Miminim	קַחַת מִנְחָה מִמִּינִים
Shishah. Vehigbir Avi Shishah	שִׁשָּׁה. וְהִגְבִּיר אֲבִי שִׁשָּׁה
Hamevorachim Beshishah.	הַמְבוֹרָכִים בְּשִׁשָּׁה.
Hoshi'enu Behakafat Pe'amim	הוֹשִׁיעֵנוּ בְּהַקָּפַת פְּעָמִים
Shishah:	שִׁשָּׁה:

Please, remember the innocent [Ya'akov] who begot from the firstborn [Leah] six [sons]. He commanded to take an offering [to Yosef] of six types. And strengthened the father of six who were blessed six [times]. Save us in this sixth hakafah:

Ana Hamechaber La'efod	אָנָּא הַמְחַבֵּר לָאֵפוֹד
Shemot Shishah. Hamatzil	שְׁמוֹת שִׁשָּׁה. הַמַּצִּיל
Nefashot Be'arei Miklat Shishah.	נְפָשׁוֹת בְּעָרֵי מִקְלָט שִׁשָּׁה.
Hamorishenu Chachemat	הַמּוֹרִישֵׁנוּ חָכְמַת

Sedarim Shishah. Hoshi'enu   סְדָרִים שִׁשָּׁה. הוֹשִׁיעֵנוּ

Behakafat Pe'amim Shishah: בְּהַקָּפַת פְּעָמִים שִׁשָּׁה:

Please, the One Who [commanded to] attached to the ephod six names. The One Who saves souls in six refuge cities. The One Who gives us wisdom [the Mishnah] of six orders. Save us in this sixth hakafah:

Hosha'ana. Hosha'ana: הוֹשַׁעְנָא. הוֹשַׁעְנָא:

Please, save us. Please, save us:

Zechut Nishmar. Berit Shamar.   זְכוּת נִשְׁמַר. בְּרִית שָׁמַר.

Bemidat Hayesod Chatum.   בְּמִדַּת הַיְסוֹד חָתוּם.

Limloch Zachah. Uvimluchah.   לִמְלֹךְ זָכָה. וּבִמְלוּכָה.

Lo Niglah Kol-Satum.   לוֹ נִגְלָה כָּל־סָתוּם.

Uvizchuto. Le'umato. Galeh   וּבִזְכוּתוֹ. לְאֻמָּתוֹ. גַּלֵּה

Ketz Hechatum. Vetirdof. Vegam   קֵץ הֶחָתוּם. וְתִרְדֹּף. וְגַם

Tahadof. Laresha'im Yesitum.   תֶּהְדֹּף. לָרְשָׁעִים יְסִיתוּם.

Zechut Avot. Rochev Aravot.   זְכוּת אָבוֹת. רוֹכֵב עֲרָבוֹת.

Zechor Hayom   זְכֹר הַיּוֹם

Leromemecha. Zacherenu   לְרוֹמְמֶךָ. זָכְרֵנוּ

Adonai Birtzon Amecha: יְהֹוָה בִּרְצוֹן עַמֶּךָ:

Merit of the guarded-one. He kept the covenant. With the attribute of Yesod (foundation), he was sealed. He merited to reign, and in his monarchy, all hidden things were revealed to him. And in his merit, for his nation, reveal the sealed end. Pursue and also repel those who incite the wicked. Merit of the fathers, Rider of the heavens, remember today for those who elevate You. Remember us, Hashem, in favoring Your people:

Bizchut Yosef. Heyeh Me'assef.	בִּזְכוּת יוֹסֵף. הֱיֵה מְאַסֵּף.
Nachalatecha Beveit	נַחֲלָתְךָ בְּבֵית
Kodshecha. Uretzeh El Chai.	קָדְשְׁךָ. וּרְצֵה אֵל חַי.
Benichochai. Tefilat Am	בְּנִיחוֹחַי. תְּפִלַּת עַם
Mekudashecha. Uverito.	מְקֻדָּשְׁךָ. וּבְרִיתוֹ.
Uzechuto. Zechor Le'am	וּזְכוּתוֹ. זְכֹר לְעַם
Megorashecha Chatemem	מְגֹרָשְׁךָ חָתְמֵם
Legilah. Vetzoholah.	לְגִילָה. וְצָהֳלָה.
Vekabetzem Lemigrashecha	וְקַבְּצֵם לְמִגְרָשֶׁךָ
Hosha'na. Verachem Na.	הוֹשַׁעְנָא. וְרַחֵם נָא.
Bizchuto Le'umecha. Zacherenu	בִּזְכוּתוֹ לְאֻמֶּךָ. זָכְרֵנוּ
Adonai Birtzon Amecha:	יְהֹוָה בִּרְצוֹן עַמֶּךָ:

In the merit of Yosef, be the Gatherer of Your inheritance in Your holy house. And favor, Living God, the fragrance of my sacrifices, the prayer of Your sanctified people. And by his covenant and his merit, remember the exiled people. Seal them for joy and gladness and gather them to Your courtyard. Save us, have mercy on us, in his merit for Your people. Remember us, Hashem, in favoring Your people:

Zechut Pinchas. Hameyuchas.	זְכוּת פִּינְחָס. הַמְיֻחָס.
Lemidat Tzadik Yesod Olam.	לְמִדַּת צַדִּיק יְסוֹד עוֹלָם.
Livrit Kine. Vayfallel Im Koneh.	לִבְרִית קִנֵּא. וַיְפַלֵּל עִם קוֹנֶה.
Hamevi Bemishpat Al Kol-	הַמֵּבִיא בְּמִשְׁפָּט עַל כָּל-
Ne'lam. Vate'atzar. Mishlachat	נֶעְלָם. וַתֵּעָצַר. מִשְׁלַחַת

Tzar. Vehu Nitbatzar. Berum	צָר. וְהוּא נִתְבַּצָּר. בְּרוּם
Olam. Hagam Halom. Berit	עוֹלָם. הֲגַם הֲלוֹם. בְּרִית
Shalom. Chayim Le'eilom.	שָׁלוֹם. חַיִּים לְעֵילוֹם.
Lichunat Olam. Uvizchuto.	לִכְהֻנַּת עוֹלָם. וּבִזְכוּתוֹ.
La'adato. Karev Ketz	לַעֲדָתוֹ. קָרֵב קֵץ
Yeminecha. Zacherenu	יְמִינֶךָ. זָכְרֵנוּ
Adonai Birtzon Amecha:	יְהוָה בִּרְצוֹן עַמֶּךָ:

The merit of Pinchas, the distinguished-one, in the attribute of the righteous foundation of the world. He was zealous for the covenant and prayed with his Creator, Who brings judgment on all hidden things. And it was stopped, the sending of trouble. And he fortified himself in the heights of the world. Even now, the covenant of peace, life everlasting, for the eternal Priesthood. And in his merit for his congregation, bring closer the end of days. Remember us, Hashem, in favoring Your people:

Bizchut Mekane Heyeh Oneh.	בִּזְכוּת מְקַנֵּא הֱיֵה עוֹנֶה.
Leshav'at Am Mekudashecha.	לְשַׁוְעַת עַם מְקֻדָּשֶׁךָ.
Retzeh El Chai. Benichochai.	רְצֵה אֵל חַי. בְּנִיחוֹחַי.
Chelef Karebani Lachmi	חֵלֶף קָרְבָּנִי לַחְמִי
Le'ishecha. Veseh Fezurah. Shai	לְאִשֶּׁךָ. וְשֶׂה פְזוּרָה. שַׁי
Lamora. Yovilu El Neveh	לְמוֹרָא. יוֹבִילוּ אֶל נְוֵה
Kodshecha. Chatemem Legilah.	קָדְשֶׁךָ. חָתְמֵם לְגִילָה.
Vetzoholah. Vekabetzem	וְצָהֳלָה. וְקַבְּצֵם
Lemigrashecha. Hosha'na.	לְמִגְרָשֶׁךָ. הוֹשַׁעְנָא.
Verachem Na. Lechanah Asher	וְרַחֵם נָא. לְכַנָּה אֲשֶׁר
Nate'ah Yeminecha. Zacherenu	נָטְעָה יְמִינֶךָ. זָכְרֵנוּ
Adonai Birtzon Amecha:	יְהוָה בִּרְצוֹן עַמֶּךָ:

In the merit of the zealous one, answer the outcry of Your sanctified people. Accept, O Living God, the fragrance of my sacrifices instead of "my bread for Your fire-offering". And the scattered flock, a gift for the Awesome, will lead them to Your holy abode. Seal them for joy and gladness and gather them to Your courtyard. Save us, have mercy on us, for the planting of Your right hand. Remember us, Hashem, in favoring Your people:

Rachamana Idkar Lan Zechuteh
Deyosef Tzadika:

רַחֲמָנָא אִדְכַּר לָן זְכוּתֵהּ
דְּיוֹסֵף צַדִּיקָא:

Merciful One, remember for us the merit of Yosef the righteous.

Rachamana Idkar Lan Keyameh
Definchas Kana'ah:

רַחֲמָנָא אִדְכַּר לָן קְיָמֵהּ
דְּפִינְחָס קַנָּאָה:

Merciful One, remember for us the zeal of Pinchas.

Rachamana Vela Titpera
Ke'ovadana Bishin Minan:

רַחֲמָנָא וְלָא תִתְפְּרַע
כְּעוֹבָדָנָא בִּישִׁין מִנָּן:

Merciful One, do not repay us according to our evil deeds.

Rachamana Chatminan Besifra
Dechayei:

רַחֲמָנָא חַתְמִנָן בְּסִפְרָא
דְּחַיֵּי:

Merciful One, inscribe us in the Book of Life.

Rachamana Chatminan Besifra
Derachamei:

רַחֲמָנָא חַתְמִנָן בְּסִפְרָא
דְּרַחֲמֵי:

Merciful One, inscribe us in the Book of Mercy.

Rachamana Chatminan Besifra
Detzadikei Vachasidei:

רַחֲמָנָא חַתְמִנָן בְּסִפְרָא
דְּצַדִּיקֵי וַחֲסִידֵי:

Merciful One, inscribe us in the Book of the Righteous and the Devout.

Rachamana Chatminan Besifra
Disharei Utemimei:

רַחֲמָנָא חַתְמִנָן בְּסִפְרָא
דִישָׁרֵי וּתְמִימֵי:

Merciful One, inscribe us in the Book of the Upright and the Perfect.

Rachamana Chatminan Besifra
Defarnasata Tavta Umezonei
Tavei:

רַחֲמָנָא חַתְמִנָן בְּסִפְרָא
דְפַרְנָסָתָא טַבְתָא וּמְזוֹנֵי
טָבֵי:

Merciful One, inscribe us in the Book of Good Sustenance and Provisions.

Rachamana Petach Shemaya
Litzlotin:

רַחֲמָנָא פְּתַח שְׁמַיָּא
לִצְלוֹתִין:

Merciful One, open the heavens to our prayers.

Rachamana Tuv Merugzach:

רַחֲמָנָא תוּב מֵרָגְזָךְ:

Merciful One, turn back from Your anger.

Rachamana Vela Nehdar
Reikam Min-Kamach:

רַחֲמָנָא וְלָא נֶהְדָּר
רֵיקָם מִן־קַמָּךְ:

Merciful One, do not let us return empty-handed from before You.

Shema Yisra'el Adonai Eloheinu   שְׁמַע יִשְׂרָאֵל יְהֹוָה אֱלֹהֵינוּ

Adonai Echad.   יְהֹוָה אֶחָד:

Hear, O Yisrael: Hashem is our God, Hashem is One.

Adonai Hu Ha'elohim   יְהֹוָה הוּא הָאֱלֹהִים

Adonai Hu Ha'elohim. **(say two**   (שתי פעמים) יְהֹוָה הוּא הָאֱלֹהִים:

times)

Hashem, He is God. Hashem, He is God. (say two times)

Adonai Melech.   יְהֹוָה מֶלֶךְ.

Adonai Malach.   יְהֹוָה מָלָךְ.

Adonai Yimloch Le'olam Va'ed.   (שתי) יְהֹוָה יִמְלֹךְ לְעֹלָם וָעֶד:

(say two times)   פעמים

Hashem reigns, Hashem has reigned, Hashem will reign forever and ever. (say two times)

Loheinu Shebashamayim   אֱלֹהֵינוּ שֶׁבַּשָּׁמַיִם

Venikra Ve'atah Ta'anenu: וְנִקְרָא וְאַתָּה תַעֲנֵנוּ:

Our God in heaven, we call and You will answer us:

Eloheinu Shebashamayim   אֱלֹהֵינוּ שֶׁבַּשָּׁמַיִם

Chatemenu Besefer Chayim   חָתְמֵנוּ בְּסֵפֶר חַיִּים

Tovim: טוֹבִים:

Our God in heaven, inscribe us in the Book of Good Life:

Chatemenu Besefer Tzadikim
Vachasidim:

חָתְמֵנוּ בְּסֵפֶר צַדִּיקִים
וַחֲסִידִים:

Inscribe us in the Book of the Righteous and the Devout:

Chatemenu Besefer Yesharim
Utemimim:

חָתְמֵנוּ בְּסֵפֶר יְשָׁרִים
וּתְמִימִים:

Inscribe us in the Book of the Upright and the Perfect:

Chatemenu Besefer Mezonot
Ufarnasah Tovah:

חָתְמֵנוּ בְּסֵפֶר מְזוֹנוֹת
וּפַרְנָסָה טוֹבָה:

Inscribe us in the Book of Sustenance and Good Livelihood:

Eloheinu Shebashamayim
Karevenu La'avodatecha:

אֱלֹהֵינוּ שֶׁבַּשָּׁמַיִם
קָרְבֵנוּ לַעֲבוֹדָתֶךָ:

Our God in heaven, draw us near to Your service:

Eloheinu Shebashamayim Refa
Kol-Cholei Amecha Yisra'el:

אֱלֹהֵינוּ שֶׁבַּשָּׁמַיִם רְפָא
כָּל־חוֹלֵי עַמְּךָ יִשְׂרָאֵל:

Our God in heaven, heal all the sick of Your people Yisrael:

Anenu Ha'oneh Be'et Ratzon
Anenu:

עֲנֵנוּ הָעוֹנֶה בְּעֵת רָצוֹן
עֲנֵנוּ:

Answer us, the One who responds at a favorable time, answer us:

Anenu Rachum Vechanun

עֲנֵנוּ רַחוּם וְחַנּוּן

Anenu:

עֲנֵנוּ:

Answer us, Merciful and Gracious One, answer us:

Adonai Chonenu

יְהֹוָה חָנֵּנוּ

Vahakimenu. Uvesefer Chayim

וַהֲקִימֵנוּ. וּבְסֵפֶר חַיִּים

Zacherenu Vechatemenu:

זָכְרֵנוּ וְחָתְמֵנוּ:

Hashem, be gracious to us and establish us. And in the Book of Life, remember and inscribe us:

Adonai Heitivah Acharitenu

יְהֹוָה הֵיטִיבָה אַחֲרִיתֵנוּ

Mereshitenu. Uvesefer Chayim

מֵרֵאשִׁיתֵנוּ. וּבְסֵפֶר חַיִּים

Zacherenu Vechatemenu:

זָכְרֵנוּ וְחָתְמֵנוּ:

Hashem, make our end better than our beginning. And in the Book of Life, remember and inscribe us:

Adonai Aseh Lema'an

יְהֹוָה עֲשֵׂה לְמַעַן

Shemecha. Vechusah Al Yisra'el

שְׁמֶךָ. וְחוּסָה עַל יִשְׂרָאֵל

Amecha:

עַמֶּךָ:

Hashem, act for the sake of Your name. And have mercy on Yisrael, Your people:

Adonai Aseh Lema'an Zechut

יְהֹוָה עֲשֵׂה לְמַעַן זְכוּת

Yosef Asir Tzadikecha. Vechusah

יוֹסֵף אַסִּיר צַדִּיקֶךָ. וְחוּסָה

Al Yisra'el Amecha:

עַל יִשְׂרָאֵל עַמֶּךָ:

Hashem, act for the merit of Yosef, Your righteous captive, and have mercy on Yisrael, Your people:

Adonai Aseh Lema'an Pinchas
Zach Kine Lishmecha. Vechusah
Al Yisra'el Amecha:

יְהֹוָה עֲשֵׂה לְמַעַן פִּינְחָס
זַךְ קִנֵּא לִשְׁמֶךָ. וְחוּסָה
עַל יִשְׂרָאֵל עַמֶּךָ:

Hashem, act for the merit of Pinchas, who was zealous for Your name, and have mercy on Yisrael, Your people:

Adonai Aseh Lema'an Harugim
Userufim Al Yichud Kedushat
Shemecha. Vechusah Al Yisra'el
Amecha:

יְהֹוָה עֲשֵׂה לְמַעַן הֲרוּגִים
וּשְׂרוּפִים עַל יִחוּד קְדֻשַּׁת
שְׁמֶךָ. וְחוּסָה עַל יִשְׂרָאֵל
עַמֶּךָ:

Hashem, act for the sake of those killed and burned for the sanctification of Your holy name, and have mercy on Yisrael, Your people:

De'anei Leyosef Beveit
Asirei. Aneinan:

דְּעָנֵי לְיוֹסֵף בְּבֵית
אֲסִירֵי. עֲנֵינָן:

The One who answered Yosef in the prison, answer us:

De'anei Lefinchas
Bashitim. Aneinan:

דְּעָנֵי לְפִינְחָס
בַּשִּׁטִּים. עֲנֵינָן:

The One who answered Pinchas in Shitim, answer us:

De'anei Letzadikei Vachasidei

דְּעָנֵי לְצַדִּיקֵי וַחֲסִידֵי

Utemimei Di Bechol-Dor

וּתְמִימֵי דִי בְּכָל־דָר

Vedor. Aneinan:

וְדָר. עֲנֵינָן:

The One who answered the righteous, the devout, and the perfect in every generation, answer us:

Todi'eni Orach Chayim Sova

תּוֹדִיעֵנִי אֹרַח חַיִּים שֹׂבַע

Semachot Et-Paneicha Ne'imot

שְׂמָחוֹת אֶת־פָּנֶיךָ נְעִמוֹת

Bimincha Netzach.

בִּימִינְךָ נֶצַח:

You will show me the path of life; in Your presence is the fullness of joy; at Your right hand, there are pleasures forever.

Yachid Ge'eh. Le'amecha

יָחִיד גֵּאֶה. לְעַמְּךָ פְּנֵה. זוֹכְרֵי

Feneh. Zocherei Kedushatecha.

קְדֻשָּׁתֶךָ:

Supreme God, turn to Your people who are mindful of Your holiness.

Continue on the next page with the Seventh Hakafah.

Hoshanah Rabbah: Seventh Hakafah

Hosha'ana. Hosha'ana: הוֹשַׁעֲנָא. הוֹשַׁעֲנָא:

Please, save us. Please, save us:

Ana Hamakdim La'olam   אָנָּא הַמַּקְדִּים לְעוֹלָם

Devarim Shiv'ah. Hasoder   דְּבָרִים שִׁבְעָה. הַסּוֹדֵר

Bereshit Leyamim Shiv'ah.   בְּרֵאשִׁית לְיָמִים שִׁבְעָה.

Hanoteh Shamayim Shiv'ah.   הַנֹּטֶה שָׁמַיִם שִׁבְעָה.

Veroka Aratzot   וְרוֹקַע אֲרָצוֹת

Shiv'ah. Hoshi'enu Bachagigat   שִׁבְעָה. הוֹשִׁיעֵנוּ בַּחֲגִיגַת

Yamim Shiv'ah Uvehakafat   יָמִים שִׁבְעָה וּבְהַקָּפַת

Pe'amim Shiv'ah: פְּעָמִים שִׁבְעָה:

Please, Who precedes the world with seven things. Who arranged
the creation in seven days. Who stretched out the heavens in seven
layers. And spread out the lands with seven names. Save us in the
celebration of seven days and in the seventh hakafah:

Ana Zechor Av Hivtachto   אָנָּא זְכֹר אָב הִבְטַחְתּוֹ

Lareshet Artzot Amamim   לָרֶשֶׁת אַרְצוֹת עֲמָמִים

Shiv'ah. Banah Bayit   שִׁבְעָה. בָּנָה בַּיִת

Lachochmah Vechatzav   לַחָכְמָה וְחָצַב

Amudeiha Shiv'ah. Karat Berit   עַמּוּדֶיהָ שִׁבְעָה. כָּרַת בְּרִית

Lenagid Bichvasot   לְנָגִיד בְּכְבָשׂוֹת

Shiv'ah. Hoshi'enu Bachagigat   שִׁבְעָה. הוֹשִׁיעֵנוּ בַּחֲגִיגַת

Yamim Shiv'ah Uvehakafat   יָמִים שִׁבְעָה וּבְהַקָּפַת

Pe'amim Shiv'ah: פְּעָמִים שִׁבְעָה:

Please, remember the father to whom You promised to inherit the lands of seven nations. Who built a house for wisdom and hewed its seven pillars. Who made a covenant with a leader with seven lambs. Save us in the celebration of seven days and in the seventh hakafah:

Ana Zechor Yachid Bisarto	אָנָּא זְכֹר יָחִיד בְּשָׂרְתּוֹ
Leketz Yamim Shiv'ah. Ho'alah	לְקֵץ יָמִים שִׁבְעָה. הֶעֱלָה
Al Har Shevi'i Leharim Shiv'ah.	עַל הַר שְׁבִיעִי לְהָרִים שִׁבְעָה.
Samach Bemotz'o Mayim	שָׂמַח בְּמָצְאוֹ מַיִם
Vayikra Otah	וַיִּקְרָא אוֹתָהּ
Shiv'ah. Hoshi'enu Bachagigat	שִׁבְעָה. הוֹשִׁיעֵנוּ בַּחֲגִיגַת
Yamim Shiv'ah Uvehakafat	יָמִים שִׁבְעָה וּבְהַקָּפַת
Pe'amim Shiv'ah:	פְּעָמִים שִׁבְעָה:

Please, remember the only one [Yitzchak] whom You proclaimed to at the end of seven days. He was offered up on the seventh mountain of seven mountains. Who rejoiced in finding water and named it "Shiv'a" ("Seven"). Save us in the celebration of seven days and in the seventh hakafah:

Ana Zechor Tam	אָנָּא זְכֹר תָּם
Hamishtachaveh Artzah	הַמִשְׁתַּחֲוֶה אַרְצָה
Pe'amim Shiv'ah. Al Shem	פְּעָמִים שִׁבְעָה. עַל שֵׁם
Sheva Yipol Tzadik Vekam	שֶׁבַע יִפּוֹל צַדִּיק וְקָם
Shiv'ah. Tzerafto Bishnei Sava	שִׁבְעָה. צְרַפְתּוֹ בִּשְׁנֵי שָׂבַע
Shiv'ah Vera'av	שִׁבְעָה וְרָעָב
Shiv'ah. Hoshi'enu Bachagigat	שִׁבְעָה. הוֹשִׁיעֵנוּ בַּחֲגִיגַת
Yamim Shiv'ah Uvehakafat	יָמִים שִׁבְעָה וּבְהַקָּפַת
Pe'amim Shiv'ah:	פְּעָמִים שִׁבְעָה:

Please, remember the perfect one [Ya'akov] who bowed to the ground seven times. For "a righteous person falls seven times and rises." You tested him with seven years of plenty and seven years of famine. Save us in the celebration of seven days and in the seventh hakafah:

Ana Hamanchilenu Shabat	אָנָּא הַמַּנְחִילֵנוּ שַׁבָּת
Leyamim Shiv'ah. Ushenat	לְיָמִים שִׁבְעָה. וּשְׁנַת
Hashemitah Leshanim Shiv'ah.	הַשְּׁמִטָּה לְשָׁנִים שִׁבְעָה.
Ushenat Hayovel Leketz	וּשְׁנַת הַיּוֹבֵל לְקֵץ
Shavu'im Shiv'ah. Hoshi'enu	שָׁבוּעִים שִׁבְעָה. הוֹשִׁיעֵנוּ
Bachagigat Yamim Shiv'ah	בַּחֲגִיגַת יָמִים שִׁבְעָה
Uvehakafat Pe'amim Shiv'ah:	וּבְהַקָּפַת פְּעָמִים שִׁבְעָה:

Please, You who gave us the Shabbat for seven days. And the Shemitah for seven years. And the Yovel at the end of seven cycles of seven. Save us in the celebration of seven days and in the seventh hakafah:

Ana Hachokek Zeman	אָנָּא הַחוֹקֵק זְמַן
Cherutenu Yamim Shiv'ah.	חֵרוּתֵנוּ יָמִים שִׁבְעָה.
Vechag Habikurim Leshavu'im	וְחַג הַבִּכּוּרִים לְשָׁבוּעִים
Shiv'ah. Velulav Vechag	שִׁבְעָה. וְלוּלָב וְחַג
Vesukkah Venisuch Hamayim	וְסֻכָּה וְנִסּוּךְ הַמַּיִם
Shiv'ah. Hoshi'enu Bachagigat	שִׁבְעָה. הוֹשִׁיעֵנוּ בַּחֲגִיגַת
Yamim Shiv'ah Uvehakafat	יָמִים שִׁבְעָה וּבְהַקָּפַת
Pe'amim Shiv'ah:	פְּעָמִים שִׁבְעָה:

Please, You who ordained the time of our freedom [Pesach] for seven days. And the Shavuot after seven weeks. And the lulav and the festival and Sukkah, and the water libation for seven days. Save us in the celebration of seven days and in the seventh hakafah:

Zechor Segen. Asher Nigen. Alei	זְכוֹר סֶגֶן. אֲשֶׁר נִגֵּן. עֲלֵי
Asor Vegam Nevel. Beshirotav.	עָשׂוֹר וְגַם נֶבֶל. בְּשִׁירוֹתָיו.
Uzemirotav. Yehodun Lach	וּזְמִירוֹתָיו. יְהוֹדוּן לָךְ
Bechol-Tevel. Lach Nimshach.	בְּכָל־תֵּבֵל. לָךְ נִמְשַׁח.
Venegdach Shach. Neso Lach	וְנֶגְדָּךְ שָׁח. נְשׂוֹא לָךְ
Ol Vegam Sevel. Pedeh	עוֹל וְגַם סֵבֶל. פְּדֵה
Neche'ah. Mekora'ah. Lecha	נְכֵאָה. מְקוֹרָאָה. לָךְ
Nachalah Vegam Chevel.	נַחֲלָה וְגַם חֵבֶל.
Lehoshi'ah. Lehargi'ah. Tigaleh	לְהוֹשִׁיעָה. לְהַרְגִּיעָה. תִּגָּלֶה
Mimeromecha. Zacherenu	מִמְּרוֹמֶךָ. זָכְרֵנוּ
Adonai Birtzon Amecha:	יְהֹוָה בִּרְצוֹן עַמֶּךָ:

Remember the deputy [David] who played on the harp and the lyre. With his songs and his praises, they will honor You in all the world. He was anointed for You, and before You, he bowed. He bore a yoke for You and also suffering. Redeem the afflicted, called to You, an inheritance and a portion. To save her, to calm her, reveal Yourself from Your heights. Remember us, Hashem, in favoring Your people:

Bizchut David. Ish Yedid.	בִּזְכוּת דָּוִד. אִישׁ יְדִיד.
Nechtam Becheter Malchutecha.	נֶחְתָּם בְּכֶתֶר מַלְכוּתֶךָ.
Terachem. Vegam Tenachem.	תְּרַחֵם. וְגַם תְּנַחֵם.
Amecha Venachalatecha.	עַמְּךָ וְנַחֲלָתֶךָ.
Bizchuto Har'eh. Le'am Nich'eh.	בִּזְכוּתוֹ הַרְאֵה. לְעַם נִכְאֶה.
Binyan Beitcha Unevatecha.	בִּנְיַן בֵּיתְךָ וּנְוָתֶךָ.
Uzechut Avot. Me'aravot.	וּזְכוּת אָבוֹת. מֵעֲרָבוֹת.

Zechor-Na La'adatecha.   זְכָר־נָא לַעֲדָתֶךָ.

Venatelem Venase'em. Bizchut   וְנַטְלֵם וְנַשְּׂאֵם. בִּזְכוּת

Shiv'ah Temimeicha. Zacherenu   שִׁבְעָה תְמִימֶיךָ. זָכְרֵנוּ

Adonai Birtzon Amecha: יְהֹוָה בִּרְצוֹן עַמֶּךָ:

By the merit of David, the beloved man, sealed with the crown of Your kingdom. Have mercy, and also comfort, Your people and Your inheritance. By his merit, show the afflicted people the rebuilding of Your house and Your dwelling. And the merit of the patriarchs from the heavens, remember for Your congregation. And take them and carry them in the merit of Your seven perfect ones. Remember us, Hashem, in favoring Your people:

Zechor-Lanu Eloheinu. Zechut   זְכָר־לָנוּ אֱלֹהֵינוּ. זְכוּת

David Beno Yishai. Umigiz'o   דָּוִד בְּנוֹ יִשָׁי. וּמִגִּזְעוֹ

Tetzav Choter. Lekabetz Et-   תְּצַו חֹטֶר. לְקַבֵּץ אֶת־

Megorashai. Uvizchuto. Esof   מְגֹרָשַׁי. וּבִזְכוּתוֹ. אֱסוֹף

Nidcho. Ve'et-Banai Ve'et-   נִדְחוֹ. וְאֶת־בָּנַי וְאֶת־

Nashai. Venagilah   נָשַׁי. וְנָגִילָה

Bemalchutecha. Vedivrei   בְּמַלְכוּתֶךָ. וְדִבְרֵי

Nifle'oteicha. Zacherenu   נִפְלְאֹתֶיךָ. זָכְרֵנוּ

Adonai Birtzon Amecha: יְהֹוָה בִּרְצוֹן עַמֶּךָ:

Remember for us, our God, the merit of David son of Yishai, and from his offspring, command a branch to gather my exiled-ones. And by his merit, gather his scattered, and my sons and my daughters, and we will rejoice in Your kingship and Your wondrous deeds. Remember us, Hashem, in favoring Your people:

Rachamana Idkar Lan Keyameh
Dedavid Malka Meshicha:
רַחֲמָנָא אִדְכַּר לָן קְיָמֵה
דְּדָוִד מַלְכָּא מְשִׁיחָא:

Merciful One, remember for us the merit of David, the anointed king.

Rachamana Idkar Lan Tzeloteh
Dishlomoh Malka:
רַחֲמָנָא אִדְכַּר לָן צְלוֹתֵה
דִּשְׁלֹמֹה מַלְכָּא:

Merciful One, remember for us the prayer of King Shlomo.

Rachamana Zachvan Chapes
Lan:
רַחֲמָנָא זַכְוָן חַפֵּשׂ
לָן:

Merciful One, seek out merits for us.

Rachamana Zivach Ashrei Alan:
רַחֲמָנָא זִיוָךְ אַשְׁרֵי עֲלָן:

Merciful One, let Your radiance shine upon us.

Rachamana Chatminan Besifra
Dechayei:
רַחֲמָנָא חַתְמִנָן בְּסִפְרָא
דְּחַיֵּי:

Merciful One, inscribe us in the Book of Life.

Rachamana Chatminan Besifra
Derachamei:
רַחֲמָנָא חַתְמִנָן בְּסִפְרָא
דְּרַחֲמֵי:

Merciful One, inscribe us in the Book of Mercy.

Rachamana Chatminan Besifra
Detzadikei Vachasidei:
רַחֲמָנָא חַתְמִנָן בְּסִפְרָא
דְּצַדִּיקֵי וַחֲסִידֵי:

Merciful One, inscribe us in the Book of the Righteous and the Devout.

Rachamana Chatminan Besifra
Disharei Utemimei:

רַחֲמָנָא חַתְמִנָן בְּסִפְרָא
דִישָׁרֵי וּתְמִימֵי:

Merciful One, inscribe us in the Book of the Upright and the Perfect.

Rachamana Chatminan Besifra
Defarnasata Tavta Umezonei
Tavei:

רַחֲמָנָא חַתְמִנָן בְּסִפְרָא
דְּפַרְנָסָתָא טַבְתָא וּמְזוֹנֵי
טָבֵי:

Merciful One, inscribe us in the Book of Good Sustenance and Provisions.

Rachamana Chashov Alan
Tavan:

רַחֲמָנָא חֲשׁוֹב עֲלָן
טָבָן:

Merciful One, think of us for good.

Rachamana Tavan Sagi'an Aytei
Alan:

רַחֲמָנָא טַבְוָן סַגִיאָן אַיְתֵי
עֲלָן:

Merciful One, bring abundant goodness upon us.

Rachamana Yitgalgelun
Rachamach Alan:

רַחֲמָנָא יִתְגַּלְגְּלוּן
רַחֲמָךְ עֲלָן:

Merciful One, let Your mercy be upon us.

Rachamana Kevosh Chemta
Verugza Minan:

רַחֲמָנָא כְּבֹשׁ חֶמְתָא
וְרֻגְזָא מִנָּן:

Merciful One, subdue Your anger and wrath from us.

Rachamana La Ta'beid Gemira
Lan:

רַחֲמָנָא לָא תַעֲבֵיד גְּמִירָא
לָן:

Merciful One, do not repay us in full.

Rachamana Mechol Ushevok
Lechovin Vela'avayan:

רַחֲמָנָא מְחֹל וּשְׁבֹק
לְחוֹבִין וְלַעֲוָיָן:

Merciful One, forgive and pardon our sins and transgressions.

Rachamana Nehor Tuvach
Anhar Alan:

רַחֲמָנָא נְהוֹר טוּבָךְ
אַנְהַר עֲלָן:

Merciful One, let the light of Your goodness shine upon us.

Rachamana Se'id Usemich
Hevei Lan:

רַחֲמָנָא סְעִיד וּסְמִיךְ
הֱוֵי לָן:

Merciful One, be our Help and Support.

Rachamana Aveid Imana Ata
Letav:

רַחֲמָנָא עֲבֵיד עִמָּנָא אָתָא
לְטָב:

Merciful One, make for us a sign for good.

Rachamana Petach Shemaya
Litzlotin:

רַחֲמָנָא פְּתַח שְׁמַיָּא
לִצְלוֹתִין:

Merciful One, open the heavens to our prayers.

Rachamana Tzelotana Kabel
Bera'ava:

רַחֲמָנָא צְלוֹתָנָא קַבֵּל
בְּרַעֲוָא:

Merciful One, accept our prayers with favor.

Rachamana Kabel Tzelotin
Uva'utin Be'idan Aktin:

רַחֲמָנָא קַבֵּל צְלוֹתִין
וּבָעוּתִין בְּעִדָן עָקָתִין:

Merciful One, accept our prayers and supplications in times of distress.

Rachamana Rachem Al
Nishmatin:

רַחֲמָנָא רַחֵם עַל
נִשְׁמָתִין:

Merciful One, have mercy on souls.

Rachamana Shata Tavta Aytei
Alan:

רַחֲמָנָא שַׁתָּא טַבְתָּא אַיְיתֵי
עֲלָן:

Merciful One, bring a good year upon us.

Rachamana Tuv Merugzach:

רַחֲמָנָא תּוּב מֵרָגְזָךְ:

Merciful One, turn back from Your anger.

Rachamana Vela Nehdar
Reikam Min-Kamach:

רַחֲמָנָא וְלָא נֶהְדַּר
רֵיקָם מִן־קַמָּךְ:

Merciful One, do not let us return empty-handed from before You.

Shema Yisra'el Adonai Eloheinu
Adonai Echad.

שְׁמַע יִשְׂרָאֵל יְהוָה אֱלֹהֵינוּ
יְהוָה אֶחָד:

Hear, O Yisrael: Hashem is our God, Hashem is One.

Adonai Hu Ha'elohim
Adonai Hu Ha'elohim. (say two times)

יְהוָה הוּא הָאֱלֹהִים
יְהוָה הוּא הָאֱלֹהִים: (שתי פעמים)

Hashem, He is God. Hashem, He is God. (say two times)

Adonai Melech.
Adonai Malach.
Adonai Yimloch Le'olam Va'ed. (say two times)

יְהוָה מֶלֶךְ.
יְהוָה מָלָךְ.
יְהוָה יִמְלֹךְ לְעֹלָם וָעֶד: (שתי פעמים)

Hashem reigns, Hashem has reigned, Hashem will reign forever and ever. (say two times)

Eloheinu Shebashamayim
Shema Kolenu Vekabel
Tefilatenu Beratzon:

אֱלֹהֵינוּ שֶׁבַּשָּׁמַיִם שְׁמַע קוֹלֵנוּ
וְקַבֵּל תְּפִלָּתֵנוּ בְּרָצוֹן:

Our God in Heaven, hear our voice and accept our prayers with favor.

Eloheinu Shebashamayim
Zacherenu Bezichron Tov
Milefaneicha:

אֱלֹהֵינוּ שֶׁבַּשָּׁמַיִם
זָכְרֵנוּ בְּזִכְרוֹן טוֹב
מִלְּפָנֶיךָ:

Our God in heaven, remember us for good before You:

Eloheinu Shebashamayim

Chatemenu Besefer Chayim

Tovim:

אֱלֹהֵינוּ שֶׁבַּשָּׁמַיִם
חָתְמֵנוּ בְּסֵפֶר חַיִּים
טוֹבִים:

Our God in heaven, inscribe us in the Book of Good Life:

Chatemenu Besefer Tzadikim

Vachasidim:

חָתְמֵנוּ בְּסֵפֶר צַדִּיקִים
וַחֲסִידִים:

Inscribe us in the Book of the Righteous and the Devout:

Chatemenu Besefer Yesharim

Utemimim:

חָתְמֵנוּ בְּסֵפֶר יְשָׁרִים
וּתְמִימִים:

Inscribe us in the Book of the Upright and the Perfect:

Chatemenu Besefer Mezonot

Ufarnasah Tovah:

חָתְמֵנוּ בְּסֵפֶר מְזוֹנוֹת
וּפַרְנָסָה טוֹבָה:

Inscribe us in the Book of Sustenance and Good Livelihood:

Chamol Aleinu Ve'al Tapeinu

Ve'al Olaleinu:

חֲמֹל עָלֵינוּ וְעַל טַפֵּינוּ
וְעַל עוֹלָלֵינוּ:

Have compassion on us, our children, and our infants:

Eloheinu Shebashamayim

Taharenu Me'avoneinu:

אֱלֹהֵינוּ שֶׁבַּשָּׁמַיִם
טַהֲרֵנוּ מֵעֲוֹנֵינוּ:

Our God in heaven, purify us from our iniquities:

Eloheinu Shebashamayim

Yehemu-Na Rachameicha

Aleinu:

אֱלֹהֵינוּ שֶׁבַּשָּׁמַיִם

יֶהֱמוּ־נָא רַחֲמֶיךָ

עָלֵינוּ:

Our God in heaven, arouse Your mercy upon us:

Eloheinu Shebashamayim

Kevosh Et-Koveshenu:

אֱלֹהֵינוּ שֶׁבַּשָּׁמַיִם

כְּבֹשׁ אֶת־כּוֹבְשֵׁנוּ:

Our God in heaven, subdue our those who subdue us:

Kalah Al-Ta'as Imanu:

כַּלֵּה אַל־תַּעַשׂ עִמָּנוּ:

Do not destroy us completely:

Eloheinu Shebashamayim

Lema'anach Aseh Im Lo

Lema'anenu:

אֱלֹהֵינוּ שֶׁבַּשָּׁמַיִם

לְמַעַנְךָ עֲשֵׂה אִם לֹא

לְמַעֲנֵנוּ:

Our God in heaven, act for Your sake, if not for ours:

Lechatz Et Lochatzeinu:

לְחַץ אֶת לוֹחֲצֵינוּ:

Oppress those who oppress us:

Eloheinu Shebashamayim Malle

Mish'alot Libenu Letovah

La'avodatecha:

אֱלֹהֵינוּ שֶׁבַּשָּׁמַיִם מַלֵּא

מִשְׁאֲלוֹת לִבֵּנוּ לְטוֹבָה

לַעֲבוֹדָתֶךָ:

Our God in heaven, fulfill the desires of our hearts for good, for Your service:

Eloheinu Shebashamayim
Nekom Et-Nikmatenu: אֱלֹהֵינוּ שֶׁבַּשָּׁמַיִם נְקֹם אֶת־נִקְמָתֵנוּ:

Our God in heaven, avenge our vengeance:

Eloheinu Shebashamayim
Semoch Et-Nefilatenu: אֱלֹהֵינוּ שֶׁבַּשָּׁמַיִם סְמֹךְ אֶת־נְפִילָתֵנוּ:

Our God in heaven, support our fallen:

Eloheinu Shebashamayim Aneh
Et-Atiratenu: אֱלֹהֵינוּ שֶׁבַּשָּׁמַיִם עֲנֵה אֶת־עֲתִירָתֵנוּ:

Our God in heaven, answer our pleas:

Eloheinu Shebashamayim
Pedenu Midei Chol-Oyeveinu: אֱלֹהֵינוּ שֶׁבַּשָּׁמַיִם פְּדֵנוּ מִידֵי כָל־אוֹיְבֵינוּ:

Our God in heaven, redeem us from the hands of all our enemies:

Eloheinu Shebashamayim
Tzaveh Itanu Birchoteicha: אֱלֹהֵינוּ שֶׁבַּשָּׁמַיִם צַוֵּה אִתָּנוּ בִּרְכוֹתֶיךָ:

Our God in heaven, command Your blessings upon us:

Tzaveh Itanu Yeshu'oteicha: צַוֵּה אִתָּנוּ יְשׁוּעוֹתֶיךָ:

Command Your salvation upon us:

Tzadekenu Bemishpateicha: צַדְּקֵנוּ בְּמִשְׁפָּטֶיךָ:

Justify us with Your judgments:

Eloheinu Shebashamayim   אֱלֹהֵינוּ שֶׁבַּשָּׁמַיִם
Karev-Lanu Ketz Hage'ulah: קָרֶב־לָנוּ קֵץ הַגְּאֻלָּה:

Our God in heaven, bring close for us the end of the redemption:

Karev-Lanu Yom Hayeshu'ah: קָרֶב־לָנוּ יוֹם הַיְשׁוּעָה:

Bring close the day of salvation for us:

Karevenu La'avodatecha: קָרְבֵנוּ לַעֲבוֹדָתֶךָ:

Draw us near to Your service:

Eloheinu Shebashamayim Rivah   אֱלֹהֵינוּ שֶׁבַּשָּׁמַיִם רִיבָה
Rivenu Uge'alenu: רִיבֵנוּ וּגְאָלֵנוּ:

Our God in heaven, plead our cause and redeem us:

Re'eh Bo'oni Amecha Yisra'el: רְאֵה בָעֳנִי עַמְּךָ יִשְׂרָאֵל:

See the affliction of Your people Yisrael:

Refa Kol-Cholei Amecha   רְפָא כָּל־חוֹלֵי עַמְּךָ
Yisra'el: יִשְׂרָאֵל:

Heal all the sick of Your people Yisrael:

Re'eh Bedochak Hasha'ah: רְאֵה בְּדֹחַק הַשָּׁעָה:

See the distress of the moment:

Eloheinu Shebashamayim   אֱלֹהֵינוּ שֶׁבַּשָּׁמַיִם
She'eh Et-Shav'atenu: שְׁעֵה אֶת־שַׁוְעָתֵנוּ:

Our God in heaven, regard our cry:

Shiyt Shalom Beineinu:

שִׁית שָׁלוֹם בֵּינֵינוּ:

Establish peace among us:

Shiyt Shalvah Be'armenoteinu:

שִׁית שַׁלְוָה בְּאַרְמְנוֹתֵינוּ:

Establish tranquility in our palaces:

Eloheinu Shebashamayim Ten
Shalom Ba'aretz:

אֱלֹהֵינוּ שֶׁבַּשָּׁמַיִם תֵּן
שָׁלוֹם בָּאָרֶץ:

Our God in heaven, grant peace in the land:

Ten Sava Ba'olam:

תֵּן שָׂבָע בָּעוֹלָם:

Grant abundance in the world:

Ten Shalom Bamalchut:

תֵּן שָׁלוֹם בַּמַּלְכוּת:

Grant peace in the government:

Ten Tal Umatar Livrachah Be'ito
Ba'aretz:

תֵּן טַל וּמָטָר לִבְרָכָה בְּעִתּוֹ
בָּאָרֶץ:

Grant dew and rain for a blessing in their time upon the land:

Ten Zera Lazorea' Velechem
La'ochel:

תֵּן זֶרַע לַזּוֹרֵעַ וְלֶחֶם
לָאוֹכֵל:

Grant seed to the sower and bread to the eater:

Ten Lechem Lefi Hataf Lasva: תֵּן לֶחֶם לְפִי הַטַף לָשֹׂבַע:

Grant bread to the mouth of the infants for satisfaction:

Eloheinu Shebashamayim Tikon   אֱלֹהֵינוּ שֶׁבַּשָּׁמַיִם תִּכּוֹן

Tefilatenu Ketoret Lefaneicha: תְּפִלָּתֵנוּ קְטֹרֶת לְפָנֶיךָ:

Our God in heaven, may our prayer be established as incense before You:

Anenu Magen David Anenu: עֲנֵנוּ מָגֵן דָּוִד עֲנֵנוּ:

Anenu Elohei Hamerkavah   עֲנֵנוּ אֱלֹהֵי הַמֶּרְכָּבָה

Anenu: Anenu Rachum   עֲנֵנוּ: עֲנֵנוּ רַחוּם

Vechanun Anenu: וְחַנּוּן עֲנֵנוּ:

Answer us, Shield of David, answer us: Answer us, God of the Chariot, answer us: Answer us, Merciful and Gracious One, answer us:

Adonai Chonenu   יְהֹוָה חָנֵּנוּ

Vahakimenu. Uvesefer Chayim   וַהֲקִימֵנוּ. וּבְסֵפֶר חַיִּים

Zacherenu Vechatemenu: זָכְרֵנוּ וְחָתְמֵנוּ:

Hashem, be gracious to us and establish us. And in the Book of Life, remember and inscribe us:

Adonai Kachotam Al Lev Hayom   יְהֹוָה כַּחוֹתָם עַל לֵב הַיּוֹם

Simenu. Uvesefer Chayim   שִׂימֵנוּ. וּבְסֵפֶר חַיִּים זָכְרֵנוּ

Zacherenu Vechatemenu: וְחָתְמֵנוּ:

Hashem, place us as a seal upon Your heart today, and in the Book of Life, remember and inscribe us:

Adonai Rivah Rivenu Ulecham
Lochameinu. Uvesefer Chayim
Zacherenu Vechatemenu:

יְהֹוָה רִיבָה רִיבֵנוּ וּלְחַם לוֹחֲמֵינוּ. וּבְסֵפֶר חַיִּים זָכְרֵנוּ וְחָתְמֵנוּ:

Hashem, plead our cause and fight our battles, and in the Book of Life, remember and inscribe us:

Adonai Barech Et-Lachmenu
Ve'et-Meimeinu. Uvesefer
Chayim Zacherenu
Vechatemenu:

יְהֹוָה בָּרֵךְ אֶת־לַחְמֵנוּ וְאֶת־מֵימֵינוּ. וּבְסֵפֶר חַיִּים זָכְרֵנוּ וְחָתְמֵנוּ:

Hashem, bless our bread and our water, and in the Book of Life, remember and inscribe us:

Adonai Aseh Lema'an
Shemecha. Vechusah Al Yisra'el
Amecha:

יְהֹוָה עֲשֵׂה לְמַעַן שְׁמֶךָ. וְחוּסָה עַל יִשְׂרָאֵל עַמֶּךָ:

Hashem, act for the sake of Your name, and have mercy on Yisrael, Your people:

Adonai Aseh Lema'an David
Ne'im Zemiroteicha. Vechusah
Al Yisra'el Amecha:

יְהֹוָה עֲשֵׂה לְמַעַן דָּוִד נְעִים זְמִירוֹתֶיךָ. וְחוּסָה עַל יִשְׂרָאֵל עַמֶּךָ:

Hashem, act for the sake of David, the sweet singer of Your praises, and have mercy on Yisrael, Your people:

Adonai Aseh Lema'an Melech
Shelomoh Banah Bayit
Lishmecha. Vechusah Al Yisra'el
Amecha:

יְהֹוָה עֲשֵׂה לְמַעַן מֶלֶךְ
שְׁלֹמֹה בָּנָה בַּיִת
לִשְׁמֶךָ. וְחוּסָה עַל יִשְׂרָאֵל
עַמֶּךָ:

Hashem, act for the sake of King Shlomo, who built a house for Your name, and have mercy on Yisrael, Your people:

Adonai Aseh Lema'an Harugim
Userufim Al Yichud Kedushat
Shemecha. Vechusah Al Yisra'el
Amecha:

יְהֹוָה עֲשֵׂה לְמַעַן הֲרוּגִים
וּשְׂרוּפִים עַל יִחוּד קְדֻשַׁת
שְׁמֶךָ. וְחוּסָה עַל יִשְׂרָאֵל
עַמֶּךָ:

Hashem, act for the sake of those killed and burned for the sanctification of Your holy name, and have mercy on Yisrael, Your people:

De'anei Ledavid Velishlomoh
Beno Birushalayim. Aneinan:

דְּעָנֵי לְדָוִד וְלִשְׁלֹמֹה
בְּנוֹ בִּירוּשָׁלַיִם. עֲנֵינָן:

The One who answered David and Shlomo, his son, in Yerushalayim, answer us:

De'anei Letzadikei Vachasidei
Utemimei Di Bechol-Dor
Vedor. Aneinan:

דְּעָנֵי לְצַדִּיקֵי וַחֲסִידֵי
וּתְמִימֵי דִי בְּכָל־דָר
וְדָר. עֲנֵינָן:

The One who answered the righteous, the devout, and the perfect in every generation, answer us:

Todi'eni Orach Chayim Sova
Semachot Et-Paneicha Ne'imot
Bimincha Netzach.

תּוֹדִיעֵנִי אֹרַח חַיִּים שֹׂבַע
שְׂמָחוֹת אֶת־פָּנֶיךָ נְעִמוֹת
בִּימִינְךָ נֶצַח:

You make known to me the path of life; in Your presence is fullness of joy; at Your right hand are pleasures forevermore.

Shav'ateinu Kabel. Ushema
Tza'akateinu. Yodea Ta'alumot.

שַׁוְעָתֵנוּ קַבֵּל. וּשְׁמַע
צַעֲקָתֵנוּ. יוֹדֵעַ תַּעֲלוּמוֹת:

Accept our prayer, hear our cry, You Who knows secret thoughts.

Hosha'ana. Hosha'ana:

הוֹשַׁעֲנָא. הוֹשַׁעֲנָא:

Please, save us. Please, save us:

Ana Hoshi'ah Na.
Ana Hoshi'ah Na:

אָנָּא הוֹשִׁיעָה נָּא.
אָנָּא הוֹשִׁיעָה נָּא:

Please, save us now. Please, save us now:

Ana Yasher Am Ba. Behosha'ana
Rabba. Lesalselach Bechibah. El
Mvoshi'i. Chish Na Pidyom. El
Nora Ve'ayom. Uvirushalayim

אָנָּא יַשֵּׁר עַם בָּא. בְּהוֹשַׁעֲנָא
רַבָּא. לְסַלְסְלָךְ בְּחִבָּה. אֵל
מוֹשִׁיעִי. חִישׁ נָא פִּדְיוֹם. אֵל
נוֹרָא וְאָיוֹם. וּבִירוּשָׁלַיִם

Kehayom. Nehalach Beyom   כְּהַיּוֹם. נְהַלְלָךְ בְּיוֹם

Shevi'i. Hoshi'ah Na. Ana   שְׁבִיעִי. הוֹשִׁיעָה נָא. אָנָּא

Hoshi'ah Na. Ana Hoshi'ah Na: הוֹשִׁיעָה נָא. אָנָּא הוֹשִׁיעָה נָא:

Please, straighten the people that come, on Hoshanah Rabbah, to cherish You with affection, God my Savior. Quickly redeem, Mighty and Awesome God, and in Yerushalayim today, we will praise You on the seventh day. Please, save us now. Please, save us now. Please, save us now:

Ana Secheh Na Kalil.   אָנָּא סְחֵה נָא כָּלִיל.

Mamlechot Ha'elil. Ve'aron Alei   מַמְלְכוֹת הָאֱלִיל. וְאָרוֹן עֲלֵי

Chalil. Bechag Sha'ashu'i.   חָלִיל. בְּחַג שַׁעֲשׁוּעִי.

Peduti Ra'ah. Vegam Ga'oh   פְּדוּתִי רָאָה. וְגַם גָּאֹה

Ga'ah. Uvirushalayim Leshanah   גָּאָה. וּבִירוּשָׁלַיִם לְשָׁנָה

Haba'ah. Nehalach Beyom   הַבָּאָה. נְהַלְלָךְ בְּיוֹם

Shevi'i. Hoshi'ah Na. Ana   שְׁבִיעִי. הוֹשִׁיעָה נָא. אָנָּא

Hoshi'ah Na. Ana Hoshi'ah   הוֹשִׁיעָה נָא. אָנָּא הוֹשִׁיעָה

Na: נָא:

Please, bring down the idolatrous kingdoms. And I will sing upon the flute, in my joyous festival. He saw my redemption, and is also greatly exalted, and in Yerushalayim next year, we will praise You on the seventh day. Please, save us now. Please, save us now. Please, save us now:

Ana Beneh Sha'ar Hashir.   אָנָּא בְּנֵה שַׁעַר הַשִּׁיר.

Vesham Lecha Ashir. Vegam Shai   וְשָׁם לְךָ אָשִׁיר. וְגַם שַׁי

Lecha Atshir. El Margo'i.   לְךָ אַתְשִׁיר. אֵל מַרְגּוֹעִי.

Bekabetzcha Ne'enakim.   בְּקַבֶּצְךָ נֶאֱנָקִים.

Mimerchakim. Vesukatecha
Takim. Nehalach Beyom Shevi'i.
Hoshi'ah Na. Ana Hoshi'ah Na.
Ana Hoshi'ah Na:

מִמֶּרְחַקִים. וְסֻכָּתְךָ
תָּקִים. נְהַלֶּלְךָ בְּיוֹם שְׁבִיעִי.
הוֹשִׁיעָה נָא. אָנָּא הוֹשִׁיעָה נָא.
אָנָּא הוֹשִׁיעָה נָא:

Please, build the gate of the song, and there I will sing to You, and also a gift I will dedicate to You, my comforting God. When You gather the groaning from distant places, and raise up Your sukkah, we will praise You on the seventh day. Please, save us now. Please, save us now. Please, save us now:

Ana Retzeh Na Vekomem. Har
Hashamem. Umigdalecha
Teromem. Vegaleh Ketz Yish'i.
Romemutecha Har'eh. Le'am
Hanich'eh. Umulecha Yera'eh.
Nehalach Beyom Shevi'i.
Hoshi'ah Na. Ana Hoshi'ah
Na. Ana Hoshi'ah Na:

אָנָּא רְצֵה נָא וְקוֹמֵם. הַר
הַשָּׁמֵם. וּמִגְדָּלְךָ
תְרוֹמֵם. וְגַלֵּה קֵץ יִשְׁעִי.
רוֹמְמוּתְךָ הַרְאֵה. לְעַם
הַנִּכְאֶה. וּמוּלְךָ יֵרָאֶה.
נְהַלֶּלְךָ בְּיוֹם שְׁבִיעִי.
הוֹשִׁיעָה נָא. אָנָּא הוֹשִׁיעָה
נָא. אָנָּא הוֹשִׁיעָה נָא:

Please, now favor and establish the desolate mountain, and raise up Your tower, and reveal the end of my salvation. Show Your exaltation to the broken people. And from before You will be seen, we will praise You on the seventh day. Please, save us now. Please, save us now. Please, save us now:

Ana Yedidim Betuvecha Raveh.
Vehodecha Alav Teshaveh.
Vetuvecha Achaveh. Betoch Am

אָנָּא יְדִידִים בְּטוּבְךָ רַוֵּה.
וְהוֹדְךָ עָלָיו תְּשַׁוֶּה.
וְטוּבְךָ אֲחַוֶּה. בְּתוֹךְ עַם

Nosha'i. Tziyon Malle. Me'am   נוֹשָׁעִי. צִיּוֹן מַלֵּא. מֵעַם

Eleh. Vesham Lecha Nechaleh.   אֵלֶּה. וְשָׁם לְךָ נְחַלֶּה.

Nehalach Beyom Shevi'i.   נְהַלֶּךְ בְּיוֹם שְׁבִיעִי.

Hoshi'ah Na. Ana Hoshi'ah Na.   הוֹשִׁיעָה נָא. אָנָּא הוֹשִׁיעָה נָא.

Ana Hoshi'ah Na: אָנָּא הוֹשִׁיעָה נָא:

Please, satisfy Your beloved ones with Your goodness, and set Your glory over them, and I will declare Your goodness among the delivered people. Fill Tziyon with these people, and there we will serve You. We will praise You on the seventh day. Please, save us now. Please, save us now. Please, save us now:

Ana Cheilcha Hanchel. Chomot   אָנָּא חֵילְךָ הַנְחֵל. חוֹמוֹת

Vachel. Vekamim Gachel   וָחֵל. וְקָמִים גַּחֵל

Vehatzmach Yish'i. Kehali   וְהַצְמַח יִשְׁעִי. קְהָלִי

Konen. Vetuvecha Ashanen.   כּוֹנֵן. וְטוּבְךָ אֲשַׁנֵּן.

Uleshimcha Aranen. Nehalach   וּלְשִׁמְךָ אֲרַנֵּן. נְהַלֶּךְ

Beyom Shevi'i. Hoshi'ah   בְּיוֹם שְׁבִיעִי. הוֹשִׁיעָה

Na. Ana Hoshi'ah Na. Ana   נָא. אָנָּא הוֹשִׁיעָה נָא. אָנָּא

Hoshi'ah Na: הוֹשִׁיעָה נָא:

Please, to Your army grant walls and the rampart. And let the embers rise and spring forth my salvation. Establish my congregation, and I will declare Your goodness, and I will sing to Your name. We will praise You on the seventh day. Save us now. Please, save us now. Please, save us now:

Ani Vahu Hoshi'ah Na.   אֲנִי וָהוּ הוֹשִׁיעָה נָא.

Ani Vahu Hoshi'ah Na: אֲנִי וָהוּ הוֹשִׁיעָה נָא:

Ani VaHu, please save us now. Ani VaHu, please save us now.

Kehosha'ta Yedidim. Mikaf	כְּהוֹשַׁעְתָּ יְדִידִים. מִכַּף
Ma'avidim. Vatimchatz Ludim.	מַעֲבִידִים. וַתִּמְחַץ לוּדִים.
Atzim Lehachni'i. Aluvei Olev.	אָצִים לְהַכְנִיעִי. עֲלוּבֵי עוֹלֵב.
Hamehalim Bechol-Lev.	הַמְהַלְלִים בְּכָל־לֵב.
Be'etrog Hadomeh Lalev.	בְּאֶתְרוֹג הַדּוֹמֶה לַלֵּב.
Nehalach Beyom Shevi'i. Ken	נְהַלֶּלְךָ בְּיוֹם שְׁבִיעִי. כֵּן
Hosha'ana. Ani Vahu Hoshi'ah	הוֹשַׁעְנָא. אֲנִי וָהוּ הוֹשִׁיעָה
Na. Ani Vahu Hoshi'ah Na:	נָא. אֲנִי וָהוּ הוֹשִׁיעָה נָא:

As You saved the beloved ones from the hand of enslavers, and struck the Ludim [Egyptians] who rushed to subdue me. The downtrodden ones who praise with all their heart, with the etrog that resembles the heart, we will praise You on the seventh day, so please save us. Ani VaHu, please, save us now. Ani VaHu, please, save us now:

Kehosha'ta Vata'azor. Anushei	כְּהוֹשַׁעְתָּ וַתַּעֲזוֹר. אֱנוּשֵׁי
Mazor. Vate'ezor Azor. Lishpot	מָזוֹר. וַתֶּאֱזוֹר אָזוֹר. לִשְׁפּוֹט
Marshi'i. Yeter Pezurah. Sovevei	מַרְשִׁיעִי. יֶתֶר פְּזוּרָה. סוֹבְבֵי
Torah. Belulav Hadomeh	תוֹרָה. בְּלוּלָב הַדּוֹמֶה
Lashidrah. Nehalach Beyom	לַשִּׁדְרָה. נְהַלֶּלְךָ בְּיוֹם
Shevi'i. Ken Hosha'ana. Ani	שְׁבִיעִי. כֵּן הוֹשַׁעֲנָא. אֲנִי
Vahu Hoshi'ah Na. Ani Vahu	וָהוּ הוֹשִׁיעָה נָא. אֲנִי וָהוּ
Hoshi'ah Na:	הוֹשִׁיעָה נָא:

As You saved and helped the afflicted ones, and girded Yourself in might to judge the wicked. The scattered remnant who encircle the Torah, with the lulav resembling the spine, we will praise You on the seventh day, so please save us. Ani VaHu, please, save us now. Ani VaHu, please, save us now:

Kehosha'ta Segurei Tzinok.	כְּהוֹשַׁעְתָּ סְגוּרֵי צִנוֹק.
No'akim Anok. Vata'anik Anok.	נוֹאֲקִים אָנוֹק. וַתַּעֲנִיק עָנוֹק.
Vehishka'ta Mashki'i. Sovevim	וְהִשְׁקַעְתָּ מַשְׁקִיעִי. סוֹבְבִים
Bemachanayim. Bemazal	בְּמַחֲנַיִם. בְּמַזַּל
Moznayim. Bahadas Hadomeh	מֹאזְנַיִם. בַּהֲדַס הַדּוֹמֶה
La'einayim. Nehalach Beyom	לָעֵינַיִם. נְהַלֶּךְ בְּיוֹם
Shevi'i. Ken Hosha'ana. Ani	שְׁבִיעִי. כֵּן הוֹשַׁעֲנָא. אֲנִי
Vahu Hoshi'ah Na. Ani Vahu	וָהוּ הוֹשִׁיעָה נָא. אֲנִי וָהוּ
Hoshi'ah Na:	הוֹשִׁיעָה נָא:

As You saved those imprisoned in confinement, groaning in their anguish, You granted them relief and sank those who sought to drown me. Encircling in camps, under the mazal of Moznayim (Libra), with hadas (myrtle) resembling eyes, we will praise You on the seventh day, so please save us. Ani VaHu, please, save us now. Ani VaHu, please, save us now:

Kehosha'ta Peduyei Am Zeh.	כְּהוֹשַׁעְתָּ פְּדוּיֵי עַם זֶה.
Beyad Chozeh Umazeh.	בְּיַד חוֹזֶה וּמַזֶּה.
Vatashet Nemivzeh. Choshek	וַתָּשֶׁת נְמִבְזֶה. חוֹשֶׁק
Lehatbi'i. Potechei Delatayim.	לְהַטְבִּיעִי. פּוֹתְחֵי דְלָתָיִם.
Letzaltzel Bimtziltayim.	לְצַלְצֵל בִּמְצִלְתַּיִם.
Ba'aravah Hadomah Lisfatayim.	בַּעֲרָבָה הַדּוֹמָה לִשְׂפָתַיִם.
Nehalach Beyom Shevi'i. Ken	נְהַלֵּךְ בְּיוֹם שְׁבִיעִי. כֵּן
Hosha'ana. Ani Vahu Hoshi'ah	הוֹשַׁעֲנָא. אֲנִי וָהוּ הוֹשִׁיעָה
Na. Ani Vahu Hoshi'ah Na:	נָא. אֲנִי וָהוּ הוֹשִׁיעָה נָא:

As You saved the redeemed of this people by the hand of Moshe and Aharon, You laid low the despicable, eager to drown me. Openers of doors to sound the cymbals. With the arava (willow) resembling lips, we will praise You on the seventh day, so please save us. Ani VaHu, please, save us now. Ani VaHu, please, save us now:

Ana El Na Hosha'ana

Vehoshi'ah Na: (Say Two Times)

אָנָּא אֵל נָא הוֹשַׁעְנָא

וְהוֹשִׁיעָה נָּא: (שתי פעמים)

Please, God, now please save and save us now: (say two times)

El Na Otzarecha Hatov Tiftach Mizevulah. Veha'aretz Titen Yevulah. Hosha'ana Vehoshi'ah Na:

אֵל נָא אוֹצָרְךָ הַטּוֹב תִּפְתַּח מִזְּבוּלָה. וְהָאָרֶץ תִּתֵּן יְבוּלָה. הוֹשַׁעְנָא וְהוֹשִׁיעָה נָּא:

God, please open Your storehouse of goodness from Your dwelling place, and the land will yield its produce. Please save and save us now.

El Na Nitfei Nedavot Yerav'u Dish'ei Chatzir. Vehisig Lachem Dayish Et-Batzir. Hosha'ana Vehoshi'ah Na:

אֵל נָא נִטְפֵי נְדָבוֹת יְרַוּוּ דִּשְׁאֵי חָצִיר. וְהִשִּׂיג לָכֶם דַּיִשׁ אֶת־בָּצִיר. הוֹשַׁעְנָא וְהוֹשִׁיעָה נָּא:

God, please let the generous drops of rain moisten the grassy vegetation, and threshing will catch up with the vintage. Please save and save us now.

El Na Yevul Ha'aretz Levarech   אֵל נָא יְבוּל הָאָרֶץ לְבָרֵךְ

He'ater. Achol Vesavoa'   הֶעָתֵר. אָכוֹל וְשָׂבוֹעַ

Vehoter. Hosha'ana Vehoshi'ah   וְהוֹתֵר. הוֹשַׁעְנָא וְהוֹשִׁיעָה

Na: נָא:

God, please bless the produce of the land abundantly, I will eat and be satisfied and have leftovers. Please save and save us now.

El Na Yom Zeh Chatom Na   אֵל נָא יוֹם זֶה חֲתוֹם נָא

Chotemet. Uvarech Chitah   חוֹתֶמֶת. וּבָרֵךְ חִטָּה

Use'orah   וּשְׂעוֹרָה

Vechusemet. Hosha'ana   וְכֻסֶּמֶת. הוֹשַׁעְנָא

Vehoshi'ah Na: וְהוֹשִׁיעָה נָא:

God, please stamp this day with a seal, and bless wheat, barley, and spelt. Please save and save us now.

El Na Vegeshem Nedavot   אֵל נָא וְגֶשֶׁם נְדָבוֹת

Techolel Ruach Tzafon. Uvarech   תְּחוֹלֵל רוּחַ צָפוֹן. וּבָרֵךְ

Shibolet Shu'al   שִׁבֹּלֶת שׁוּעָל

Veshifon. Hosha'ana Vehoshi'ah   וְשִׁיפוֹן. הוֹשַׁעְנָא וְהוֹשִׁיעָה

Na: נָא:

God, please bring generous rain from the north wind, and bless oat and rye. Please save and save us now.

El Na Sapek Sefek Bechol-   אֵל נָא סַפֵּק סְפֵק בְּכָל־

Chodesh Vachodesh. Uvarech   חֹדֶשׁ וָחֹדֶשׁ. וּבָרֵךְ

Orez Vedochan Ufol   אֹרֶז וְדֹחַן וּפוֹל

Ve'edesh. Hosha'ana Vehoshi'ah
Na:

וְעֵדֶשׁ. הוֹשַׁעֲנָא וְהוֹשִׁיעָה
נָא:

God, please provide supply every month, and bless rice, millet, beans, and lentils. Please save and save us now.

El Na Petzeh Shanah Zo

Mishamir Vashait. Uvarech Etz

Shemen Vazayit. Hosha'ana

Vehoshi'ah Na:

אֵל נָא פְּצֵה שָׁנָה זוֹ
מִשָּׁמִיר וָשָׁיִת. וּבָרֵךְ עֵץ
שֶׁמֶן וָזַיִת. הוֹשַׁעֲנָא
וְהוֹשִׁיעָה נָא:

God, please protect this year from thorns and thistles, and bless the olive tree and the olives. Please save and save us now.

El Na Bematar Raveh Charvonei

Yeshimon. Uvarech Gefen

Ute'enah Verimon. Hosha'ana

Vehoshi'ah Na:

אֵל נָא בְּמָטָר רַוֵּה חַרְבֹנֵי
יְשִׁימוֹן. וּבָרֵךְ גֶּפֶן
וּתְאֵנָה וְרִמּוֹן. הוֹשַׁעֲנָא
וְהוֹשִׁיעָה נָא:

God, please let the rain moisten the dry wilderness, and bless the vine, fig, and pomegranate. Please save and save us now.

El Na Romem Atzeret Olelei

Tipuchim. Uvarech Egoz

Vetamar

Vetapuchim. Hosha'ana

Vehoshi'ah Na:

אֵל נָא רוֹמֵם עֲצֶרֶת עוֹלְלֵי
טִפּוּחִים. וּבָרֵךְ אֱגוֹז
וְתָמָר
וְתַפּוּחִים. הוֹשַׁעֲנָא
וְהוֹשִׁיעָה נָא:

God, please exalt the assembly of nurtured children, and bless walnut, date, and apple. Please save and save us now.

El Na Yadecha Harchev Verabeh

Chazizei Me'onim. Uvarech

Batenim Ushekedim

Ve'armonim. Hosha'ana

Vehoshi'ah Na:

אֵל נָא יָדְךָ הַרְחֵב וְרַבֵּה
חֲזִיזֵי מְעוֹנִים. וּבָרֵךְ
בָּטְנִים וּשְׁקֵדִים
וְעַרְמוֹנִים. הוֹשַׁעֲנָא
וְהוֹשִׁיעָה נָא:

God, please open Your hand and multiply the thunderous clouds in the sky, and bless almonds, chestnuts, and hazelnuts. Please save and save us now.

El Na Tzidkecha Me'amecha Bal

Yipasek. Uvarech Charuv

Ukerustemal

Va'afarsek. Hosha'ana

Vehoshi'ah Na:

אֵל נָא צִדְקְךָ מֵעַמְּךָ בַּל
יִפָּסֵק. וּבָרֵךְ חָרוּב
וּקְרִסְטְמַל
וַאֲפַרְסֵק. הוֹשַׁעֲנָא
וְהוֹשִׁיעָה נָא:

God, please do not let Your righteousness be withheld from Your people, and bless carob, lotus, and peach. Please save and save us now.

El Na Chaletz Kehilah Asher

Seviveicha Ta'arog. Uvarech

Hatut Veha'egoz

Veha'etrog. Hosha'ana

Vehoshi'ah Na:

אֵל נָא חַלֵּץ קְהִלָּה אֲשֶׁר
סְבִיבֶיךָ תַּעֲרֹג. וּבָרֵךְ
הַתּוּת וְהָאֱגוֹז
וְהָאֶתְרוֹג. הוֹשַׁעֲנָא
וְהוֹשִׁיעָה נָא:

God, please deliver the congregation that longs for You, and bless the mulberry, walnut, and etrog. Please save and save us now.

El Na Kera Na Sava

Bemitrot Reki'im. Uvarech

Kol-Minei Yerakot

Uzera'im. Hosha'ana

Vehoshi'ah Na:

אֵל נָא קְרָא נָא שָׂבַע
בְּמִטְרוֹת רְקִיעִים. וּבָרֵךְ
כָּל־מִינֵי יְרָקוֹת
וּזְרָעִים. הוֹשַׁעֲנָא
וְהוֹשִׁיעָה נָא:

God, please call for abundance from the rains of the heavens, and bless all kinds of vegetables and seeds. Please save and save us now.

Ana El Na Hosha'ana

Vehatzlichah Na: (say two times)

אָנָּא אֵל נָא הוֹשַׁעֲנָא
וְהַצְלִיחָה נָא: (שתי פעמים)

Please, God, please save us now and grant success now: (say two times)

El Na Yom Zeh Al Ketz Tafsia'.

Vechaletz Shesu'ah Mikaf

Mashsia'. Gefen Mimitzrayim

Tassia'. Hosha'ana Vehatzlichah

Na:

אֵל נָא יוֹם זֶה עַל קֵץ תַּפְסִיעַ.
וְחַלֵּץ שְׁסוּעָה מִכַּף
מַשְׁסִיעַ. גֶּפֶן מִמִּצְרַיִם
תַּסִּיעַ. הוֹשַׁעֲנָא וְהַצְלִיחָה
נָא:

God, please, take a long stride this day towards the end swiftly. Deliver the torn from the hand of the oppressor. Transport a vine from Mitzrayim. Save us and grant success now:

El Na Uminof Nehalta Giz'eiha.

Vatafriach Zemorei Zeru'eiha.

Tegaresh Goyim

Vatita'eha. Hosha'ana

Vehatzlichah Na:

אֵל נָא וּמִנּוֹף נֶהֱלַתָ גִּזְעֶיהָ.
וַתַּפְרִיחַ זְמוֹרֵי זְרוּעֶיהָ.
תְּגָרֵשׁ גּוֹיִם
וַתִּטָּעֶהָ. הוֹשַׁעֲנָא
וְהַצְלִיחָה נָא:

God, please, You led its stock from Nof [Mitzrayim]. You made its planted branches blossom. You expelled nations and implanted it. Save us and grant success now:

El Na Semadareiha Henitzota	אֵל נָא סְמָדָרֶיהָ הֵנִיצֽוֹתָ
Bemeretz. Ufinita Lefaneiha	בְּמֶֽרֶץ. וּפִנִֽיתָ לְפָנֶֽיהָ
Shiv'ah Goyim Be'eretz.	שִׁבְעָה גוֹיִם בְּאֶֽרֶץ.
Vatashresh Sharasheiha	וַתַּשְׁרֵשׁ שָׁרָשֶֽׁיהָ
Vatemalle-Aretz. Hosha'ana	וַתְּמַלֵּא־אָֽרֶץ. הוֹשַֽׁעְנָא
Vehatzlichah Na:	וְהַצְלִֽיחָה נָא:

God, please, Who made her blossoms to bloom with vigor. You cleared before her seven nations with force. You rooted her roots, and You filled the land. Save us and grant success now:

El Na Pe'erot Hifrachta Piryam.	אֵל נָא פֵּארוֹת הִפְרַֽחְתָּ פִּרְיָם.
Uvatov Hisba'ta Edyam.	וּבְטוֹב הִשְׂבַּֽעְתָּ עֶדְיָם.
Teshalach Ketzireiha Ad-	תְּשַׁלַּח קְצִירֶֽיהָ עַד־
Yam. Hosha'ana Vehatzlichah	יָם. הוֹשַֽׁעְנָא וְהַצְלִֽיחָה
Na:	נָא:

God, please, You made its branches blossom fruit, and satisfied them in old age with goodness, and spread its harvest to the sea. Save us and grant success now:

El Na Halo Attah Neta'tah	אֵל נָא הֲלֹא אַתָּה נְטַעְתָּה
Vatitzereha. Ume'az Netzartah	וַתִּצְּרֶֽהָ. וּמֵאָז נְצַרְתָּה
Vatishmereh. Lamah Paratzta	וַתִּשְׁמְרָה. לָֽמָּה פָרַֽצְתָּ
Gedereiha. Hosha'ana	גְדֵרֶֽיהָ. הוֹשַֽׁעְנָא

Vehatzlichah Na: וְהַצְלִיחָה נָא:

God, please, is it not You Who planted it and protected it? You guarded it and watched over it from the beginning. Why have You broken down its walls? Save us and grant success now:

El Na Kadosh Rav Ezuzot. Habet   אֵל נָא קָדוֹשׁ רַב עֱזוּזוֹת. הַבֶּט
Mishamayim Lachazot. Ufekod   מִשָּׁמַיִם לַחֲזוֹת. וּפְקֹד
Gefen Zot. Hosha'ana   גֶּפֶן זֹאת. הוֹשַׁעֲנָא
Vehatzlichah Na: וְהַצְלִיחָה נָא:

God, please, Holy One with abundant power, look from the heavens to see and remember this vine. Save us and grant success now:

El Na Tuvecha Galeh La'amusei   אֵל נָא טוּבְךָ גַּלֵּה לַעֲמוּסֵי
Me'ayim. Yisbe'u Tuvecha   מֵעִים. יִשְׂבְּעוּ טוּבְךָ
Nochalei Dat Yomayim.   נוֹחֲלֵי דָת יוֹמָיִם.
Umima'aynei Hayeshu'ah   וּמִמַּעְיְנֵי הַיְשׁוּעָה
Yish'avun Mayim. Hosha'ana   יִשְׁאֲבוּן מָיִם. הוֹשַׁעֲנָא
Vehatzlichah Na: וְהַצְלִיחָה נָא:

God, please, reveal Your goodness to those carried from birth. Let the inheritors of the Law of two days be satisfied with Your goodness and draw water from the fountains of salvation. Save us and grant success now:

Ana El Na Hosha'ana   אָנָּא אֵל נָא הוֹשַׁעֲנָא
Veharvichah Na Avinu   וְהַרְוִיחָה נָא אָבִינוּ
Atah: (say twice)   אָתָּה: (שתי פעמים)

Please, God, please save us and grant relief now. You are our Father:
(say twice)

El Na Lema'an Av Umatz	אֵל נָא לְמַעַן אָב אָמֵץ
Mimotze'ei Alilah Al Mayim.	מִמּוֹצְאֵי עֲלִילָה עַל מָיִם.
Betzillecha Gonanto Vehitzalto	בְּצִלְּךָ גּוֹנַנְתּוֹ וְהִצַּלְתּוֹ
Mishetifat Mayim. Biglalo	מִשְּׁטִיפַת מָיִם. בִּגְלָלוֹ
Nishba'ta Shelo Lehavi Mabul	נִשְׁבַּעְתָּ שֶׁלֹּא לְהָבִיא מַבּוּל
Mayim. Ba'avuro Lo Timna	מָיִם. בַּעֲבוּרוֹ לֹא תִמְנַע
Mayim. Hosha'ana Veharvichah	מָיִם. הוֹשַׁעְנָא וְהַרְוִיחָה
Na:	נָא:

God, please, for the sake of the father [Noach] who was strengthened from those slandering him about waters. In Your shade, You protected him and saved him from the flood-waters. Because of him, You swore not to bring a flood of waters. For his sake, do not withhold water. Please save us and grant relief now:

El Na Lema'an Av Na'am	אֵל נָא לְמַעַן אָב נָאַם
Yukach-Na Me'at-Mayim.	יֻקַּח־נָא מְעַט־מָיִם.
Bogedim Himshich Achareicha	בּוֹגְדִים הִמְשִׁיךְ אַחֲרֶיךָ
El Moded Besho'olo Mayim.	אֵל מוֹדֵד בְּשָׁעֳלוֹ מָיִם.
Bitek Zarim Ovedei Esh	בִּתֵּק זָרִים עוֹבְדֵי אֵשׁ
Umayim. Ba'avuro Lo Timna	וּמָיִם. בַּעֲבוּרוֹ לֹא תִמְנַע
Mayim. Hosha'ana Veharvichah	מָיִם. הוֹשַׁעְנָא וְהַרְוִיחָה
Na:	נָא:

God, please, for the sake of the father [Avraham] who said, "Please take some water." He drew the rebellious after You, God, Who measures with His hand, the waters. Who speared the strangers, worshippers of fire and water. For his sake, do not withhold water. Please save us and grant relief now:

<table>
<tr><td>El Na Lema'an Ben Hane'ekad</td><td>אֵל נָא לְמַעַן בֶּן הַנֶּעֱקַד</td></tr>
<tr><td>Vechafar Be'er Mayim. Gar</td><td>וְחָפַר בְּאֵר מָיִם. גָּר</td></tr>
<tr><td>Bigrar Veravu Al Hamayim.</td><td>בִּגְרָר וְרָבוּ עַל הַמָּיִם.</td></tr>
<tr><td>Biseruhu Avadav Matzanu</td><td>בִּשְׂרוּהוּ עֲבָדָיו מָצָאנוּ</td></tr>
<tr><td>Mayim. Ba'avuro Lo Timna</td><td>מָיִם. בַּעֲבוּרוֹ לֹא תִמְנַע</td></tr>
<tr><td>Mayim. Hosha'ana Veharvichah</td><td>מָיִם. הוֹשַׁעֲנָא וְהַרְוִיחָה</td></tr>
<tr><td>Na:</td><td>נָא:</td></tr>
</table>

God, please, for the sake of the son [Yitzchak] who was bound and dug a well of water. He lived in Gerar, and they quarreled over water. His servants reported, "We have found water." For his sake, do not withhold water. Please save us and grant relief now:

<table>
<tr><td>El Na Lema'an Tam Gal Even</td><td>אֵל נָא לְמַעַן תָּם גָּל אֶבֶן</td></tr>
<tr><td>Me'al Be'er Mayim. Dalah</td><td>מֵעַל בְּאֵר מָיִם. דָּלָה</td></tr>
<tr><td>Vehishkah Tzon Lavan Mayim.</td><td>וְהִשְׁקָה צֹאן לָבָן מָיִם.</td></tr>
<tr><td>Vehitzig Maklot Beshikatot</td><td>וְהִצִּיג מַקְלוֹת בְּשִׁקֲתוֹת</td></tr>
<tr><td>Hamayim. Ba'avuro Lo Timna</td><td>הַמָּיִם. בַּעֲבוּרוֹ לֹא תִמְנַע</td></tr>
<tr><td>Mayim. Hosha'ana Veharvichah</td><td>מָיִם. הוֹשַׁעֲנָא וְהַרְוִיחָה</td></tr>
<tr><td>Na:</td><td>נָא:</td></tr>
</table>

God, please, for the sake of the perfect one [Ya'akov] who rolled the stone off a well of water. He drew and watered Laban's flock with water. He set up rods in the troughs of water. For his sake, do not withhold water. Please save us and grant relief now:

El Na Lema'an Dagul Mashui	אֵל נָא לְמַעַן דָּגוּל מָשׁוּי
Mimayim. He'evir Chevlach	מִמַּיִם. הֶעֱבִיר חֲבָלְךָ
Betoch Gallei Mayim. Patach	בְּתוֹךְ גַּלֵּי מָיִם. פָּתַח
Tzur Vayazuvu Mayim. Ba'avuro	צוּר וַיָּזוּבוּ מָיִם. בַּעֲבוּרוֹ
Lo Timna Mayim. Hosha'ana	לֹא תִמְנַע מָיִם. הוֹשַׁעֲנָא
Veharvichah Na:	וְהַרְוִיחָה נָא:

God, please, for the sake of the distinguished one [Moshe] drawn from water, who led Your people through the midst of waves of water, and struck the rock from which flowed water. For his sake, do not withhold water. Please save us and grant us relief:

Ana El Na. Refa Na. Selach	אָנָּא אֵל נָא. רְפָא נָא. סְלַח
Na. Hosha'ana Vehoshi'ah Na.	נָא. הוֹשַׁעֲנָא וְהוֹשִׁיעָה נָא.
Avinu Atah: (say two times)	אָבִינוּ אָתָּה: (שתי פעמים)

Please, God, heal us, forgive us, please save us, and save now. You are our Father: (say two times)

Lema'an Av Nifkad Vayibachen.	לְמַעַן אָב נִפְקַד וַיִּבָּחֵן.
Kichlot Dor Tzochen. Venoach	כִּכְלוֹת דּוֹר צוֹחֵן. וְנֹחַ
Matza Chen. Ba'avuro Talbish	מָצָא חֵן. בַּעֲבוּרוֹ תַּלְבִּישׁ
Tehilah. Le'orechei Lecha	תְּהִלָּה. לְעוֹרְכֵי לָךְ
Tefilah. Hosha'ana Vehoshi'ah	תְּפִלָּה. הוֹשַׁעֲנָא וְהוֹשִׁיעָה
Na:	נָא:

For the sake of the father [Noach] who was commanded and tested, when the scoffing generation ended, and Noah found favor. Because of him, You adorned praise to those who offer prayer. Please save us and bring success now:

Lema'an Ne'eman Amitz Beli
Cheshel. Venitzal Mikeshel.
Vayita Eshel. Ba'avuro Hayom
Tachlel. Gomerei Lecha
Hallel. Hosha'ana Vehoshi'ah
Na:

לְמַעַן נֶאֱמָן אַמִּיץ בְּלִי
חֶשֶׁל. וְנִצַּל מִכֶּשֶׁל.
וַיִּטַּע אֵשֶׁל. בַּעֲבוּרוֹ הַיּוֹם
תְּכַלֵּל. גּוֹמְרֵי לְךָ
הַלֵּל. הוֹשַׁעְנָא וְהוֹשִׁיעָה
נָא:

For the sake of the faithful one [Avraham], strong without weakness. He was saved from stumbling and planted a tamarisk tree. Because of him, crown those today who complete the Hallel to You. Please save us and bring success now:

Lema'an Yachid Mekora'i.
Berecho El Ro'i. Biv'er Lechai
Ro'i. Ba'avuro Hayom Yuchsaf.
Yosefei Lecha Musaf. Hosha'ana
Vehoshi'ah Na:

לְמַעַן יָחִיד מְקוֹרָאִי.
בֵּרְכוֹ אֵל רוֹאִי. בִּבְאֵר לְחַי
רוֹאִי. בַּעֲבוּרוֹ הַיּוֹם יֻכְסַף.
יוֹסְפֵי לְךָ מוּסָף. הוֹשַׁעְנָא
וְהוֹשִׁיעָה נָא:

For the sake of the one called "the only one" [Yitzchak], my source, blessed by the God Who sees at Be'er Lachai Ro'i. For his sake, may those who add a Musaf prayer be endeared to You. Please save us and bring success now:

Lema'an Yashan Betabur Olam.
Vesof Ne'lam Chalam.
Vayachalom Vehineh Sulam.
Ba'avuro Tevarech Rova.
Sovevei Sheva. Hosha'ana
Vehoshi'ah Na:

לְמַעַן יָשַׁן בְּטַבּוּר עוֹלָם.
וְסוֹף נֶעְלָם חָלָם.
וַיַּחֲלֹם וְהִנֵּה סֻלָּם.
בַּעֲבוּרוֹ תְּבָרֵךְ רֹבַע.
סוֹבְבֵי שֶׁבַע. הוֹשַׁעְנָא
וְהוֹשִׁיעָה נָא:

For the sake of the one who slept at the navel of the world [Ya'akov] and he dreamed of an end that disappeared. "He dreamt, and behold there was a ladder." Because of him, bless his offspring who encircle seven times. Please save us and bring success now:

Lema'an Vatik Karan Or Panav	לְמַעַן וָתִיק קָרַן עוֹר פָּנָיו
Ve'or Einav. Veha'ish Mosheh	וְאוֹר עֵינָיו. וְהָאִישׁ מֹשֶׁה
Me'od Anav. Ba'avuro Tevarech	מְאֹד עָנָיו. בַּעֲבוּרוֹ תְּבָרֵךְ
Shanah. Letzo'akei	שָׁנָה. לְצוֹעֲקֵי
Hosha'ana. Hosha'ana	הוֹשַׁעֲנָא. הוֹשַׁעֲנָא
Vehoshi'ah Na:	וְהוֹשִׁיעָה נָא:

For the sake of the humble one [Moshe], whose face shone and eyes lit up radiantly. "...and the man Moshe, was exceedingly humble." Because of him, bless the year, for those who cry out, "Save us." Please save us and bring success now:

Lema'an Po'alei Ra Halam.	לְמַעַן פּוֹעֲלֵי רַע הָלַם.
Veshalom Lo Hushlam. Berit	וְשָׁלוֹם לוֹ הֻשְׁלַם. בְּרִית
Kehunat Olam. Ba'avuro Ge'on	כְּהֻנַּת עוֹלָם. בַּעֲבוּרוֹ גְּאוֹן
Aritz Techaser. Vetashmia'	עָרִיץ תְּחַסֵּר. וְתַשְׁמִיעַ
Mevaser. Hosha'ana Vehoshi'ah	מְבַשֵּׂר. הוֹשַׁעֲנָא וְהוֹשִׁיעָה
Na:	נָא:

For the sake of the one who struck evil [Pinchas], and peace was repaid to him, a covenant of Kehuna (priesthood) forever. Because of him, break the pride of the tyrant and let us hear the herald. Please save us and bring success now:

Hoshi'enu Moshi'enu. Ki Lecha
Eineinu. Ulechah Lishu'atenu:

הוֹשִׁיעֵנוּ מוֹשִׁיעֵנוּ. כִּי לְךָ
עֵינֵינוּ. וּלְךָ לִישׁוּעָתֵנוּ:

Save us, our Savior. For our eyes are toward You, and come to our salvation:

Yoshev Kedem Ayom Venora.
Yom Zeh Te'ametz Sovevei
Torah. Veshanah Zo Tehe Shenat
Orah. Ki Lecha Eineinu.
Ulechah Lishu'atenu:

יוֹשֵׁב קֶדֶם אָיוֹם וְנוֹרָא.
יוֹם זֶה תְּאַמֵּץ סוֹבְבֵי
תוֹרָה. וְשָׁנָה זוֹ תְּהֵא שְׁנַת
אוֹרָה. כִּי לְךָ עֵינֵינוּ.
וּלְךָ לִישׁוּעָתֵנוּ:

He Who is enthroned from ancient days, fearsome and awesome, on this day strengthen those encircling the Torah. Let this year be a year of light. For our eyes are toward You, and come to our salvation:

Venofef Kore'eicha Beruch
Nemuchah. Sovevim Shiv'ah
Hayom Nesuvah. Veshanah Zo
Tehe Shenat Berachah. Ki Lecha
Eineinu. Ulechah Lishu'atenu:

וְנוֹפֵף קוֹרְאֶיךָ בְּרוּחַ
נְמוּכָה. סוֹבְבִים שִׁבְעָה
הַיּוֹם נְסוּבָה. וְשָׁנָה זוֹ
תְּהֵא שְׁנַת בְּרָכָה. כִּי לְךָ
עֵינֵינוּ. וּלְךָ לִישׁוּעָתֵנוּ:

Elevate those who call to You with a humble spirit, who encircle seven times today. Let this year be a year of blessing. For our eyes are toward You, and come to our salvation:

Shagev Shanah Zo Mikol-
Machalah. Veshitah Geshumah
Deshunah Utelulah. Veshanah

שַׂגֵּב שָׁנָה זוֹ מִכָּל-
מַחֲלָה. וְשִׁיתָה גְּשׁוּמָה
דְשׁוּנָה וּטְלוּלָה. וְשָׁנָה

Zo Tehe Shenat Gilah. Ki Lecha
Eineinu. Ulechah Lishu'atenu:

זוֹ תְּהֵא שְׁנַת גִּילָה. כִּי לְךָ
עֵינֵינוּ. וּלְכָה לִישׁוּעָתֵנוּ:

Protect this year from all illness, and make it rainy, plentiful and dewy. Let this year be a year of rejoicing. For our eyes are toward You, and come to our salvation:

Petacheicha Harchev Le'om

Yafah Ketirtzah. Mitchanenet

Lefaneicha Vehegyon Melitzah.

Veshanah Zo Tehe Shenat

Ditzah. Ki Lecha Eineinu.

Ulechah Lishu'atenu:

פְּתָחֶיךָ הַרְחֵב לְאוֹם
יָפָה כְּתִרְצָה. מִתְחַנֶּנֶת
לְפָנֶיךָ בְּהֶגְיוֹן מְלִיצָה.
וְשָׁנָה זוֹ תְּהֵא שְׁנַת
דִּיצָה. כִּי לְךָ עֵינֵינוּ.
וּלְכָה לִישׁוּעָתֵנוּ:

Your doors open wide for a nation beautiful as Tirtzah, who pleads before You with poetic prayer. Let this year be a year of delight. For our eyes are toward You, and come to our salvation:

Ha'el Lemosha'ot. Am Nosha

B'Adonai. Hosha'ana

Bechasdecha Meyachalim

L'Adonai. Ki Lishu'atecha

Kivinu Adonai. Adam

Uvehemah Toshia' Adonai. Ki

Lishu'atecha Kivinu Adonai:

הָאֵל לְמוֹשָׁעוֹת. עַם נוֹשַׁע
בַּיהוָה. הוֹשַׁעֲנָא
בְּחַסְדְּךָ מְיַחֲלִים
לַיהוָה. כִּי לִישׁוּעָתְךָ
קִוִּינוּ יְהוָה. אָדָם
וּבְהֵמָה תּוֹשִׁיעַ יְהוָה. כִּי
לִישׁוּעָתְךָ קִוִּינוּ יְהוָה:

(say two times)

(שתי פעמים)

The God Who saves a people saved by Hashem, please save in Your kindness, those who hope in Hashem. For it is for Your salvation we wait, Hashem. Man and beast You save, Hashem. For it is for Your salvation we wait, Hashem: (say two times)

Tiftach Eretz Veyifru Yesha.

Le'am Asher Bechipuram

Peditam Mipesha. Ta'avat

Anavim Shama'ta Adonai. Ki

Lishu'atecha Kivinu Adonai:

תִּפְתַּח אֶרֶץ וְיִפְרוּ יֶשַׁע.
לְעַם אֲשֶׁר בְּכִפּוּרָם
פְּדִיתָם מִפֶּשַׁע. תַּאֲוַת
עֲנָוִים שָׁמַעְתָּ יְהֹוָה. כִּי
לִישׁוּעָתְךָ קִוִּינוּ יְהֹוָה:

Open up the earth and let them be fruitful in deliverance, for the people whom You redeemed from sin on Yom Kippur. You have heard the desire of the humble, Hashem. For it is for Your salvation we wait, Hashem:

Mipeleg Male Raveh

Le'umecha. Keyom Asher

Yatzata Leyesha Amecha. Yom

Asher Ne'emar Bo Vayosha

Adonai. Ki Lishu'atecha Kivinu

Adonai:

מִפֶּלֶג מָלֵא רַוֶּה
לְאֻמֶּךָ. כְּיוֹם אֲשֶׁר
יָצָאתָ לְיֵשַׁע עַמֶּךָ. יוֹם
אֲשֶׁר נֶאֱמַר בּוֹ וַיּוֹשַׁע
יְהֹוָה. כִּי לִישׁוּעָתְךָ קִוִּינוּ
יְהֹוָה:

From a full stream, quench Your nation, as on the day You went forth to save Your people. The day when it was said, "And Hashem saved." For it is for Your salvation we wait, Hashem:

Heyeh Na Lishu'ah Tzur Oneh

Vatzar. Peduti Karev Ki Yadecha

Lo Tiktzar. Re'eh Ki Ta'avti

Yeshu'atecha Adonai. Ki

Lishu'atecha Kivinu Adonai:

הֱיֵה נָא לִישׁוּעָה צוּר עוֹנֶה
בַצָּר. פְּדוּתִי קָרֵב כִּי יָדְךָ
לֹא תִקְצָר. רְאֵה כִּי תָאַבְתִּי
יְשׁוּעָתְךָ יְהֹוָה. כִּי
לִישׁוּעָתְךָ קִוִּינוּ יְהֹוָה:

Please be for a salvation, Rock, Who answers in distress. Bring near my redemption, for Your hand is not limited. See that I long for Your salvation, Hashem. For it is for Your salvation we wait, Hashem:

Hoshi'ah Asir Tzo'ek Mibeit	הוֹשִׁיעָה אַסִיר צוֹעֵק מִבֵּית
Kele. Leshav'i Himatze Tzur	כֶּלֶא. לְשַׁוְעִי הִמָּצֵא צוּר
Oseh Fele. Petach Peleg Malle.	עוֹשֵׂה פֶלֶא. פְּתַח פֶּלֶג מָלֵא.
Yisbe'u Atzei Adonai. Ki	יִשְׂבְּעוּ עֲצֵי יְהֹוָה. כִּי
Lishu'atecha Kivinu Adonai:	לִישׁוּעָתְךָ קִוִּינוּ יְהֹוָה:

Save the imprisoned who cry out from the prison. Be attentive to my plea, Rock, Who performs wonders. Open a full stream and let the trees of Hashem be satiated. For it is for Your salvation we wait, Hashem:

Hateh Oznecha Shema Na	הַטֵּה אָזְנְךָ שְׁמַע נָא
Vehosha Na. Nefashot	וְהוֹשַׁע נָא. נְפָשׁוֹת
Hateruchot Bema'arichei	הַטְּרוּחוֹת בְּמַאֲרִיכֵי
Techinah. Siftotam Taba'nah	תְּחִנָּה. שִׂפְתוֹתָם תַּבַּעְנָה
Yeshu'atah L'Adonai. Ki	יְשׁוּעָתָה לַיהֹוָה. כִּי
Lishu'atecha Kivinu Adonai:	לִישׁוּעָתְךָ קִוִּינוּ יְהֹוָה:

Incline Your ear, please hear us and save us now. Troubled souls, pouring out lengthy supplications. Their lips express the salvation of Hashem. For it is for Your salvation we wait, Hashem:

Retzeh Shav'at Amelim.	רְצֵה שַׁוְעַת אֲמֵלִים.
Yeshu'atecha Meyachalim.	יְשׁוּעָתְךָ מְיַחֲלִים.
Umezonam Sho'alim. Beyom	וּמְזוֹנָם שׁוֹאֲלִים. בְּיוֹם
Lulav Notelim. Geshamim	לוּלָב נוֹטְלִים. גְּשָׁמִים
Utelalim. Tazil Mizevulim.	וּטְלָלִים. תַּזִּיל מִזְּבוּלִים.
Vechish Yelechu Ge'ulim.	וְחִישׁ יֵלְכוּ גְאוּלִים.
Ufeduyei Adonai. Ki	וּפְדוּיֵי יְהֹוָה. כִּי
Lishu'atecha Kivinu Adonai:	לִישׁוּעָתְךָ קִוִּינוּ יְהֹוָה:

Favor the cry of the afflicted. They yearn for Your salvation and ask for their sustenance on the day they take the Lulav. Rains and dew, pour from the heavens. Quickly, let the redeemed and the ransomed of Hashem go. For it is for Your salvation we wait, Hashem:

Kol Mevaser Mevaser

Ve'omer: (say seven times)

קוֹל מְבַשֵּׂר מְבַשֵּׂר

וְאוֹמֵר: (ז' פעמים)

The voice of the herald proclaims and declares: (say seven times)

Yefeh Nof Anofef Bechezyon

Te'udah. Yismach Har-Tziyon

Tagelenah Benot Yehudah.

Mevaser Mevaser Ve'omer:

יְפֵה נוֹף אֲנוֹפֵף בְּחֶזְיוֹן

תְּעוּדָה. יִשְׂמַח הַר־צִיּוֹן

תָּגֵלְנָה בְּנוֹת יְהוּדָה.

מְבַשֵּׂר מְבַשֵּׂר וְאוֹמֵר:

Beautiful sight, I raise up in a vision of prophecy. Mount Tziyon rejoices, the daughters of Yehudah are glad. The herald proclaims and declares:

Vavei Navech Afaseg Ve'archiv

Gevulech. Ki Adonai Yihyeh-

Lache Le'or Olam Veshalemu

Yemei Evlech. Mevaser Mevaser

Ve'omer:

וָוֵי נָוֵךְ אֲפַסֵּג וְאַרְחִיב

גְּבוּלֵךְ. כִּי יְהֹוָה יִהְיֶה־

לָךְ לְאוֹר עוֹלָם וְשָׁלֵמוּ

יְמֵי אֶבְלֵךְ. מְבַשֵּׂר מְבַשֵּׂר

וְאוֹמֵר:

I will raise up and expand your border. For Hashem will be for you an everlasting light, and your days of mourning will end. The herald proclaims and declares:

Sobu Tziyon Vehakifuha Sifru   סֹבּוּ צִיּוֹן וְהַקִּיפוּהָ סִפְרוּ

Migdaleiha. Sisu Itah Masos   מִגְדָלֶיהָ. שִׂישׂוּ אִתָּה מָשׂוֹשׂ

Kol-Hamit'abelim Aleiha.   כָּל־הַמִּתְאַבְּלִים עָלֶיהָ.

Mevaser Mevaser Ve'omer: מְבַשֵּׂר מְבַשֵּׂר וְאוֹמֵר:

Surround Tziyon and encircle her, count her towers. Rejoice in her exultation, all who mourned for her. The herald proclaims and declares:

Peta Ashlich Al Edom   פֶּתַע אַשְׁלִיךְ עַל אֱדוֹם

Na'alayim. Pitzchu Ranenu   נַעֲלָיִם. פִּצְחוּ רַנְּנוּ

Yachdav Charevot   יַחְדָּו חָרְבוֹת

Yerushalayim. Mevaser Mevaser   יְרוּשָׁלָיִם. מְבַשֵּׂר מְבַשֵּׂר

Ve'omer: וְאוֹמֵר:

I will suddenly cast my shoes on Edom. Burst forth and sing together, ruins of Yerushalayim. The herald proclaims and declares:

Ketz Yeshu'ati Chashti Mime'on   קֵץ יְשׁוּעָתִי חַשְׁתִּי מִמְּעוֹן

Shachak. Keravti Tzidkati Lo   שַׁחַק. קֵרַבְתִּי צִדְקָתִי לֹא

Tirchak. Mevaser Mevaser   תִרְחָק. מְבַשֵּׂר מְבַשֵּׂר

Ve'omer: וְאוֹמֵר:

I hastened the end of My salvation from the heavenly abode. I brought near My righteousness; it is not far off. The herald proclaims and declares:

Hit'oreri Mimizrach Uvo'i   הִתְעוֹרְרִי מִמִּזְרָח וּבֹאִי

Mima'arav. Har-Tziyon Yarketei   מִמַּעֲרָב. הַר־צִיּוֹן יַרְכְּתֵי

Tzafon Kiryat Melech — צָפוֹן קִרְיַת מֶלֶךְ

Rav. Mevaser Mevaser Ve'omer: — רָב. מְבַשֵּׂר מְבַשֵּׂר וְאוֹמֵר:

Awake from the east and come from the west, Mount Tziyon, the northern sides, the city of the great king. The herald proclaims and declares.

Kol Mevaser Mevaser — קוֹל מְבַשֵּׂר מְבַשֵּׂר

Ve'omer: (say two times) — וְאוֹמֵר: ((שתי פעמים))

The voice of the herald proclaims and declares: (say two times)

Kakatuv: Mah-Navu Al-Heharim — כַּכָּתוּב: מַה־נָּאווּ עַל־הֶהָרִים

Raglei Mevaser Mashmia' — רַגְלֵי מְבַשֵּׂר מַשְׁמִיעַ

Shalom Mevaser Tov Mashmia' — שָׁלוֹם מְבַשֵּׂר טוֹב מַשְׁמִיעַ

Yeshu'ah Omer Letziyon Malach — יְשׁוּעָה אֹמֵר לְצִיּוֹן מָלַךְ

Elohayich. Vene'emar: Kol — אֱלֹהָיִךְ: וְנֶאֱמַר: קוֹל

Tzofayich Nase'u Kol Yachdav — צֹפַיִךְ נָשְׂאוּ קוֹל יַחְדָּו

Yeranenu Ki Ayin Be'ayin Yir'u — יְרַנֵּנוּ כִּי עַיִן בְּעַיִן יִרְאוּ

Beshuv Adonai Tziyon. — בְּשׁוּב יְהֹוָה צִיּוֹן:

Vene'emar: Pitzchu Ranenu — וְנֶאֱמַר: פִּצְחוּ רַנְּנוּ

Yachdav Chorvot Yerushalaim Ki- — יַחְדָּו חָרְבוֹת יְרוּשָׁלָ͏ם כִּי־

Nicham Adonai Amo Ga'al — נִחַם יְהֹוָה עַמּוֹ גָּאַל

Yerushalaim. Vene'emar: Ki- — יְרוּשָׁלָ͏ם: וְנֶאֱמַר: כִּי־

Nicham Adonai Tziyon Nicham — נִחַם יְהֹוָה צִיּוֹן נִחַם

Kol-Chorvoteiha Vayasem — כָּל־חָרְבֹתֶיהָ וַיָּשֶׂם

Midbarah Ke'eden Ve'arvatah — מִדְבָּרָהּ כְּעֵדֶן וְעַרְבָתָהּ

Kegan-Adonai Sason Vesimchah — כְּגַן־יְהֹוָה שָׂשׂוֹן וְשִׂמְחָה

Yimatze Vah Todah Vekol	יִמָּצֵא בָהּ תּוֹדָה וְקוֹל
Zimrah. Vene'emar: Ranu	זִמְרָה: וְנֶאֱמַר: רָנּוּ
Shamayim Vegili Aretz Ufitzchu	שָׁמַיִם וְגִילִי אָרֶץ וּפִצְחוּ
Harim Rinah Ki-Nicham	הָרִים רִנָּה כִּי־נִחַם
Adonai Amo Va'aniyav	יְהֹוָה עַמּוֹ וַעֲנִיָּיו
Yerachem. Vene'emar: Vehalechu	יְרַחֵם: וְנֶאֱמַר: וְהָלְכוּ
Amim Rabim Ve'ameru Lechu	עַמִּים רַבִּים וְאָמְרוּ לְכוּ
Vena'aleh El-Har-Adonai El-Beit	וְנַעֲלֶה אֶל־הַר־יְהֹוָה אֶל־בֵּית
Elohei Ya'akov Veyorenu	אֱלֹהֵי יַעֲקֹב וְיֹרֵנוּ
Miderachav Venelechah	מִדְּרָכָיו וְנֵלְכָה
Be'orechotav Ki Mitziyon Tetze	בְּאֹרְחֹתָיו כִּי מִצִּיּוֹן תֵּצֵא
Torah Udevar-Adonai	תוֹרָה וּדְבַר־יְהֹוָה
Mirushalaim. Vene'emar:	מִירוּשָׁלָם: וְנֶאֱמַר:
Ufeduyei Adonai Yeshuvun	וּפְדוּיֵי יְהֹוָה יְשֻׁבוּן
Uva'u Tziyon Berinah Vesimchat	וּבָאוּ צִיּוֹן בְּרִנָּה וְשִׂמְחַת
Olam Al-Rosham Sason	עוֹלָם עַל־רֹאשָׁם שָׂשׂוֹן
Vesimchah Yassigu Venasu Yagon	וְשִׂמְחָה יַשִּׂיגוּ וְנָסוּ יָגוֹן
Va'anachah. Vene'emar: Chasaf	וַאֲנָחָה: וְנֶאֱמַר: חָשַׂף
Adonai Et-Zeroa' Kodsho	יְהֹוָה אֶת־זְרוֹעַ קָדְשׁוֹ
Le'einei Kol-Hagoyim Vera'u Kol-	לְעֵינֵי כָּל־הַגּוֹיִם וְרָאוּ כָּל־
Afsei-Aretz Et Yeshu'at	אַפְסֵי־אָרֶץ אֵת יְשׁוּעַת
Eloheinu. Vene'emar: Veyihyu	אֱלֹהֵינוּ: וְנֶאֱמַר: וְיִהְיוּ
Devarai Eleh Asher Hitchananti	דְבָרַי אֵלֶּה אֲשֶׁר הִתְחַנַּנְתִּי
Lifnei Adonai Kerovim El-	לִפְנֵי יְהֹוָה קְרֹבִים אֶל־
Adonai Eloheinu Yomam	יְהֹוָה אֱלֹהֵינוּ יוֹמָם
Valayelah La'asot Mishpat Avdo	וָלָיְלָה לַעֲשׂוֹת מִשְׁפַּט עַבְדּוֹ
Umishpat Amo Yisra'el Devar-	וּמִשְׁפַּט עַמּוֹ יִשְׂרָאֵל דְּבַר־
Yom Beyomo. Lema'an Da'at	יוֹם בְּיוֹמוֹ: לְמַעַן דַּעַת

Kol-Amei Ha'aretz Ki Adonai Hu
Ha'elohim Ein Od.

כָּל־עַמֵּי הָאָרֶץ כִּי יְהֹוָה הוּא
הָאֱלֹהִים אֵין עוֹד:

As it is written: "How beautiful upon the mountains are the feet of the messenger of good news, That announces peace, the harbinger of good news, That announces salvation; That says to Tziyon: 'Your God reigns.'" And it is said: "Your watchmen lift up their voice, with one voice they will sing together: for face to face they will see when Hashem returns to Tziyon." And it is said: "Burst forth and sing together, ruins of Yerushalayim, for Hashem has comforted His people, He has redeemed Yerushalayim." And it is said: "For Hashem has comforted Tziyon, He has comforted all her waste places, and has made her wilderness like Eden, and her desert like the garden of Hashem. Joy and gladness will be found in her, thanksgiving and the voice of song." And it is said: "Sing, heavens, and be joyful, earth, And break out into singing, mountains; For Hashem has comforted His people, And has compassion on His afflicted." And it is said: "And many peoples shall go and say: 'Come and let us go up to the mountain of Hashem, To the house of the God of Ya'akov; And He will teach us of His ways, And we will walk in His paths.' For out of Tziyon shall the Torah go forth, and the word of Hashem from Yerushalayim." And it is said: "And the ransomed of Hashem will return, and come to Tziyon with singing, and everlasting joy shall be upon their heads; They shall obtain gladness and joy, and sorrow and sighing shall flee." And it is said: "Hashem has made bare His holy arm in the eyes of all the nations, and all the ends of the earth will see the salvation of our God." And it is said: "Let these words of mine, with which I have pleaded before Hashem, be near to Hashem our God day and night, that He may maintain the cause of His servant and the cause of His people Yisrael, as each day requires; so that all the peoples of the earth may know that Hashem is God; there is no other."

Hoshanot for Shabbat Day

הושענות ליום שבת

The Geonim were divided on reciting Hoshanot on Shabbat, with some forbidding it to avoid confusion regarding taking the lulav, while others permitted it without circling. Different customs exist today. Some communities recite Hoshanot after Hallel, others after Musaf, and some omit it entirely on Shabbat. These variations reflect traditions across different Sephardic and Ashkenazi communities.

Erchatz Benikayon Kapai   אֶרְחַץ בְּנִקָּיוֹן כַּפָּי

Va'asovevah Et-Mizbachacha   וַאֲסֹבְבָה אֶת־מִזְבַּחֲךָ

Adonai: Lashmia' Bekol Todah   יְהוָה: לַשְׁמִעַ בְּקוֹל תּוֹדָה

Ulesaper Kol-Nifle'oteicha.   וּלְסַפֵּר כָּל־נִפְלְאוֹתֶיךָ:

I will wash my hands in innocence, and I will encircle your altar, Hashem. That I may make the voice of thanksgiving to be heard, and tell of all Your wondrous works. (Ps. 26:6-7)

Hosha'ana. Hosha'ana: הוֹשַׁעְנָא. הוֹשַׁעְנָא:

Please save us. Please save us:

Lema'anach Eloheinu.   לְמַעַנְךָ אֱלֹהֵינוּ.

Lema'anach Bore'enu.   לְמַעַנְךָ בּוֹרְאָנוּ.

Lema'anach Go'alenu.   לְמַעַנְךָ גּוֹאֲלֵנוּ.

Lema'anach Doreshenu: לְמַעַנְךָ דּוֹרְשֵׁנוּ:

For Your sake, our God. For Your sake, our Creator. For Your sake, our Redeemer. For Your sake, our Seeker.

Lema'anach Adir Adirim.   לְמַעַנְךָ אַדִּיר אַדִּירִים.

Lema'anach Boreiruach Veyotzer   לְמַעַנְךָ בּוֹרֵא רוּחַ וְיוֹצֵר

Harim. Lema'anach Gedol   הָרִים. לְמַעַנְךָ גָּדוֹל

Ha'etzah Mashpil Umerim.	הָעֵצָה מַשְׁפִּיל וּמֵרִים.
Lema'anach Dover Tzedek	לְמַעַנְךָ דּוֹבֵר צֶדֶק
Magid Meisharim.	מַגִּיד מֵישָׁרִים.
Lema'anach Hayodea' Va'ed Im	לְמַעַנְךָ הַיּוֹדֵעַ וָעֵד אִם
Yisater Ish Bemistarim.	יִסָּתֵר אִישׁ בְּמִסְתָּרִים.
Lema'anach Vehu Be'echad Umi	לְמַעַנְךָ וְהוּא בְּאֶחָד וּמִי
Yeshivenu Amarim.	יְשִׁיבֵנוּ אֲמָרִים.
Lema'anach Zach Venaki	לְמַעַנְךָ זַךְ וְנָקִי
Umitbarer Im Barim.	וּמִתְבָּרֵר עִם בָּרִים.
Lema'anach Chofes Matzpun	לְמַעַנְךָ חוֹפֵשׂ מַצְפּוּן
Vechoker Kol-Chadarim.	וְחוֹקֵר כָּל־חֲדָרִים.
Lema'anach Tipechah Yemino	לְמַעַנְךָ טִפְּחָה יְמִינוֹ
Shamayim Ve'asah Me'orim.	שָׁמַיִם וְעָשָׂה מְאוֹרִים.
Lema'anach Yasad Eretz Batzurot	לְמַעַנְךָ יָסַד אֶרֶץ בַּצּוּרוֹת
Bika Ye'orim. Lema'anach Kabir	בִּקַּע יְאוֹרִים. לְמַעַנְךָ כַּבִּיר
Koach Mechubad Ba'urim.	כֹּחַ מְכֻבָּד בָּאוּרִים.
Lema'anach Lo Yitamu Shenotav	לְמַעַנְךָ לֹא יִתַּמּוּ שְׁנוֹתָיו
Ledor Dorim:	לְדוֹר דּוֹרִים:

For Your sake, Mightiest of the mighty. For Your sake, Creator of the wind and the Former of mountains. For Your sake, Great in counsel, Who humbles and lifts high. For Your sake, Speaker of righteousness, declaring uprightness. For Your sake, Knower and Witness, whether a person hides in secret places. For Your sake, He Who is One, and Who will return us with utterances. For Your sake, Pure and Innocent and Who is pure with the pure. For Your sake, Liberator of the hidden and Searcher of all chambers. For Your sake, He Who spread out the sky with His right hand and made the luminaries. For Your sake, He Who founded the earth with its boundaries, carving the rivers in rocks. For Your sake, the Great in

Power, honored with lights. For Your sake, His years will never end for generations of generations:

Hosha'ana. Hosha'ana:

הוֹשַׁעְנָא. הוֹשַׁעְנָא:

Please save us. Please save us:

Om Netzurah Kevavat. Banah	אִם נְצוּרָה כְּבָבַת. בָּנָה
Behilchot Shabbat. Gomeret Dat	בְּהִלְכוֹת שַׁבָּת. גוֹמֶרֶת דַּת
Nefesh Meshivat. Doreshet	נֶפֶשׁ מְשִׁיבַת. דּוֹרֶשֶׁת
Yetzi'ot Shabbat.	יְצִיאוֹת שַׁבָּת.

A nation guarded like the apple of the eye, built upon the laws of Shabbat, studies the law that restores the soul, expounds [upon the laws of] carrying on Shabbat.

Hakova'at Alafim Techum	הַקּוֹבַעַת אֲלָפִים תְּחוּם
Shabbat. Ve'al-Shetei Kikarot	שַׁבָּת. וְעַל־שְׁתֵּי כִּכָּרוֹת
Botza'at Beshabbat. Zachor	בּוֹצַעַת בְּשַׁבָּת. זָכוֹר
Veshamor Mekayemet	וְשָׁמוֹר מְקַיֶּמֶת
Beshabbat.	בְּשַׁבָּת.

Who establishes the Shabbat boundary of two thousand [cubits], and breaks two loaves of bread on Shabbat. They observe [the commandments] to "Remember" and "Keep" on Shabbat.

Choshevet Vetorachat Behilchot	חוֹשֶׁבֶת וְטוֹרַחַת בְּהִלְכוֹת
Shabbat. To'emet Shalosh	שַׁבָּת. טוֹעֶמֶת שָׁלוֹשׁ
Se'udot Beshabbat.	סְעוּדוֹת בְּשַׁבָּת.

They ponder and toil in the laws of Shabbat, while eating three meals on Shabbat.

Yosher Sheva Berachot Orechet
Beshabbat. Kolelet Shir Mizmor
Veshevach Beshabbat.

יוֹשֶׁר שֶׁבַע בְּרָכוֹת עוֹרֶכֶת
בְּשַׁבָּת. כּוֹלֶלֶת שִׁיר מִזְמוֹר
וְשֶׁבַח בְּשַׁבָּת.

Arranging the seven blessings on Shabbat, reciting psalms and praises on Shabbat.

Lehallel Leshimcha Matmedet
Beshabbat. Mo'eset Kol-Chefetz
Beyom Hashabbat.

לְהַלֵּל לְשִׁמְךָ מַתְמֶדֶת
בְּשַׁבָּת. מוֹאֶסֶת כָּל־חֵפֶץ
בְּיוֹם הַשַּׁבָּת.

To praise Your name constantly on Shabbat. Despising all commerce on the day of Shabbat.

No'emet Milechalel Et-Yom
Hashabbat. Sovelet Al Kaved
Ba'avur Yom Hashabbat.

נוֹאֶמֶת מִלְחַלֵּל אֶת־יוֹם
הַשַּׁבָּת. סוֹבֶלֶת עַל כָּבֵד
בַּעֲבוּר יוֹם הַשַּׁבָּת.

They speak out against desecrating the day of Shabbat, and endure burdens in honor of Shabbat.

Orechet Mizmor Shir Leyom
Hashabbat. Potachat Yad
Lameyachadim Beshabbat.

עוֹרֶכֶת מִזְמוֹר שִׁיר לְיוֹם
הַשַּׁבָּת. פּוֹתַחַת יָד
לַמְיַחֲדִים בְּשַׁבָּת.

They prepare a psalm [to recite] for the day of Shabbat, and open their hand to those devoted on Shabbat.

Tze'akah Uvichyah Meracheket
Beshabbat. Kofetzet Kaf
Milischor Beshabbat.

צְעָקָה וּבְכִיָּה מְרַחֶקֶת
בְּשַׁבָּת. קוֹפֶצֶת כַּף
מִלִּסְחוֹר בְּשַׁבָּת.

Cries and laments they distance from on Shabbat. And stop their hands from doing business on Shabbat.

Roshemet Bichtav Ve'al-Peh	רוֹשֶׁמֶת בִּכְתָב וְעַל־פֶּה
Beshabbat. Shomeret Oneg	בְּשַׁבָּת. שׁוֹמֶרֶת עֹנֶג
Kedushat Shabbat. Tamid Ken	קְדֻשַּׁת שַׁבָּת. תָּמִיד כֵּן
Tanchilenah Olam Shekulo	תַּנְחִילֶנָּה עוֹלָם שֶׁכֻּלּוֹ
Shabbat:	שַׁבָּת:

Referring to the Written and Oral [Torah] on Shabbat. And guards the delight in sanctity of Shabbat. May You always grant them a world that is entirely Shabbat.

Hosha'ana. Hosha'ana:	הוֹשַׁעְנָא. הוֹשַׁעְנָא:

Please save us. Please save us:

El Na'aratz. Besod Kedoshim	אֵל נַעֲרָץ. בְּסוֹד קְדוֹשִׁים
Rabat. Mizmor Shir Leyom	רַבָּת. מִזְמוֹר שִׁיר לְיוֹם
Hashabbat:	הַשַּׁבָּת:

Revered God, in the assembly of the holy. A psalm, a song for the Sabbath day:

Borei Niv Sefatayim. Mistater	בּוֹרֵא נִיב שְׂפָתַיִם. מִסְתַּתֵּר
Beshafrir Chevyon. Tov Lehodot	בְּשַׁפְרִיר חֶבְיוֹן. טוֹב לְהוֹדוֹת
L'Adonai. Ulezamer Leshimcha	לַיהוה. וּלְזַמֵּר לְשִׁמְךָ
Elyon:	עֶלְיוֹן:

Creator of the utterance of lips. Who is hidden in the shelter of seclusion. It is good to give thanks to Hashem, and to sing praises to Your name, Most High:

Gadol Adonai Umehulal Me'od.

Tzur Nora Alilot. Lehagid

Baboker Chasdecha.

Ve'emunatecha Baleilot:

גָּדוֹל יְהוָה וּמְהֻלָּל מְאֹד.

צוּר נוֹרָא עֲלִילוֹת. לְהַגִּיד

בַּבֹּקֶר חַסְדֶּךָ.

וֶאֱמוּנָתְךָ בַּלֵּילוֹת:

Great is Hashem and greatly to be praised. A Rock of awesome deeds. To declare Your kindness in the morning, and Your faithfulness at night:

Dover Tzedek Umagid

Meisharim. Mehulal Besha'ar

Nikanor. Alei-Asor Va'alei-

Navel. Alei Higayon Bechinor:

דּוֹבֵר צֶדֶק וּמַגִּיד

מֵישָׁרִים. מְהֻלָּל בְּשַׁעַר

נִקָנוֹר. עֲלֵי-עָשׂוֹר וַעֲלֵי-

נָבֶל. עֲלֵי הִגָּיוֹן בְּכִנּוֹר:

He speaks righteousness and declares uprightness. Praised in the gate of Nikanor. With the ten-stringed instrument and the lyre. With a voice of song on the kinor:

Horeni Adonai Darkecha.

Utzedoktecha Ashanen. Ki

Simachtani Adonai Befo'olecha.

Bema'asei Yadeicha Aranen:

הוֹרֵנִי יְהוָה דַּרְכֶּךָ.

וּצְדָקָתְךָ אֲשַׁנֵּן. כִּי

שִׂמַּחְתַּנִי יְהוָה בְּפָעֳלֶךָ.

בְּמַעֲשֵׂי יָדֶיךָ אֲרַנֵּן:

Teach me Your way, Hashem. And I will follow Your righteousness. For You have gladdened me, Hashem, with Your deeds. I will sing for joy at the works of Your hands:

Va'ani Tefilati Lecha Adonai. Ki

Gavehu Sodoteicha. Mah-

Gadelu Ma'aseicha Adonai.

וַאֲנִי תְפִלָּתִי לְךָ יְהוָה. כִּי

גָּבְהוּ סוֹדוֹתֶיךָ. מַה-

גָּדְלוּ מַעֲשֶׂיךָ יְהוָה.

Me'od Ameku Machshevoteicha: מְאֹד עָמְקוּ מַחְשְׁבֹתֶיךָ:

But as for me, my prayer is to You, Hashem. For Your secrets are lofty. How great are Your deeds, Hashem. Very deep are Your thoughts:

Zechor Rachameicha Adonai. Ki   זְכֹר רַחֲמֶיךָ יְהוָה. כִּי

Ein Od Milevadecha. Kumah   אֵין עוֹד מִלְּבַדֶּךָ. קוּמָה

Ezratah Lanu. Ufedenu Lema'an   עֶזְרָתָה לָּנוּ. וּפְדֵנוּ לְמַעַן

Chasdecha: חַסְדֶּךָ:

Remember Your mercies, Hashem. For there is none besides You. Arise to help us, and redeem us for the sake of Your kindness:

Chonenu Ki Tzar Achalanu.   חָנֵּנוּ כִּי צַר אֲכָלָנוּ.

Har'enu Adonai Chasdecha.   הַרְאֵנוּ יְהוָה חַסְדֶּךָ.

Viyesh'acha Titen-Lanu: Tov   וְיֶשְׁעֲךָ תִּתֶּן־לָנוּ: טוֹב

Adonai Lakol. Yeshivuni   יְהוָה לַכֹּל. יְשִׁיבוּנִי

Ra'yonai. Yihyu Leratzon Imrei-   רַעְיוֹנַי. יִהְיוּ לְרָצוֹן אִמְרֵי־

Fi Vehegyon Libi Lefaneicha   פִי וְהֶגְיוֹן לִבִּי לְפָנֶיךָ

Adonai: יְהוָה:

Be gracious to us, for our enemy has consumed us. Show us, Hashem, Your kindness and grant us Your salvation: Hashem is good to all. My thoughts return me. May the words of my mouth and the meditation of my heart be acceptable before You, Hashem.

Hosha'ana. Hosha'ana: הוֹשַׁעְנָא. הוֹשַׁעְנָא:

Please save us. Please save us:

Beyom Shabbat Kodesh. Hashev
Am Segulah. El-Hamenuchah
Ve'el-Hanachalah:

בְּיוֹם שַׁבָּת קֹדֶשׁ. הָשֵׁב
עַם סְגֻלָּה. אֶל־הַמְּנוּחָה
וְאֶל־הַנַּחֲלָה:

On the holy day of Shabbat, return the chosen nation to rest and to inheritance:

Beyom Shabbat Kodesh. Kayem
Adonai Ma'amar Chuzecha.
Kumah Adonai Limnuchatecha.
Attah Va'aron Uzecha:

בְּיוֹם שַׁבָּת קֹדֶשׁ. קַיֵּם
יְהֹוָה מַאֲמַר חֻזֶּךָ.
קוּמָה יְהֹוָה לִמְנוּחָתֶךָ.
אַתָּה וַאֲרוֹן עֻזֶּךָ:

On the holy Shabbat day, fulfill, Hashem, the promise of Your strength. "Arise, Hashem, to Your resting place, You and the Ark of Your might.":

Beyom Shabbat Kodesh. Ta'aneh
Edah Pezurah Venidachah. Yiten
Adonai Lachem. Umetzena
Menuchah:

בְּיוֹם שַׁבָּת קֹדֶשׁ. תַּעֲנֶה
עֵדָה פְּזוּרָה וְנִדָּחָה. יִתֵּן
יְהֹוָה לָכֶם. וּמְצֶאןָ
מְנוּחָה:

On the holy Shabbat day, proclaim to the scattered and exiled congregation. "May Hashem grant you and may you find rest.":

Beyom Shabbat Kodesh.
Hamtze Le'amecha Manoach.
Vesham Yanuchu Yegi'ei
Choach:

בְּיוֹם שַׁבָּת קֹדֶשׁ.
הַמְצֵא לְעַמְּךָ מָנוֹחַ.
וְשָׁם יָנוּחוּ יְגִיעֵי
כֹחַ:

On the holy Shabbat day, grant rest to Your people, and there the weary will find strength:

Beyom Shabbat Kodesh. Tikra   בְּיוֹם שַׁבַּת קֹדֶשׁ. תִּקְרָא

Letzorer Verodef. Zot   לְצוֹרֵר וְרוֹדֵף. זֹאת

Hamenuchah. Hanichu Le'ayef: הַמְּנוּחָה. הָנִיחוּ לְעָיֵף:

On the holy Shabbat day, call to the oppressor and pursuer. "This is the resting place — give respite to the weary.":

Beyom Shabbat Kodesh.   בְּיוֹם שַׁבַּת קֹדֶשׁ.

Avarech Tzur Fodeh Vego'el.   אֲבָרֵךְ צוּר פּוֹדֶה וְגוֹאֵל.

Baruch Adonai. Asher Natan   בָּרוּךְ יְהוָה. אֲשֶׁר נָתַן

Menuchah Le'amo Yisra'el: מְנוּחָה לְעַמּוֹ יִשְׂרָאֵל:

On the holy Shabbat day, I will bless the Rock, Redeemer and Savior. Blessed is Hashem who has granted rest to His people Yisrael:

Hosha'ana. Hosha'ana: הוֹשַׁעְנָא. הוֹשַׁעְנָא:

Please save us. Please save us:

Ana Hoshi'ah Na.   אָנָּא הוֹשִׁיעָה נָּא.

Ana Hoshi'ah Na: אָנָּא הוֹשִׁיעָה נָּא:

Please save us now. Please save us now:

Ana Chish Na Yish'i. Beyom   אָנָּא חִישׁ נָא יִשְׁעִי. בְּיוֹם

Hashevi'i. Ushe'eh Na Shav'i.   הַשְּׁבִיעִי. וּשְׁעֵה נָא שַׁוְעִי.

Keminchat Machavat. Vechon   כְּמִנְחַת מַחֲבַת. וְחֹן

Shokedei Amor. Zachor   שׁוֹקְדֵי אָמוֹר. זְכוֹר

Veshamor. Hamezamerim   וְשָׁמוֹר. הַמְזַמְּרִים

Mizmor. Shir Leyom Hashabbat.

(Hayom Beyom Shabbat.)

Hoshi'ah Na:

מִזְמוֹר. שִׁיר לְיוֹם הַשַּׁבָּת.

(הַיּוֹם בְּיוֹם שַׁבָּת.)

הוֹשִׁיעָה נָּא:

Please hasten my salvation on the seventh day. And hear my cry like the pan-offering. Show favor to those who diligently observe, to "remember" and "keep", singing the psalm, a song for the Shabbat day. (Today, on the day of Shabbat,) please save us:

Ana Hoshi'ah Na.

Ana Hoshi'ah Na:

אָנָּא הוֹשִׁיעָה נָּא.

אָנָּא הוֹשִׁיעָה נָּא:

Please save us now. Please save us now:

Ana Sovev Hashevi'i. Tuvecha

Mabi'i. Umalle Gevi'i. Chok

Bal-Yushbat. Pezureicha

Shechol. Kodesh Mechol.

Lesalselach Alei Machol.

Hayom Beyom Shabbat.

Hoshi'ah Na:

אָנָּא סוֹבֵב הַשְּׁבִיעִי. טוּבְךָ

מָבִיעִי. וּמַלֵּא גְבִיעִי. חֹק

בַּל־יִשְׁבַּת. פְּזוּרֶיךָ

שֶׁחֹל. קֹדֶשׁ מֵחֹל.

לְסַלְסְלָךְ עֲלֵי מָחוֹל.

הַיּוֹם בְּיוֹם שַׁבָּת.

הוֹשִׁיעָה נָּא:

Please, circle the seventh day, expressing Your goodness. Fill my cup with an unbroken decree. Gather Your scattered ones, the sanctified from the mundane, to glorify You with joyous dance. Today on Shabbat, please save us:

Ana Hoshi'ah Na.

Ana Hoshi'ah Na:

אָנָּא הוֹשִׁיעָה נָּא.

אָנָּא הוֹשִׁיעָה נָּא:

Please save us now. Please save us now:

Ani Vahu Hoshi'ah Na.	אֲנִי וָהוּ הוֹשִׁיעָה נָּא.
Ani Vahu Hoshi'ah Na:	אֲנִי וָהוּ הוֹשִׁיעָה נָּא:

Ani VaHu. please save us now. Ani VaHu. please save us now:

Kehosha'ta Yotze'ei Patros.	כְּהוֹשַׁעְתָּ יוֹצְאֵי פַתְרוֹס.
Vera'atzta Arotz. Vataharos	וְרָעַצְתָּ עָרוֹץ. וַתַּהֲרֹס
Haros. Lesarisei Rabbat.	הָרוֹס. לְסָרִיסֵי רַבַּת.
Shorerei Lecha Shirot. Venotenei	שׁוֹרְרֵי לָךְ שִׁירוֹת. וְנוֹתְנֵי
Zemirot. Amarot Tehorot.	זְמִירוֹת. אֲמָרוֹת טְהוֹרוֹת.
Nehalelach Beyom Shabbat.	נְהַלֶּלָךְ בְּיוֹם שַׁבָּת.
Ken Hosha'ana:	כֵּן הוֹשַׁעֲנָא:

As You saved those who left Patros [Egypt] and crushed the oppressor, and destroyed the officers of Rabbat, so too please save Your servants who sing songs to You and offer pure words of praise, we will glorify You on Shabbat:

Kehosha'ta Sechufei Sochef.	כְּהוֹשַׁעְתָּ סְחוּפֵי סוֹחֵף.
Vatesagel Rochef. Yedid	וַתְּסַגֵּל רוֹחֵף. יְדִיד
Shochen Vechofef. Vatitzor	שׁוֹכֵן וְחוֹפֵף. וַתִּצּוֹר
Kevavat. Potzechei Renanot.	כְּבָבַת. פּוֹצְחֵי רְנָנוֹת.
Umenagenei Neginot. Bitfilah	וּמְנַגְּנֵי נְגִינוֹת. בִּתְפִלָּה
Uvitchinot. Nehalelach Beyom	וּבִתְחֲנוֹת. נְהַלֶּלָךְ בְּיוֹם
Shabbat. Ken Hosha'ana:	שַׁבָּת. כֵּן הוֹשַׁעֲנָא:

As You saved those storm-tossed and protected the wanderer, Beloved One, Who dwells and shelters, You guarded them as the apple of Your eye. So too please save those who sing of joyful songs, and play melodies with prayer and supplication—we will praise You on the Shabbat day:

Ani Vahu Hoshi'ah Na.

Ani Vahu Hoshi'ah Na:

Ani VaHu. please save us now. Ani VaHu. please save us now:

אֲנִי וָהוּ הוֹשִׁיעָה נָּא.

אֲנִי וָהוּ הוֹשִׁיעָה נָּא:

Banu Leyached Shem Ha'el.

Hayom Behallel Ushevachah.

Ein Lanu Lehalelo. Beminim

Arba'ah. Tzur Podeh Vego'el.

Yotzi'enu Lirvachah. Yiten

Adonai Lachem. Umetzena

Menuchah:

בָּאנוּ לְיַחֵד שֵׁם הָאֵל.

הַיּוֹם בְּהַלֵּל וּשְׁבָחָה.

אֵין לָנוּ לְהַלְלוֹ. בְּמִינִים

אַרְבָּעָה. צוּר פּוֹדֶה וְגוֹאֵל.

יוֹצִיאֵנוּ לִרְוָחָה. יִתֵּן

יְהוָה לָכֶם. וּמְצָאן

מְנוּחָה:

We come to declare the unity of God's name today in praise and song. We cannot praise Him with the four species. Our Rock, Redeemer and Savior will bring us relief. May Hashem give you and grant you rest:

Yom Kadosh Venora. Nichbad

Mikol-Yamim. Hinchilo Le'am

Kodesh Oneg Lishnei Olamim.

Bo Shavat Mimelachah. Roka

Eretz Al-Hamayim. Limtzo-Vo

Margoa' Venefesh Semechah.

Yiten Adonai Lachem.

Umetzena Menuchah:

יוֹם קָדוֹשׁ וְנוֹרָא. נִכְבָּד

מִכָּל־יָמִים. הִנְחִילוֹ לְעַם

קֹדֶשׁ עֹנֶג לִשְׁנֵי עוֹלָמִים.

בּוֹ שָׁבַת מִמְּלָאכָה. רָקַע

אֶרֶץ עַל־הַמָּיִם. לִמְצוֹא־בוֹ

מַרְגּוֹעַ וְנֶפֶשׁ שְׂמֵחָה.

יִתֵּן יְהוָה לָכֶם.

וּמְצָאן מְנוּחָה:

A holy and awesome day, more honored than all other days. He bestowed it upon His holy nation as a delight for both worlds. On it, He ceased from work, spreading the earth upon the waters, to find rest and a joyous soul. May Hashem give you and grant us rest.

Kehosha'ta Me'az Adatecha.   כְּהוֹשַׁעְתָּ מֵאָז עֲדָתֶךָ.

Ken Hoshi'ah Et Amecha.   כֵּן הוֹשִׁיעָה אֶת עַמֶּךָ.

Uvarech Et Nachalatecha.   וּבָרֵךְ אֶת נַחֲלָתֶךָ.

Nehalelach Beyom Shabbat.   נְהַלְלָךְ בְּיוֹם שַׁבָּת.

Ken Hosha'ana: כֵּן הוֹשַׁעֲנָא:

As You have saved Your congregation in the past, so save Your people now, and bless Your inheritance. We will praise You on the day of Shabbat, so please save us.

Ani Vahu Hoshi'ah Na.   אֲנִי וָהוּ הוֹשִׁיעָה נָא.

Ani Vahu Hoshi'ah Na: אֲנִי וָהוּ הוֹשִׁיעָה נָא:

 Ani VaHu. please save us now. Ani VaHu. please save us now:

Kakatuv: Hoshi'ah. Et-Amecha.   כַּכָּתוּב: הוֹשִׁיעָה. אֶת־עַמֶּךָ.

Uvarech Et-Nachalatecha   וּבָרֵךְ אֶת־נַחֲלָתֶךָ וּרְעֵם

Ure'em Venase'em Ad-Ha'olam: וּנְשָׂאֵם עַד־הָעוֹלָם:

As it is written: "Save Your people and bless Your inheritance; tend them and carry them forever."

Some conclude with the following page, others skip to Yehi Shem:

Vene'emar: Veyihyu Devarai	וְנֶאֱמַר: וְיִהְיוּ דְבָרַי
Eleh Asher Hitchananti Lifnei	אֵלֶה אֲשֶׁר הִתְחַנַּנְתִּי לִפְנֵי
Adonai Kerovim El-Adonai	יְהֹוָה קְרֹבִים אֶל־יְהֹוָה
Eloheinu Yomam Valayelah	אֱלֹהֵינוּ יוֹמָם וָלַיְלָה
La'asot Mishpat Avdo Umishpat	לַעֲשׂוֹת מִשְׁפַּט עַבְדּוֹ וּמִשְׁפַּט
Amo Yisra'el Devar-Yom	עַמּוֹ יִשְׂרָאֵל דְּבַר־יוֹם
Beyomo: Lema'an Da'at Kol-	בְּיוֹמוֹ: לְמַעַן דַּעַת כָּל־
Ammei Ha'aretz Ki Adonai Hu	עַמֵּי הָאָרֶץ כִּי יְהֹוָה הוּא
Ha'elohim Ein Od: Lo-Yamush	הָאֱלֹהִים אֵין עוֹד: לֹא־יָמוּשׁ
Sefer Hatorah Hazeh Mipicha	סֵפֶר הַתּוֹרָה הַזֶּה מִפִּיךָ
Vehagita Bo Yomam Valaylah	וְהָגִיתָ בּוֹ יוֹמָם וָלַיְלָה
Lema'an Tishmor La'asot	לְמַעַן תִּשְׁמֹר לַעֲשׂוֹת
Kechol-Hakatuv Bo Ki-Az	כְּכָל־הַכָּתוּב בּוֹ כִּי־אָז
Tatzliach Et-Derachecha Ve'az	תַּצְלִיחַ אֶת־דְּרָכֶךָ וְאָז
Taskil: Halo Tziviticha Chazak	תַּשְׂכִּיל: הֲלוֹא צִוִּיתִיךָ חֲזַק
Ve'ematz Al-Ta'arotz Ve'al-	וֶאֱמָץ אַל־תַּעֲרֹץ וְאַל־
Techat Ki Imecha Adonai	תֵּחָת כִּי עִמְּךָ יְהֹוָה
Eloheicha Bechol Asher Telech:	אֱלֹהֶיךָ בְּכֹל אֲשֶׁר תֵּלֵךְ:

And it is said: May these words of mine, with which I have pleaded before Hashem, be near to Hashem our God day and night, that He may maintain the cause of His servant and the cause of His people Yisrael, as each day requires. So that all the peoples of the earth may know that Hashem is God, there is none else. This book of the Torah shall not depart from your mouth, but you shall meditate on it day and night, so that you may observe to do according to all that is written in it; for then you will make your way prosperous, and then you will have good success. Have I not commanded you? Be strong and courageous. Do not be afraid or dismayed, for Hashem your God is with you wherever you go.

Yehi Shem

Yehi Shem Adonai Mevorach;
Me'attah. Ve'ad-'Olam.
Mimizrach-Shemesh Ad-
Mevo'o; Mehulal. Shem Adonai
Ram Al-Chol-Goyim Adonai Al
Hashamayim Kevodo. Adonai
Adoneinu; Mah-'Adir Shimcha.
Bechol-Ha'aretz.

יְהִי שֵׁם יְהֹוָה מְבֹרָךְ
מֵעַתָּה וְעַד־עוֹלָם:
מִמִּזְרַח־שֶׁמֶשׁ עַד־
מְבוֹאוֹ מְהֻלָּל שֵׁם יְהֹוָה:
רָם עַל־כָּל־גּוֹיִם ו יְהֹוָה עַל
הַשָּׁמַיִם כְּבוֹדוֹ: יְהֹוָה
אֲדֹנֵינוּ מָה־אַדִּיר שִׁמְךָ
בְּכָל־הָאָרֶץ:

Blessed is the name of Hashem from this time forward and forever.
From the rising of the sun to it's going down, Hashem's name is to
be praised. Hashem, our Lord, How glorious is Your name in all of
the earth. **(Psalms 113:2-4, 8:2)**